Southern Women Playwrights

Southern Women Playwrights

New Essays in Literary History and Criticism

Edited by
Robert L. McDonald and Linda Rohrer Paige

THE UNIVERSITY OF ALABAMA PRESS
TUSCALOOSA AND LONDON

Copyright © 2002
The University of Alabama Press
Tuscaloosa, Alabama 35487-0380
All rights reserved
Manufactured in the United States of America

9 8 7 6 5 4 3 2 1
10 09 08 07 06 05 04 03 02

Typeface: Adobe Garamond

∞

The paper on which this book is printed meets the minimum requirements of American
National Standard for Information Science–Permanence of Paper for Printed Library
Materials, ANSI Z39.48–1984.

Library of Congress Cataloging-in-Publication Data

Southern women playwrights : new essays in literary history and criticism / edited by
Robert L. McDonald and Linda Rohrer Paige.
    p. cm.
Includes bibliographical references and index.
    ISBN 0-8173-1079-7 (cloth : alk. paper)—ISBN 0-8173-1080-0 (paper : alk. paper)
    1. American drama—Southern States—History and criticism. 2. Women and literature—
Southern States—History—20th century. 3. American drama—Women authors—History
and criticism. 4. American drama—20th century—History and criticism. I. McDonald,
Robert L., 1964– II. Paige, Linda Rohrer, 1948–
    PS261 .S57 2002
    812′.5099287′0975—dc21
                    2001004243

British Library Cataloguing-in-Publication Data available

Contents

Acknowledgments

Both editors freely admit how lost they would have been without the expert computer skills and the vital encouragement of Lanell VanLandingham, administrative secretary of the Department of Literature and Philosophy at Georgia Southern University. For headaches prevented and disasters averted, we thank her. We have also appreciated the guidance and generous attention of Curtis Clark, Mindy Wilson, Jennifer Horne, and others at The University of Alabama Press.

Rob McDonald wishes to thank the VMI Research Committee for a generous grant-in-aid which enabled work on his essay and on the collection in general. In the process, Christina Russell McDonald demonstrated once again just how essential she is to his ability to accomplish just about anything. He is pleased now, as always, to state publicly his gratitude for her critical insights as well as her patient accommodations of his working life.

Linda Rohrer Paige offers thanks to Bruce Krajewski, Chair of the Department of Literature and Philosophy at Georgia Southern University, who encouraged this work, allowing much needed support to bring this project to fruition, and to Julia Griffin, who kept her from creating a new dictionary. She also thanks her students Buell Wisner and Amara McGee, for their proofreading assistance and encouragement, especially when her eyes lacked focus; Cynthia Frost and the Interlibrary Loan Department of Georgia Southern for promptly and adeptly securing research materials; and last, David Paige, her husband, who enthusiastically, tirelessly, has supported her work, along with her children, Zachary and Callie, who came to see less of their mother as this volume took shape.

Introduction

We decided to initiate this collection after discovering in conversation that we had experienced similar frustrations in trying to locate either primary or secondary materials that would help us to teach and write about drama by Southern women in context, in perspective. For our courses and research in modern drama, Southern literature, and women's literature and gender studies, no collections of Southern women's plays existed. Nor could we locate much in the way of scholarship about these playwrights, despite the fact that some had very active and visible careers. We did find substantive work on Beth Henley, Marsha Norman, and, of course, Lillian Hellman—a kind of artistic Trinity, we came to feel. They apparently represent the extent to which critics and historians, with few exceptions, have acknowledged the achievements of Southern women playwrights.

Of course, we knew other voices existed. In our searches for basic information other names surfaced, some of them familiar, many not: Valetta Anderson, Sallie Bingham, Sharon Bridgeforth, Ada Jack Carver, Jo Carson, Jane Chambers, Alice Childress, Pearl Cleage, Sandra Deer, Elizabeth Dewberry, Margaret Edson, Margery Evernden, Julia Fields, Martha Ayers Fuentes, Amparo Garcia, Rebecca Gilman, Barbara Guest, Bernice Kelly Harris, Nancy Wallace Henderson, Shirlene Holmes, Zora Neale Hurston, Marsha A. Jackson-Randolph, Georgia Johnson, Gayl Jones, Barbara Lebow, Jane Martin, Carson McCullers, Sally Ordway, Regina Porter, Rebecca Ranson, Patricia Resnick, Sonia Sanchez, Nicky Silver, Regina Taylor, Naomi Wallace, Paula Vogel, Billie Jean Young, Shay Youngblood. From what we could see, some of these writers wore their Southernness like a virtue, while others tended to value it less. Certainly, though, location bound these women together—the fact of their having been born in the region or having settled there to live and write—and they were connected further by neglect. Despite their impressive collective body of work, and in some instances, considerable local acclaim, why weren't their plays being discussed to any significant degree in either Southern Studies or generic venues in literature and theater?

The idea for this collection thus had its genesis in a string of associated, though not necessarily connected, questions that we thought deserved attention. We began asking ourselves—and anyone else who would join us in the conversation—who *are* the most notable, the most interesting Southern women playwrights, past or present? What is the literary and theatrical heritage of the Southern woman playwright? Is there anything unique or special about the ways Southern women have approached the conventional modes of comedy and tragedy? How does the South, its types and stereotypes, its peculiarities, its traditions—both literary and cultural—figure in these plays? Does it matter that a play happens to be written by a woman who happens to be "Southern," especially when the play doesn't seem particularly to be about the South? Does noticing that a play is written by a Southern woman tend to affect our perception of the play's potential "universality"?

Our collection does not aim to answer any one of these questions explicitly nor to serve as an exhaustive or canon-making anatomy of the Southern Woman Playwright. Rather, our goal has been more catholic. From our earliest plans, we envisioned an eclectic forum, a place for interested parties to call attention to distinctive voices, features, and themes in drama by Southern women. As we considered the many provocative topics suggested in response to our open call for submissions for this volume, we felt pleased by the number of people who obviously had been reflecting on some of our same concerns. Representing diverse interests in English, history, theater, and performance studies, those essays selected for inclusion here present a variety of stimulating forays into literary, cultural, and theater criticism and suggest an array of opportunities for further study of Southern women's achievements in theater.

The volume opens with Robert L. McDonald's review of "The Current State of Scholarship on Southern Women Playwrights." He suggests that the neglect of drama by Southern women is due to "deep, historical prejudices" against the drama itself and against women artists, especially in the South. McDonald calls for a critical awareness of these prejudices so that Southern women playwrights, past and present, might be accorded the serious attention their works merit.

Three essays follow which illuminate important, but often overlooked or misunderstood, topics in the history of Southern women's drama. While today Zora Neale Hurston is well known and regarded as a novelist and folklorist, in "'Let the People Sing!': Zora Neale Hurston and the Dream of a Negro Theater," John Lowe assays her emerging reputation as a dramatist. Acquainting us with Hurston's life and her persistent ambitions as a folk dramatist, Lowe offers a lively assessment of the writer's career, detailing her efforts to create "an authentic Negro theatre" that might dramatize African American life in all its dimensions. Providing a helpful introduction to Hurston's entire play-writing oeuvre, Lowe discusses many works only recently discovered and being prepared for publication.

Not all Southern women playwrights have needed to have their works rescued from the oblivion of literary history, of course, and none has been so much the subject of study as Lillian Hellman. Born in New Orleans, Hellman, who achieved not just greatness, but fame, as one of the more colorful literary personalities of the 1940s and 1950s, never cared much for the label "Southern playwright." Still, as T. R. Mooney's impressive textual research in the Hellman archives reveals, the author did indeed draw upon her "Southern roots" as a fundamental resource for her plays, both in terms of characters and themes. In "These Four: Hellman's Roots Are Showing," her ties to the region have been unfortunately blurred because of a virtual recasting of her image as a "social," or "political," or "feminist" playwright, and because Hellman herself began to use, but not pronounce, details from her Southern background in her writing.

In "Carson McCullers, Lillian Smith, and the Politics of Broadway," Judith Giblin James presents another example of the ways in which literary history might be revised to account for the efforts of Southern women writers to participate in the theater. James compares the parallel, but quite different, experiences of McCullers and Smith in adapting best-selling novels for Broadway: McCullers's successful adaptation of *The Member of the Wedding* and Smith's disastrous attempt to bring *Strange Fruit* to the stage. Revealing the extent to which these two women "battled producers, directors, advisers, and collaborators for control of their artistic visions," James casts light on both the plays themselves and the special challenges that white Southern women faced in trying to present their controversial visions of their home region, particularly as concerns the issue of race.

Unlike Lillian Hellman, Carson McCullers never attempted to ignore her Southernness, but she remained in painful conflict about its effect on her life, as Betty E. McKinnie and Carlos L. Dews submit in "The Delayed Entrance of Lily Mae Jenkins: Queer Identity, Gender Ambiguity, and Southern Ambivalence in Carson McCullers's *The Member of the Wedding*." McKinnie and Dews investigate the biographical implications of a character—"an abandoned, waifish Negro homosexual"—that McCullers originally planned to integrate into *The Heart is a Lonely Hunter* but withheld and introduced later, though only in conversation, in her provocative novel and play *The Member of the Wedding*. McKinnie and Dews argue persuasively that this minor character assumes magnitude as a reflection of McCullers's vision of Southern "intolerance," particularly in terms of race and sexual difference. In the next essay, Donna Lisker demonstrates how another playwright, South Carolina native Alice Childress, addressed similar problems with her home region more directly. In "'Controversy Only Means Disagreement': Alice Childress's Activist Drama," Lisker suggests that Childress's popular success in dramatizing civil rights issues in the South was limited not only by her explicit, even confrontational, political themes, but also by her realistic bent: she was writing at precisely the historical moment, the 1950s, when "the theater was undergoing a transformation" that made the genre seem "quaint and outdated to many." Yet realism proved, in fact, the perfect artistic mode for Childress, Lisker contends. Childress pursued the uses of art for activist purposes—her characters as important and powerful as any political figure of the time—staging in vivid detail the injustices of a Jim Crow South.

In "Role-ing on the River: Actors Theatre of Louisville and the Southern Woman Playwright," Elizabeth S. Bell brings the collection to contemporary times by reviewing the famous ATL's role as a veritable incubator of women's talent in the drama. Bell explains the theater's history and mission before proceeding to underscore some of the distinguished careers of Southern women playwrights whose talents germinated there—especially those cultivated by ATL producing director, Jon Jory, whose protégés included Jane Martin, Marsha Norman, and Naomi Wallace. The next few essays that follow Bell's piece examine, in detail, works by playwrights who got their start or were nurtured at the ATL.

In "Precursor and Protégé: Lillian Hellman and Marsha Norman," Sally Burke casts the relationship between two of the South's best-known women playwrights as a feminist revision of the masculine "anxiety of influence," as articulated famously by Harold Bloom. Rather than try to "annihilate" or to reject her predecessor, Norman embraces and fully acknowledges the influence of her role model, Hellman. Through close textual readings, Burke demonstrates how Norman draws on Hellman's plays, both subtly and overtly, and, in so doing, contributes to the establishment of a coherent women's tradition of drama. Janet L. Gupton, in "'Un-ruling' the Woman: Comedy and the Plays of Beth Henley and Rebecca Gilman," delineates another relationship between women playwrights, albeit an unacknowledged one. She notes how Pulitzer winner Henley and relative newcomer Gilman have arrived at similar feminist interpolations of the conventions of comedy in order to critique aspects of Southern culture. In particular, they introduce an evolving style of comedy that "destabilize[s] the stereotype of the Southern 'lady' and explore[s] the anti-authoritarian aspects that can make comedy a socially transformative tool."

The next two essays examine the work of two playwrights associated with the ATL whose successes have been the subjects of some curiosity. In "Pseudonymy and Identity Politics: Exploring 'Jane Martin,'" J. Ellen Gainor explores the implications of a career built on a pseudonym. Martin, one of the most prolific talents cultivated (and concealed) by Jory and the ATL establishment, has received almost as much attention for "her" insistent anonymity as for "her" plays. After reviewing the controversies surrounding Martin's "true" identity—some critics speculate that Martin might be male, perhaps even Jory himself—Gainor studies several of Martin's most successful works in light of their supposed authorship by a Southern woman. Although no controversy surrounds the identity of Kentucky native (and 1999 MacArthur "genius" grant winner) Naomi Wallace, some curiosity exists regarding the fact that her plays have been far more successful in Europe, particularly England where she now lives, than at home. In "Dialectic and the Drama of Naomi Wallace," Claudia Barnett analyzes a fundamental aspect of Wallace's dramaturgy: a theoretical perspective which views history as a malleable continuum, à la Brecht, in which "time and place are both distant and present." Wallace seldom sets her plays in the South, but regional influences remain present, only cloaked as a "far-off reality" that the playwright then reveals as familiar and local. Audiences thus become "distanced" even as they are drawn into the action and themes of the play: "Her South is disguised," Barnett explains, "not so she can hide it, but so she can ultimately expose it."

The concluding essays address an assortment of topics concerning works by some of the most interesting and important voices in contemporary Southern women's theater. Displaying less overt political interest, emerging Mexicana playwright Amparo Garcia stages controversial themes important to her local community, Mexicanos living in a small town in southwest Texas. In "Amparo Garcia and the Eyes of Tejas: Texas Community through Mexicana Eyes," Carolyn Roark argues that Garcia's plays, particularly given the playwright's interest in themes of community and family, as well as in her treatment of violence, place her squarely within traditions of Southern literature. Attention to Garcia's staging of the urgency of life in small-town Texas—as evidenced in her play "Under a Western Sky," a drama about the social disruptions attending a gang rape—challenges us to expand common preconceptions about the limits of the "South." Elizabeth Brown-Guillory invites further examination of those who are marginalized—in this instance, African Americans—in her postcolonial critique, "Reconfiguring History: Migration, Memory, and (Re)Membering in Suzan-Lori Parks's Plays." Linking form and content in Parks's dramas, Brown-Guillory discusses the major themes and motifs of one of the most innovative "theoretical artists" writing for the contemporary theatre. Kentucky-born Parks has earned both a critical reputation and the respect of her peers for challenging the expectations and preconceptions of audiences with "the possibility of multiple meanings in non-linear, multidirectional works," such as those of her Obie Award–winning *The America Play* and *The Death of the Last Black Man in the Whole Entire World*.

Next, Alan Shepard and Mary Lamb contribute an essay that no doubt will surprise many in a volume on Southern women playwrights. Yet 1998 Pulitzer Prize–winner Paula Vogel, born in the border state of Maryland, proudly claims the Southernness imparted to her especially by her mother, a native of New Orleans. That influence evinces itself in "The Memory Palace in Paula Vogel's Plays," in which Shepard and Lamb compellingly map a theme that both pervades Vogel's plays and appears as a standard component in most formulations of the characteristics of Southern literature: a persistent, even obsessive, interest in history and memory. Vogel's plays operate on a number of levels in order to "create an atmosphere that opens spectators to the possibility of reimagining, and sometimes rescripting, a number of America's myths and historical 'truths,'" the two argue. Mary Resing directs us to the work of another playwright gaining the respect of critics and popular audiences alike, Savannah native Regina Porter. In "Postmodern Monologues in Regina Porter's *Tripping through the Car House*," Resing illustrates the methods by which Porter utilizes both realistic and nonrealistic elements in her most recent play, especially the monologue and interests of the domestic drama, in order to evoke the "schizophrenic" world the characters inhabit. The monologic scenes, in particular, dramatize the "multiple identities" of the characters, which "betoken the fragmented world in which they live," Resing submits.

In the final essay in the collection, "Southern Women Playwrights and the Atlanta Hub: Home Is the Place Where You Go," Linda Rohrer Paige illumines one of the most vibrant, diverse theater scenes outside New York today. Highlighting the work of four Atlanta playwrights, Shirlene Holmes, Barbara Lebow, Sandra Deer, and Pearl Cleage, Paige draws attention to the surge of women playwrights making Atlanta their home. In the theater community, they find an environment that welcomes their messages, and, in some cases, their activism. Paige examines their attitudes towards living and working in Atlanta and in the South and highlights major themes that seem to reflect their social and artistic interests. Finding the Atlanta theater community a thriving, productive environment for women playwrights, in particular, she concludes that a broad cultural and aesthetic diversity is the magnet attracting talented playwrights to the city.

In "The Discourse of Southernness," a provocative essay included in the 1996 collection entitled *The Future of Southern Letters,* Jefferson Humphries takes up the notion that to study Southern literature is to study "the South as an idea." He argues, "The South, what we mean when we talk about the South, is not a geographical place and is only related to geographical place by pure arbitrary contingency. The South is instead nothing in the world but an idea in narrative form, a discourse or rhetoric of narrative tropes, a story made out of stories, a lie, a fiction to which we have lent reality by believing in it" (120). In the afterword for a new paperback edition of his classic *Writing the South: Ideas of an American Region,* Richard Gray makes a similar point as he critiques the controlling metaphor of his study:

> Language, telling, gives us all the chance to be in history and out of it: to participate in the many levels and constant changes of our culture and to articulate them, to communicate them to others and ourselves. What this rather abstract statement means is that, if I were searching around to explain the theme of this book now, I would try somehow not to put quite so much focus on *writing* as the means by which Southerners have been actively engaged in inventing and understanding their localities; talking has been just as important, perhaps more so. If the South has emerged as one of the determining concepts of American history and culture—one of the crucial ways significant groups of Americans, past, and present, have attempted to make sense of their lives and changes—it is as a concept active in the everyday speech of communities as well as in written and published texts. (299–300)

While we might argue with Humphries's extremism—the affective "reality" of a July day in South Carolina, for example, seems undeniable—we find instructive the point both he and Gray make about the active construction of "Southernness" through *telling,* a process of *enactment.* Although it does not appear that either of these men has drama specifically in mind, plays perform precisely the function they describe. As Jindřich Honzl cogently explained a long time ago, "dramatic performance is a set of signs" expressed and interpreted (269). Viewed in this way, as performative, semiotic narratives, the plays discussed in this collection dramatize and are therefore implicated in the (re)construction of aspects of Southernness that warrant our attention. Indeed, they not only invite a reconceptualization of our understanding of Southern literature—the conventional modes and tropes of Southern storytelling—but they also challenge us to realize the ways in which regional affiliation (conscious or unconscious) might influence a writer's aesthetic and thematic choices. Whether in folk drama, conventional realism, or radical dramatic experiments linking form and idea, we believe that the contributors to this volume argue persuasively that those choices for Southern women have been bolder and more substantive than most people realize. In the spirit in which our collaboration on this project was born, then, we hope that the essays here will serve as points of departure for fresh inquiry into the ways that Southern women playwrights tell their stories and, in doing so, participate in enacting the story of their region.

Works Cited

Gray, Richard. *Writing the South: Ideas of an American Region.* 1986. Baton Rouge: Louisiana State UP, 1997.

Honzl, Jindřich. "Dynamics of the Sign in the Theatre." 1940. *Modern Theories of Drama: A Selection on Writing on Drama and Theatre, 1840–1990.* New York: Oxford UP, 1998. 269–78.

Humphries, Jefferson. "The Discourse of Southernness: Or How We Can Know There Will Still Be Such a Thing as the South and Southern Literary Culture in the Twenty-First Century." *The Future of Southern Letters.* Ed. Jefferson Humphries and John Lowe. New York: Oxford UP, 1996. 119–33.

Southern Women Playwrights

I

The Current State of Scholarship on Southern Women Playwrights

Robert L. McDonald

Indeed it will be a long time still, I think, before a woman can sit down to write a book without finding a phantom to be slain, a rock to be dashed against.
— Virginia Woolf, "Professions for Women"

The woman playwright endeavoring to communicate her vision to the world is engaged in a radical act.
— Rachel Koenig, Introduction, *Interviews with Contemporary Women Playwrights*

As Sally Burke observes at the beginning of *American Feminist Playwrights: A Critical History,* before the cultural awakenings instigated by the women's movement of the 1960s, American "women writing in any genre were given short shrift. This lack of attention was compounded for the playwright by the difficulty, even near impossibility, of getting her drama produced in a theater ruled by men" (vii). If women are now duly recognized as major voices in fiction, poetry, and such nonfiction genres as the essay, the memoir, and biography, the same still cannot be said for women dramatists. Beyond the offerings of a small number of theater groups and scholars who concentrate on plays by women, drama remains the single literary genre in which women's achievement continues to be wrought piece by piece, performance by performance, as if tradition is being invented on the spot. That American women have written interesting plays since the earliest days of the republic is not something one could know from our literary histories and the bulk of criticism. Women's drama remains conscripted to the margins, rather like a chorus surrounding the dominant voices of our decidedly "major" (i.e., male) playwrights. More attention should be devoted to the question of why.[1]

As a contribution and encouragement to future dialogue on this point, this volume is intended to upgrade the current state of scholarship on a particular group of women playwrights: those who were born or reside in and who write out of their experiences in the American South. These artists are worth our attention not only because the quality of their plays is high, but also because they have been so neglected. Despite a few occasional exceptions, such as Lillian Hellman and Pulitzer Prize–winners Beth Henley and Marsha Norman, in general women playwrights are absent from the history and criticism of Southern literature—their works not simply unremarked but unknown. A recent exchange with a friend (and former professor) who happens also to be a respected scholar of modern Southern literature is, I fear, typical. When he asked about my current research project, I wrote that a colleague and I were beginning a collection of essays on Southern women playwrights. "You're working on Southern *what?*" he replied, humorously but not altogether unseriously. "I didn't know there were any." Of course, such offhanded dismissal is not new. It originates in deep, historical prejudices against every term of the label "Southern Woman Playwright" which have combined to discourage women dramatists and to suppress acknowledgment of their achievements.

Fundamentally, Southern women playwrights, like all serious dramatists both male and female, have faced the traditional cultural and academic prejudice against the drama itself. Susan Harris Smith explains the grounds for this attitude in *American Drama: The Bastard Art,* identifying a host of complicit factors that have tended to cast the drama as "an unwanted bastard child" (2) among the major genres of American literature. The drama has been devalued, Smith argues persuasively,

> in part because of a culturally dominant puritan distaste for and suspicion of the theater; in part because of a persistent, unwavering allegiance to European models, slavish Anglophilia, and a predilection for heightened language cemented by the New Critics; in part because of a fear of populist, leftist, and experimental art; in part because of a disdain of alternative, oppositional, and vulgar performances; in part because of narrow disciplinary divisions separating drama from theater and performance; and in part because of the dominance of prose and poetry in the hierarchy of genres studied in university literature courses and reproduced in American criticism. (3)

If American dramatists have created some of the world's great plays, as they certainly have, they have done so despite a profoundly schizophrenic attitude toward their work. As mere entertainment drama might be fine, but it has always been viewed as either too commonplace or too threatening (in its capacity to disseminate radical visions) for full, comfortable acceptance by the arbiters of bourgeois culture as "art."[2]

The attitude has been no more enlightened in Southern Studies, where a disquieting silence has deemed drama as virtually inconsequential in the development of the region's literature. In his landmark history, *The South in American Literature, 1607–1900* (1954), for example, Jay B. Hubbell notes active theaters in such antebellum cities as Richmond, Annapolis, and Charleston. Concluding that "in the main the theatrical history of the United States concerns the larger cities of the North" (13), however, Hubbell devotes fewer than a dozen pages of his 879-page volume to the drama. Although the first book-length history of Southern drama appeared recently (Watson),[3] scholars concerned with the broadest outlines of Southern literature have continued to slight the genre. Our most comprehensive and authoritative history, and the most quoted, remains *The History of Southern Literature* (1985), a 600-page volume initiated and supported by the Society for the Study of Southern Literature in order to tell "*the story* of the South's literature" (Rubin 1, emphasis added). In this "story" appears a single concentrated discussion of Southern drama: a seven-page chapter in which Jacob H. Adler simply reworks and repeats, at times practically verbatim, the same observations on the same three "major" playwrights—Paul Green, Tennessee Williams, and Lillian Hellman—that he had published nearly twenty-five years earlier (Rubin and Jacobs).[4]

Add to this situation the condition of being a *woman* dramatist in American, particularly Southern, culture and the problems compound. Women who pursue forms of expression that defy norms of femininity have always met with intolerance, disapproval, and even aggressive discouragement, which can generate deep guilt and flashes of self-doubt in even the hardiest of souls. This has been especially true for the woman playwright, whose commitment to her art is so public that she becomes an easy target for critique more interested in her place as a woman than with her abilities as a dramatist. In a 1973 *New York Times* feature entitled "Where Are the Women Playwrights?" Gretchen Cryer reported an encounter with her neighbor, "a kindly old gentleman," who approached her after her new play had closed after only a few performances. "'Tell me,' he asked, 'is this the way you really want to spend your life—writing plays that are only going to close? Especially when you have children.'" Cryer said she "blanched" and walked away, but thought immediately of another recent exchange, this one with her nine-year-old daughter following an unusually late rehearsal. Crying, the child was waiting for her when she got home:

"Mommy, we don't see you any more." Even though she had considered how, "[f]or a woman in my position (an unmarried head of a household), it would seem a kind of grand self-indulgence to spend 14 hours a day away from my children doing a kind of work which may not even make a living for my family," Cryer remained committed to her writing. "But let me tell you, it takes a tremendous effort to shake my woman's guilt," she confessed ("Where" 1).

This scene was played out, we must note, a full decade after Betty Friedan challenged the limitations placed on women by the "feminine mystique" and asked her revolutionary questions about "what happens when women try to live according to an image [of femininity] that makes them deny their minds?" (66). But the cultural trappings and expectations incumbent upon imagery—those that persist as what Virginia Woolf once called the "phantoms" women writers seem ever fated to combat for their artistic freedom—die harder than any real restrictions. Apparent social evolution does not always account for assumptions of propriety, especially where gender roles are concerned. This explains both the old man's presumptive question and Cryer's uncontrollable guilt, which are grounded in ancient notions of order, decorum, and the woman's sphere. In analyzing the western attitude toward the woman playwright, British dramatist Kathleen Betsko spells out the deeply embedded cultural code that links perceptions of certain women's roles with fears about social control:

> The drama is, after all, the most public of arts. The author lurks unseen with godlike powers, able to shove living, breathing human beings around on stage, able to 'bump them off' at will, capable of making us cry or gasp out loud or otherwise embarrass ourselves in front of others. . . . And herein likes the dramatic rub. It has never been acceptable in the past (and still isn't very nice today) for women to make a fuss in public, on or off the stage. So one can understand—if not approve—the tendency to keep the ladies in the pews and out of the pulpit, where they are capable of considerable damage when out of control. (452)

And as the organizers of the First International Women Playwrights Conference, in 1988, observed: "[A]n important play often confronts the status quo, defies the establishment and shocks its audience into reconsidering accepted norms and stereotypes. As a rule, women who confront and defy and shock are judged harshly in all societies" (France and Corso xii).[5]

Such conditions pervade traditional societies, which are bound to the regulation and enforcement of social roles, and surely no segment of American culture rates as more traditional in this regard than the South. In the case of the Southern woman playwright, all of the conventional prejudices reign and are intensified by the region's peculiar problematizing of its women and their art. To speak of the Southern woman conjures a mythological type, that social icon of refinement and poise and restraint: the Southern Lady. As Anne Goodwyn Jones notes, although she bears much in common with nineteenth-century British and American notions of "true womanhood," "the Southern lady" is special in that she is a creature "at the core of a region's self-definition" (4): "The lady, with her grace and hospitality, seemed the flower of a uniquely southern civilization, the embodiment of all it prized most deeply—a generosity of spirit, a love for beauty" (3). The tradition of the Southern Lady thus establishes a unique challenge for women writers. Jones explains, "The woman writer in the South . . . participates in a tradition that defines her ideal self in ways that must inevitably conflict with her very integrity as an artist: voicelessness, passivity, ignorance" (39–40).[6] Indeed, although the mythology here perhaps dictates that we think first of *white* Southern women, the situation of the black Southern woman playwright might be cast in similar terms. Dominant Southern traditions have rendered her too as voiceless, passive, and ignorant—albeit with the difference that these expectations have never been so much veiled or euphemized as they have been made explicit.[7]

Despite the remarkable generations of women who have met this challenge and written exceptional books—including those artists, black and white, who have "refuse[d] to stay in their place [and] upset the whole shebang" by rejecting certain basic conventions of Southern literary tradition (Segrest 354)—the ironic consequence of the region's idolization of its women has been the trivialization or neglect of women's voices in Southern literature. As the editors of the recent collection *Southern Women's Writing: Colonial to Contemporary* note, standard anthologies and critical texts from the beginnings of the formal study of Southern literature to the present "all give a slim overview of the women's tradition in the South" (Weaks and Perry xiii). In fact, as absurd as it may sound to anyone entering the field today, that there *is* a "women's tradition" in Southern writing worthy of scholarly inquiry was itself a radical notion until recently. In his new book *Inventing Southern Literature,* an iconoclastic critique of the establishment of the field of Southern literary studies, Michael Kreyling observes the "gendered character" of "so many Southern literary projects" (100), and finds that even when writing by women has been admitted into colloquy—as in the cases of Ellen Glasgow or Elizabeth Madox Roberts—critics, predominately white and male, have discussed those works by measuring them according to "a paradigm that negates [the writers'] gender by appearing to transcend it" (104). Traditional criticism never takes into account that certain books were written by women, much less women of color, and that this fact might influence our readings of them. Kreyling cites Louis D. Rubin Jr.'s preface to the widely used 1979 anthology *The Literary South* as a representative expression of the field's masculine bent: " '[I]n general, the study of Southern Literature has largely involved a community of *scholars and gentlemen* who are *friends and fellow workers,* and it has been a privilege to be part of this activity,' " Rubin wrote, before going on to thank twenty-two of those "scholars and gentlemen," "friends and fellow-workers"—all male—by name (qtd. in Kreyling 100, emphasis added).

For women writers of fiction and poetry, this situation began to change in the early 1980s, inspired in large part by Jones's book, *Tomorrow is Another Day: The Woman Writer in the South, 1859–1936* (1981). Now, as even a cursory review of the scholarship will confirm, gender is one of the fundamental, thriving areas of inquiry in Southern literary studies. In his introduction to *The Future of Southern Letters,* editor John Lowe asserts, "Without question, many of the very best and/or most popular contemporary writers from the region are female, African-American, or both" (7). But in an exasperating example of the problem I am attempting to delineate here, although Lowe himself briefly mentions Beth Henley twice, his contributors do not provide a single extended observation on a single Southern woman playwright—indeed, nothing on drama at all save an occasional reference to Horton Foote.[8]

To date, the most concentrated scholarly attention ever accorded Southern women's drama is a 1987 special issue of the *Southern Quarterly* for which guest editor Milly S. Barranger assembled essays on "four generations of women writing for the American stage" (7)—Hellman, Carson McCullers, Alice Childress, Norman, Henley, and Sandra Deer—who "demonstrate an awareness of their southern roots" (8) and who "are creating [a] presence for women both real and fictive in a contemporary renascence of southern playwrighting" (9). Insightful as these essays remain, we cannot fail to notice that they are now more than ten years old; with the surge in attention to other kinds of writing by Southern women, they should have been followed by more work on the drama. Particularly at the level of regional and community theater, something of an unheralded renascence in the Southern theater has in fact occurred, and women have led the way. As Cindy Lutenbacher points out (in yet another decade-old essay), "theatre women in the South are in the very thick of a theatrical vision so compelling, potent and simple that it offers nothing less hopeful than a general overhaul of theatre in the South" (253). Some of these women have attained national as well as international prominence—how many people realize that *four* women who recently have won Pulitzers for drama claim Southern roots (Henley, Norman, Paula Vogel, and Margaret Edson)?—while many more, such as the women involved with organizations like the Atlanta-based Alternate ROOTS (Regional Organization of Theatres South), are participating in an ongoing community-oriented revival of theater arts whose vitality and influence promise to exceed that of its predecessor, the regional folk-drama movement of the 1920s and 1930s.[9]

In our scholarship and in our teaching, we have failed to acknowledge this vitality. But we should, and we must consider the ways, both historical and contemporary, that Southern women's drama has contributed to the thriving literary and cultural climate of the South. Unquestionably, it has. Consider the scores of plays written and seen into production by not just Hellman, Henley, and Norman, but by Jo Carson, Alice Childress, Pearl Cleage, Sandra Deer, Elizabeth Dewberry, Bernice Kelly Harris, Zora Neale Hurston, Georgia Johnson, Barbara Lebow, the pseudonymous Jane Martin, May Miller, Carson McCullers, Suzan-Lori Parks, Regina Porter, Rebecca Ranson, Regina Taylor, Paula Vogel, Naomi Wallace, and Billie Jean Young, to name only a very few. If many of these names are unfamiliar to us—or the familiar ones, such as Hurston and McCullers, are unknown to us in the field of drama—that is because conventional prejudices alone, not their art, have kept them and their plays out of the critical conversations that determine merit and significance. We don't know the ways and degrees to which works by these playwrights might be not just average or good but excellent, and until more regular and sustained study begins, our conversations about the South's literature will continue to be poorer for that ignorance. Let the current volume stand as an invitation to begin this work.

Notes

1. In the past few years, several excellent anthologies have been published in an attempt to recover the history of American women's drama. Notable among these are Amelia Howe Kritzer's *Plays by Early American Women, 1775–1850* (Ann Arbor: U of Michigan P, 1995); Kathy A. Perkins's *Black Female Playwrights: An Anthology of Plays before 1950* (Bloomington: Indiana UP, 1989); and Judith E. Barlow's two collections,

Plays by American Women, 1900–1930 (New York: Applause, 1985) and *Plays by American Women, 1930–1960* (New York: Applause, 1994).

2. Part of the cause for this problem is the American playwright's perennial interest in "domestic realism"—a genre which, though important, contradicts elite definitions of art as complex and therefore accessible only to those whose educations and/or cultural experiences have prepared them to "interpret" it. As Gerald Berkowitz has argued, "Whatever the deeper meanings of an American play, on one solid level it is about love and marriage, or earning a living, or dealing with a family crisis. . . . [T]he insight becomes more than merely technical. . . . A national literature of plays set in living rooms is a deeply democratic literature, one that assumes that the important subjects are those that manifest themselves in the daily lives of ordinary people" (3). In a recent essay June Schlueter finds domestic realism, with its assumption "that the nuclear family is the structural given of the American theater," outdated (12). She examines plays by Sam Shepard, Beth Henley, Arthur Miller, and Edward Albee to suggest "a readiness on the part of American playwrights to respond to social change and artistic challenge and to admit that, in the coming century, domestic realism, despite its ideological attractions, can no longer serve as the dominant paradigm" (24–25).

3. Watson's *The History of Southern Drama* (1997) is the first attempt to present "a comprehensive history of the subject . . . from the plays of Robert Munford in the 1770s to those of current dramatists such as Horton Foote and Beth Henley" (ix). Although admirable in many ways, Watson's very aspiration to comprehensiveness seems to limit his attention to lesser-known playwrights, such as the women treated in this collection. Hellman is treated in a chapter of her own, and Zora Neale Hurston, Georgia Johnson, Beth Henley, and Marsha Norman receive adequate treatment—but not Carson McCullers or Alice Childress, much less playwrights of emerging significance, like Regina Porter and Naomi Wallace, who are not discussed at all.

4. Such neglect implies that drama is absent from Southern literary history because it has not been good enough to merit attention alongside the works of our best writers of fiction and poetry. A 1930 editorial for *Theater Magazine* reads like a dramatist's echo of Mencken's indictment of the Sahara of the Bozart: "Though famous as a cradle of beautiful letters, from which its sons and daughters spring to eminence as authors, editors, and critics, the South has failed to produce so far a native playwright able to dispel the drama's cheap assumption that Dixie is a land of mammy-thumpers, monkey-baiters, and Heflins, necktie parties and julep-tossers. Its Proustian nostalgia for times past, its paradox of two civilizations, its tragical disillusion are all smothered on the stage in the cartoon of a slouch hat and tattered frock coat" (Anderson 47). A more likely explanation for the neglect—and one that many serious commentators have allowed (e.g., Watson 7–8)—is the remoteness of the South from the traditional hub of theatrical creativity, New York City. Achievements in the drama remain unknown as long as plays remain unperformed and thus undiscussed.

5. The potential for repercussions is greatest for those who challenge the conventions of a masculinist mainstream theater by writing plays that interrogate the theoreti-

cal underpinnings of realism by exploring feminist themes and dramatic techniques. (Adrienne Kennedy, Emily Mann, and Paula Vogel come immediately to mind.) More than one scholar has argued that the theater establishment's commitment to realism, or at least to less-experimental forms in general, "have contributed greatly to the repression and suppression of women's creative efforts" (Gavin 6). Burke provides an excellent overview of feminist theater; see also Sue-Ellen Case's important primer *Feminism and Theater* (New York: Methuen, 1988), and for analyses of the feminist conflict with realism, Jeanie Forte's "Realism, Narrative, and the Feminist Playwright: A Problem of Reception" (*Modern Drama* 32 [1989], 115–27) and Janet Haedicke's "Margins in the Mainstream: Contemporary Women Playwrights" (*Realism and the American Dramatic Tradition,* Ed. William W. Demastes [Tuscaloosa: U of Alabama P, 1996], 203–17).

6. Jones acknowledges historian Anne Firor Scott as a major influence on her thinking about the Southern woman writer; Scott's *The Southern Lady: From Pedestal to Politics, 1830–1930* (Chicago: U of Chicago P, 1970) remains an indispensable source on its topic.

7. For a study of the development of African American drama, see Leslie Catharine Sanders's *The Development of a Black Theater in America* (Baton Rouge: Louisiana State UP, 1988). Kathy Perkins's much-cited anthology (mentioned in note one above) includes the work of three playwrights with Southern connections (Georgia Douglas Johnson, Zora Neale Hurston, and May Miller) as well as a stimulating bibliography, "Plays and Pageants by Black Women before 1950."

8. For example, similar distortions appear in such important scholarly works as Robert Bain and Joseph M. Flora's source book *Contemporary Poets, Dramatists, Essayists, and Novelists of the South,* which includes information on three women playwrights out of just six dramatists in the total of forty-nine authors covered. And in recent anthologies of Southern women's writing (e.g., Weaks and Perry; Mee) women's drama is not under-but completely *un*represented.

9. Five of the plays in Kathie deNobriga and Valetta Anderson's anthology *Alternate Roots: Plays from the Southern Theater* (Portsmouth, NH: Heinemann, 1994) are written or coauthored by women.

Works Cited

Anderson, John. "' . . . Look Away, Dixieland.'" *Theater Magazine* 52 (Dec. 1930): 47, 62.

Barranger, Milly S. "Southern Playwrights: A Perspective on Women Writers." *Southern Quarterly* 25.3 (1987): 5–9.

Berkowitz, Gerald M. *American Drama of the Twentieth Century.* London: Longman, 1992.

Betsko, Kathleen. Afterword. Betsko and Koenig 451–61.

Betsko, Kathleen, and Rachel Koenig, eds. *Interviews with Contemporary Women Playwrights.* New York: Morrow, 1987.

Burke, Sally. *American Feminist Playwrights: A Critical History.* New York: Twayne, 1997.

France, Anna Kay, and P. J. Corso, eds. *International Women Playwrights: Voices of Identity and Transformation.* Proceedings of the First International Women Playwrights Conference, October 18–23, 1988. Metuchen, NJ: Scarecrow, 1993.

Friedan, Betty. *The Feminine Mystique.* 1963. New York: Laurel, 1984.

Gavin, Christy. *American Women Playwrights, 1964–1989: A Research Guide and Annotated Bibliography.* New York: Garland, 1993.

Hubbell, Jay B. *The South in American Literature, 1607–1900.* Durham: Duke UP, 1954.

Jones, Anne Goodwyn. *Tomorrow Is Another Day: The Woman Writer in the South, 1859–1936.* Baton Rouge: Louisiana State UP, 1981.

Kreyling, Michael. *Inventing Southern Literature.* Jackson: UP of Mississippi, 1998.

Lowe, John. Introduction. *The Future of Southern Letters.* Ed. Jefferson Humphries and John Lowe. New York: Oxford UP, 1996. 3–19.

Lutenbacher, Cindy. "'So much more than just myself': Women Theater Artists in the South." *Themes in Drama* 11 (1989): 253–63.

Mee, Susie, ed. *Downhome: An Anthology of Southern Women Writers.* San Diego: Harvest, 1995.

Rubin, Louis D., Jr., et al., eds. *The History of Southern Literature.* Baton Rouge: Louisiana State UP, 1985.

Rubin, Louis D., Jr., and Robert D. Jacobs, eds. *South: Modern Southern Literature in Its Cultural Setting.* Garden City, NY: Dolphin, 1961.

Schlueter, June. "Domestic Realism: Is It Still Possible on the American Stage?" *South Atlantic Review* 64 (Winter 1999): 11–25.

Segrest, Mab. "Southern Women Writing: Toward a Literature of Wholeness." Weaks and Perry 346–64.

Smith, Susan Harris. *American Drama: The Bastard Art.* New York: Cambridge UP, 1997.

Watson, Charles S. *The History of Southern Drama.* Lexington: U of Kentucky P, 1997.

Weaks, Mary Louise, and Carolyn Perry, eds. *Southern Women's Writing: Colonial to Contemporary.* Gainesville: UP of Florida, 1995.

"Where Are the Women Playwrights?" *New York Times* 20 May 1973: B1, 3.

Woolf, Virginia. "Professions for Women." 1942. *Daughters of the Revolution: Classic Essays by Women.* Ed. James D. Lester. Lincolnwood, IL: NTC Publishing Group, 1996. 36–42.

2

"Let the People Sing!": Zora Neale Hurston and the Dream of a Negro Theater

John Lowe

Zora Neale Hurston has recently emerged as a major figure in the American literary canon after years of obscurity. One sees her image on the murals at Barnes and Noble bookstores, alongside James Joyce and Virginia Woolf. Her stature thus far, however, has stemmed from her success as a novelist, especially as the author of *Their Eyes Were Watching God* (1937), now one of the most-taught books in American literary history. Most readers know little about her other work, except perhaps her oft-criticized autobiography, *Dust Tracks on a Road* (1942), and two often anthologized short stories.

Throughout her life, like Henry James before her, Hurston had a burning ambition to be a successful playwright. None of her plays were produced, however, during her lifetime, and only in 1991, when the play she co-authored with Langston Hughes, *Mule Bone,* had its Broadway debut, did most fans even know that she had written for the theater. One of her first publications, in fact, was a play, and she never gave up trying to mount dramatic productions that would form the opening wedge of "authentic Negro theatre."[1]

As a preacher's daughter, Hurston came by her dramatic gifts naturally. John Hurston, born a slave, overcame his humble origins by marrying Lucy Potts, the daughter of a well-to-do farmer, and by heeding a "call" from God. A strapping man, he cast a compelling figure in the pulpit and made the most of his booming voice and musical gifts. Zora Neale was born either on January 7th or January 15, 1891, in Notasulga, Alabama, not far from Booker T. Washington's Tuskegee Institute. She was the sixth of John and Lucy's brood; subsequently three more sons were born after the family relocated to Eatonville, an all-black town in central Florida, in the early 1890s. Throughout her life, Hurston boasted of having the map of Dixie on her tongue and always insisted that she was a Southerner through and through. It is hardly surprising that the plays she wrote exude many characteristics of Southern expression, in particular, and culture, in general.

Hurston's apparently happy life fell apart in 1904 when her mother died. Not getting along with her stepmother, she eventually left Florida as a lady's maid for a traveling Gilbert and Sullivan company, thus inaugurating her theatrical experiences. After a series of jobs and a sequence of college courses at Morgan State and Howard University, Hurston won a scholarship to Barnard College, where she studied with Ruth Benedict and Franz Boas, the founders of American anthropology. While in New York, she also met the leading figures of the "New Negro" literary movement, and soon became one of the leading "niggerati," as she called them herself. One of her several contributions to the "Harlem Renaissance," as it became known, was a play, *Color Struck,* which she submitted along with another play, *Spears* (since lost), to *Opportunity* magazine's annual literary contest. *Color Struck* won second prize, eventually getting published in a short-lived magazine, *Fire!!* (1926).

The next year, when asked to contribute a piece to Charles S. Johnson's *Ebony and Topaz: A Collectanea,* an anthology of black writing, Hurston provided *The First One: A Play in One Act,* an imaginative retelling of the story of Noah and his son Ham. Set in the Valley of Ararat three years after the flood, the play features Noah, his wife, their sons Shem, Japheth, and Ham, Eve (Ham's wife), and the sons' wives and children.

Meanwhile, the playwright continued her education at Columbia. Encouraged by Boas, she began a series of trips to Florida to gather folklore materials. This work was facilitated for years by the sponsorship of a wealthy white woman, Mrs. Osgood Mason, who supported the careers of a few of Hurston's gifted friends, such as writers Langston Hughes and Alain Locke, as well as the musician Hall Johnson, who was active in the Broadway theater. All of them called Mrs. Mason "Godmother."

Hurston and Hughes became close friends, and became enthused with the idea of founding a vernacular theater and opera based on "*real* Negro" life. Over a period of months, they worked on a three-act play entitled *Mule Bone,* which was based on a short story by Hurston. Eventually, however, in a complicated series of events, the authors had a permanent "falling out" and the play was never published or produced during the authors' lifetimes.

In the early thirties, Hurston constructed a series of plays depicting life in rural black communities and work camps. Written versions of these have not survived, but Hurston did write down a one-act play that was part of a performance of *From Sun to Sun* at Rollins College in 1933. Never published, "The Fiery Chariot," now in the Hurston Collection of the University of Florida, creates a seven-page drama out of an old folktale.

During the thirties, Hurston spent most of her time writing three novels, *Jonah's Gourd Vine* (1934), *Their Eyes Were Watching God* (1937), and *Moses, Man of the Mountain* (1939); and two books of folklore, *Mules and Men* (1935) and *Tell My Horse* (1938). In between novels, Hurston's intermittent theatrical ventures helped her secure a position with the Federal Theatre Project; she helped organize a Harlem division for the program, but she left New York in 1936 to gather folklore as a Guggenheim Fellow. She mostly wrote nonfiction in the forties and fifties, publishing an autobiography, *Dust Tracks on a Road* (1942), and a final novel, *Seraph on the Suwanee* (1948). Another full-length play, *Polk County: A Comedy of Negro Life on a Sawmill Camp with Authentic Negro Music in Three Acts,* was written in collaboration with Dorothy Waring and copyrighted in 1944, but has never been published or produced.[2] During this period, Hurston made several other efforts to further her yearning to succeed as a dramatist. In 1931 she was hired to write some skits for a black musical review, *Fast and Furious,* which was produced by Forbes Randolph and opened at the New York Theatre on September 15, 1931. Appearing as a pom-pom girl in a football skit, she also helped direct the show, which folded after a week. Her next theatrical adventure was writing skits for the revue *Jungle Scandals* (1931), which also closed quickly. Hurston had nothing but scorn for the white-dominated "Negro" musicals being produced on Broadway. Seeing an opportunity to correct their errors with a musical of her own, she accordingly sought out Hall Johnson, who had directed the chorus of the wildly successful *Green Pastures* (1931). Hurston thought that play, written by a white man, Marc Connelly, provided a dreadful hash of black culture. Conversely, she felt Johnson was master of his craft and could help her mount *authentic* folk narratives. She decided to set a single day in a railroad work camp to music; at first she thought of calling it *Spunk,*[3] but settled on *The Great Day.* Johnson worked on the project desultorily but finally withdrew, only to filch some of Hurston's material for his production, *Run Little Chillun,* which opened to favorable reviews in 1931.

Hurston nevertheless persevered, pawning some of her possessions to raise funds and wheedling the final backing from Godmother. Presented at New York's John Golden Theater on January 10, 1932, the musical used a concert format, and Alain Locke wrote the program notes. In Part One, the audience saw workers arising and going to the job; singing work songs as they laid track; returning to their homes where their children played folk games; and listening to a preacher's sermon accompanied by spirituals. Part Two presented an evening's entertainment at the local "jook" (nightclub), consisting mainly of blues songs, ending with half the cast doing a blues song while the other half sings *Deep River*. No theatrical producer came forward to offer an extended run, and the show lost money, even though it attracted a good crowd and favorable reviews. Godmother refused to allow Zora to produce the play again, and also forbade the theatrical use of other portions of *Mules and Men*. Hurston did succeed in mounting an edited version of *The Great Day* at Manhattan's New School on March 29, 1932; a program survives, and *Theatre Arts* published a photo of the cast.

The next year, back home in Florida, Hurston and her friend Robert Wunsch of the Rollins College English Department produced a January performance of the revised musical to great acclaim, using a new title, *From Sun to Sun*, with a second performance given in February. In this form, the musical was mounted in a number of other cities in Florida, including Eatonville. Two years later Hurston repeated the show in abbreviated concert form at Fisk University in Nashville and followed with a performance in Chicago, using still another title, *Singing Steel*, and casting it with aspiring singers from the YWCA. Once again the show got good reviews, but more importantly, officials from the Rosenwald Foundation, impressed by Hurston's research, offered to sponsor her return to Columbia to work on a Ph.D. in anthropology. We have no script for these musicals, but the Library of Congress owns tapes of many of the musical numbers. A version was pieced together for performance at the 1993 Zora Neale Hurston Festival of the Arts in Eatonville.

Hurston was hired by Bethune-Cookman College in 1934 to found a school of dramatic arts, one "based on pure Negro expression," and to write a pageant commemorating the school's anniversary. Instead, after mounting a performance of her standard, *From Sun to Sun*, she left the college after inevitable bridling under the dictates of the school's powerful president, Mary MacLeod Bethune. While attempting to organize a drama department at North Carolina College in 1939, she studied with the famous white playwright Paul Green in Chapel Hill, who suggested that they collaborate on a play based on the folk trickster High John de Conquer. Hurston also told the Carolina Dramatic Association about her dream of a Negro theater, claiming "our drama must be like us or it doesn't exist" (Hemenway, 255).

Although her novels won critical acclaim and a limited audience in the thirties, Hurston's brand of fiction gradually became eclipsed by that of black "protest" writers such as Richard Wright. In the fifties all of Hurston's books were out of print, and she drifted from job to job while working on various manuscripts. When she died in 1960, she was living in a Florida charity facility.

Never achieving her dream of founding a new "Negro" dramatic movement, the author, nonetheless, had led a highly dramatic life; despite its end, it was rich and productive.

As I have suggested, the most important Hurston play is the collaboration with Langston Hughes, *Mule Bone*. In 1985, Henry Louis Gates Jr. read the drama at Yale and began a campaign to get it produced. It almost didn't happen; a staged reading before one hundred prominent black writers and theater people in 1988 led over half of them to urge that the project be shelved, partly because its humor seemed stereotypical—it made extensive use of vernacular and racial humor, including the word "nigger." Changes duly made, *Mule Bone* finally was brought to the New York stage, opening at the Ethel Barrymore Theatre on February 14, 1991. The play, as performed, was edited and revised by George Houston Bass, Ann Cattaneo, Henry Louis Gates Jr., Arnold Rampersand, and the director Michael Schultz. Taj Mahal provided the musical numbers, which included lyrics drawn from some poems by Hughes. Bass wrote a "frame" story involving Zora herself, who pronounced to the audience that the evening's event was a result of her scientific folklore expeditions.

In both the original and revised versions, the plot stems from Hurston's unpublished short story, "The Bone of Contention," which detailed the falling out of two friends who quarrel over a turkey one of them has shot. In the three-act version, the two friends, Jim Weston, a musician, and Dave Carter, a dancer, form a musical team. They quarrel over a flirtatious local domestic worker, Daisy Taylor, who skillfully plays them off against each other. Eventually, Daisy chooses Jim and demands he take a good job as the white folks' yardman. When Jim refuses, she sidles up to Dave, but he too rejects her, and the play ends with the two men back together, determined to make the town accept them both.

Mule Bone enjoyed only moderate success at the box office, closing on April 14, 1991, after twenty-seven previews and sixty-seven performances. Although a few critics applauded it as funny and historic (Kissel), an "exuberant" theatrical event (Beaufort), and a "wonderful piece of black theatre" (Barnes), it was deemed "an amiable curiosity" (Winer), "one of the American theatre's more tantalizing might-have-beens" (Rich), "pleasant but uneventful" (Wilson), and a "theatrical curio" (Watt) by other critics, who found it charming but dramatically deficient.[4]

Aside from the material surrounding *Mule Bone*'s publication and premiere, some brief commentary by her biographer (Hemenway), and articles by Adele Newsome (on "The Fiery Chariot") and Lynda Hill (on plays that dramatize

Hurston's life and work), virtually nothing has been written on Hurston as a dramatist. One finds some insight into her dramatic program, however, by examining the nature of her few published and several unpublished plays.

Her first, *Color-Struck,* a four-scene melodrama, initially depicts a group boarding a Jim Crow railway car en route to a cake walk contest. The best performers quarrel because Emma, a dark woman, thinks brown-skinned John has been flirting with the mulatto, Effie. Throughout the play, Emma's jealousy and self-hatred keep her from accepting John's love, first at the cakewalk itself, and then later after a twenty-year separation. Recently widowed, John says he chose a dark wife because he longed for Emma, and teases her when he discovers her invalid teenage daughter is nearly white. He tells her he'll stay with the girl while Emma goes for a doctor; Emma doubles back, accusing John of lust for her daughter. John departs and the daughter dies, leaving Emma hopeless and alone. The play's melodrama makes it top-heavy, but it succeeds in suggesting the creativity and exuberance of African American culture in the highly animated cakewalk scenes and in sketching in the parameters of color prejudice within the race.

The First One, Hurston's next play, proved the first of several pieces that the author would set in biblical times, frequently in black dialect. Here, however, Hurston employs standard speech. As the play opens, Noah and everyone else stand fuming because Ham, the wayward son, once again arrives late for the annual commemoration of the delivery from the flood. Ham comes in playing a harp, in dress that links him with both Orpheus and Bacchus. Mrs. Shem criticizes him because Ham doesn't bring an offering and merely tends the flocks and sings, unlike his brothers, who toil in the fields. Noah calls upon Ham to play and sing to help them forget, while he gets drunk to efface the image of the dead faces that float by the ark.

When Ham, also inebriated, laughingly reports on his father's nakedness in the tent, Shem's jealous wife wakes Noah, reporting the deed but not the identity of the perpetrator. Noah, enraged, roars that "His skin shall be black. . . . He and his seed forever. He shall serve his brothers and they shall rule over him." Appalled, all involved try to reverse the curse, but Ham comes in laughing, unaware that he has been turned black. His son has changed color as well. Noah banishes them, fearing the contagion of blackness. Ham, rather than showing dismay, laughs cynically, saying, "Oh, remain with your flocks and fields and vineyards, to covet, to sweat, to die and know no peace. I go to the sun." Two notions here seem noteworthy: first, a race begins because of its founding father's joke, and second, the ending suggests that "The First [black]

One" surpasses whites by knowing how to lead a fully imagined and creative life. As such, Hurston's playlet embraces and inverts the traditional interpretation of the biblical passage.

Mule Bone's slight central plot concerns a love triangle formed by Jim, his partner Dave, and Daisy. The real voice in the play, however, belongs to the community. The men on Joe Clarke's porch and the women who stroll by offer a continual stream of commentary on the triangle, tell jokes and stories, and play local card games and checkers. Even children contribute, playing out classic African American folk games for the audience. A political parallel to these innocent contests emerges in the Reverend Simms's public campaign to unseat Joe Clarke as Mayor.

The triangular melodrama merges with folk spectacle when Jim (a Methodist) knocks out Dave (a Baptist) with a mule bone. The community takes sides according to their religious denominations, and Act Two largely consists of Jim's "trial," held at the Macedonia Baptist Church, presided over by Mayor Clarke. His leadership is challenged by Reverend Simms, who later spars with Reverend Childers. Their rivalry in turn finds a comic match in the hilarious duel between the Methodist Sister Lewis and the Baptist Sister Taylor, who "signify" on each other to beat the band, seemingly setting off various other quarrels. A continuing joke is the general ineffectiveness of the town marshall, Lum Boger, to coerce anyone, of any denomination. The latter proves that the mule bone is indeed a dangerous weapon by quoting Samson's story from the Bible. Clarke rules that Dave be banished for two years.

Although the love narrative of *Mule Bone* provokes slight interest, the richly detailed, boisterous interaction of the folk—especially in the "duels" of the second act—creates one of the most vibrant communal dramatizations in American theater, while simultaneously preserving for posterity the idioms, humor, and creativity of a largely vanished small-town culture.

Although *The Fiery Chariot* by contrast offers a sketch on a much reduced canvas, it too aims at presenting and preserving elements of African American folk culture. The action takes place in a slave cabin, where Ike, tired of his toil for "Massa," prays every night for God to come get him in his fiery chariot. Ole Massa overhears this and appears before the door wearing a sheet, claiming to be the Lord, and creating a series of comic maneuvers culminating in Ike's bolting out and away. Although the play builds on an old comic tradition, it has serious undertones. Ike prays for death because Ole Massa works him so hard; Ole Massa's decision to take Ike's wife Dinah instead verges toward the habit actual owners had of appropriating the bodies of their female slaves.

Finally, Ike's clever escape links him with the heroics of the legendary trickster slave, High John de Conquer.

Hurston's second three-act play, *Polk County,* lacks a compelling story line, but demonstrates that the author never gave up trying to achieve her dream of the "real Negro theatre" as she had outlined to Hughes in 1928: "we shall act out the folk tales, however short, with the abrupt angularity and naivete of the primitive 'bama Nigger." Like *Mule Bone* before it, *Polk County* attempts to meet this goal with a combination of humor, folklore, and music, and a large cast—sixteen named characters and many others play parts. Hurston, obviously profiting from her experiences with *From Sun to Sun,* included twenty-seven vocal and instrumental numbers. The first act provides exposition, first by using song and ritual to demonstrate the breaking of day in the camp, including a conversation between a rooster and his hens. Virtually all the human characters reprise roles they played in Hurston's book of folklore, *Mules and Men* (1934), and thus are presumably based in fact. The simple story line centers on a mulatto, Leafy Lee, who has wandered down from New York hoping to learn the blues; this device runs throughout the play, furnishing the rationale for the insertion of most of the musical numbers. Big Sweet, the dominant character in the camp, befriends Leafy, using her fists and knife to protect her and to maintain order when the white Bossman isn't around. Similar to Ike in "The Fiery Chariot," she finds inspiration in the example of the legendary hero, High John de Conquer. Although she can physically dispatch any enemy, her arsenal of verbal taunts makes her truly formidable and entertaining, the comic dynamo of the play.

Big Sweet's man Lonnie "friends" with My Honey, a guitar player sought after by Dicey, a sour, scheming, dark-complexioned woman. Significantly, her plans find temporary success only when she can involve the white Quarters Boss. Despite her role as villain, Dicey resembles the despairing Emma of *Color-Struck* in her bitterness over color.

When Dicey's plot to set the other characters against each other fails, Leafy and My Honey marry, setting a new standard that the other characters intend to imitate. Their courtship throughout the play has a communal dimension, affording much commentary from the cast on the nature of love. Leafy, as initiate into the community's lore, parallels the role Zora herself played in Polk County in *Mules and Men.*

As in *Mule Bone,* children play typical African American games as part of the display of everyday life in the Quarter, and central scenes are communal. While *Mule Bone* focuses on the Methodist/Baptist quarrel that accompanies

Jim's "trial," here the chief battles take place in the Quarters' jook, which Hurston describes elaborately, and in the woods, where Ella Wall's hoodoo fails to conjure Leafy and My Honey's marriage. Amazingly, the generally realistic play fuses with the expressionistic ending: a huge rainbow descends and all get on board, plates in hand, with Lonnie singing, "I ride the rainbow, when I see Jesus." The curtain falls as the rainbow ascends.

A few years ago, news came that a cache of previously unknown and un-published plays of Hurston's had been located in Washington. These plays fur-ther testify to the renegade role that the author played during the Renaissance. As she said in *Dust Tracks*, "LET THE PEOPLE SING, was and is my motto," and putting on shows such as *From Sun to Sun*, full of African American song, dance, and folk games seemed one way to do it. Her drama was to demonstrate as well that "There is no *The Negro* here. Our lives are so diversified, internal attitudes so varied, appearances and capabilities so different, that there is no possible classification so catholic that is will cover us all, except My people! My people!" (*Dust Tracks*, 237).

One of the most delightful of the new finds is *Cold Keener* (1930), a nine-skit work that begins at a filling station on the Georgia-Alabama line. Very much like one of the comedy skits in the fabled Rabbit Foot Circuit that toured the South, *Keener* features a series of jokes loosely strung together around slip-shod service at the station. The state line setting permits verbal dueling between Ala-bama and Georgia residents, such as the following:

"How's you Georgy folks starvin'?"
"Starvin'? Who ever heard tell of anybody starvin' in Georgy—people so fat in Georgy till I speck Gabriel gointuh have to knock us in de head on judgment day so we kin go long wid de rest."
Ford Driver: "He might have to knock some of them Georgy crackers in de head, but you niggers will be all ready and waitin' for de trumpet."
"How come?"
"Cause dem crackers y'all got over there sho is hard on zigaboos."
"Lemme tell *you* something, coon. We got *nice* white folks in Georgy! But them Alabama red-necks is too mean to give God a honest prayer with-out snatchin' back amen!"
"Who mean? I know you ain't talkin' 'bout them white folks in *my* state. Alabama is de best state in de world. If you can't git along there, you can't get along nowhere. But in Georgy they hates niggers so bad till one day they lynched a black mule for kickin' a white one."

Hurston also includes a classic about laughing:

"Well, they tell me they don't 'low y'all niggers to laugh on de streets in Georgy. They got laughin' barrels on certain corners for niggers, and when you gets tickled you got to hold it till you can make it to one of them barrels and stick yo' head in. Then you can cut loose. Laughin' any old place just ain't allowed."
"Well, over in Alabama, if they tell a funny joke in the theatre, y'all ain't allowed to laugh till the white folks git through."

Many of the jokes echo the old duels between slaves who bragged on how good their masters were, but as they extend into a debate about the merits of Fords and Chevrolets they perhaps gave the audience a source of pride, since both combatants own cars. They involve comic hyperbole too, such as the claim that the new Fords will have a lawyer in the tool box—"as soon as you have a collision, the lawyer will spring right out and begin to collect damages." The Chevy owner claims Lindbergh flew to Paris in a Chevy, bringing current events into the exchange. As is usual, the humor keeps the two men from coming to blows, although they pick up wrenches and jack handles as they talk. The Proprietor separates them at the end and they drive off, saying they'll be back with guns, thus leaving with honor on both sides. The tale seems meant for a black audience in the South, and it never sags—it shows Hurston at her signifying best, knitting together bits and pieces of African American humor, some topical, some classic, all of it demonstrating the man of words thinking on his feet to beat the band.

"Cock Robin," set in "any city" on a "street in colored town" depicts the shooting of Cock Robin with three arrows. Most of the characters are supposedly birds, and Cock Robin gets shot because he was messing with Mrs. Sparrow. Her husband found out because some blue eggs started appearing in the nest. Soon other birds get nervous:

Jaybird: (Begins to pick feathers violently) "Now, you done got me to scratchin' where I don't itch—come to think of it, I done seen two or three blue eggs in *my* nest." Just then Mrs. Crow lays a blue egg in front of her husband and all the others!

The "funeralizin'" arrangements demand a choice of hall, and all the "lodges" vie for the honor. It turns out that Cock Robin belonged to all of them, too. Jaybird says, for instance, "He was Superior Subordinate Exalted Contaminator in the Personal Parading Jay Birds." Fish adds, "We certainly going to put a word in, cause he was a Bottom Ruler in the order of The Never Been Caught Fishes." The debate escalates into a dueling "parade," as the orders indicate how they'll put Cock Robin away, replete with sample "struts" that show how they'll "spread their junk." Owl, the judge, decrees that whoever pays the bills wins. Profound silence ensues, and Crow offers, "Well, brothers and sisters, since we'se all here at one time, you know Sister Speckled Hen is having a grand barbecue and fish fry down on Front Street and Beale—why not let's have one grand consolidated, amalgamated fraternall parade down to her place and enjoy the consequences," and they all strut off leaving Cock Robin where he is. Hurston would set this again in her sketch "Cock Robin Beale Street."

"Heaven," the third sketch, was perhaps a small correction of the play Hurston hated, Marc Connelly's *The Green Pastures.* She draws on the old comic tradition that one finds in virtually all ethnic groups, the story of St. Peter's admitting people to heaven. Depicted at the intersection of Hallelujah Avenue and Amen Street in front of the Pearly Gates, Jim, a recent arrival killed by the Johnstown Flood, brags about the high water to an old man. "Aw shucks, you ain't seen no water," returns the old man, who turns out to be Noah. Flying recklessly around Heaven in his new wings, despite the warning of the angels, Jim soon gets his wings repossessed after several disastrous crashes. Nonetheless, he confesses, "I don't keer. I was a flyin' fool when I had 'em," a line which provides one version of a classic joke that often ends, "I flew some."

Sketches of new thematic interest coincide with threads of tales already known. For instance, with characters immersed in a Florida swamp, "Mr. Frog" is an enactment of the song of Mr. Frog marrying Miss Mousie. Most interesting of the sketches, however, is "Lenox Avenue," set at the intersection of Lenox and 135th Street, the heart of Harlem. It begins with a joking exchange between a black policeman and a stereotypical gay man with a knitting bag. The next attraction features a comic duel between an errant husband and his angry wife that ends happily, nevertheless. A street preacher/con man and his accomplice "sisters" harangue the crowd until the officer drives them away, too. Then, two men ogle a woman: "man if these new styles keep on the way they're going, we'll find out that the snake's got hips." A female duo appears, one "small and doll-like and the other . . . tall and masculine. They stroll across, arm in arm. The two men glare, then one says, Well, Bo, I still got this consolation—ain't nobody but a man and the holy ghost been the father of a family yet." Then comes a joke about a guy who's been studying at Columbia so as to find a way to get to Brooklyn, a typical New York joke still told today. The play ends with a woman leaving her husband, who tries to stop her: "If you stick your rusty foot in *my* face you going to jail. . . . Cause there's a cop right there on the corner and I'm going to holler like a pretty white woman!"

The sketch ends there—not much to it—but it proudly runs through the litany of Harlem "types," as they all parade before the policeman, a kind of impresario of entertainers. The scene offers a comic rendition of the panorama King Solomon Gillis sees when he emerges for the first time from the subway's womb in Rudolph Fisher's paradigmatic Harlem tale, "City of Refuge," as Hurston initially set her play on this very same street corner.

"House that Jack Built" introduces a comic sketch of a rural school featuring De Otis Blunt, an unruly student who nevertheless "caps" all the other students after they recite folk rhymes (many of them comic) with a heroic rendition of the repeating cycle, "House that Jack Built." In addition to featuring the rich rhymes of African American culture, the skit makes the students look quite crafty, and the "bad boy" tops them all with his masterful memory and performance, a classic of oral culture.

"Bahamas" is another Harlem sketch, also set, initially, at 135th Street and Lenox Avenue, where Good Black hears from Joe Wiley about the latter's planned voyage to Africa with The Emperor Jones via the Bahamas. The sketch appears to be a satire of Marcus Garvey. The Emperor, surrounded by a pretentious court, proclaims he's going to kick Britain, France, and Belgium out of Africa and install ambassadors in Europe *and* a "black house" side by side with the White House in Washington. The second scene, in a grove in the Bahamas, features Bahamian songs, chants, and dancing, all taken from Hurston's research there. The sketch ends with the announcement that the boat is now leaving for Africa.

"Railroad Camp" features many of the work songs and dramatic scenes Hurston would use in her various musicals, especially *Sun to Sun*. Although there is some comic exchange with the water boy, most of the skit is devoted to songs, mostly about work and women.

"Jook" is set in a sawmill club. Nunkie plays the piano as couples dance; Draw-leg enters and starts dancing with Bunk's woman Planchita. Other characters, interestingly, are figures in the Harlem story "Muttsy," namely Bluefront, Muttsy himself, and others such as Stack-of-Dollars. Muttsy has just returned from three months on the chain gang that he got for a trumped-up charge. The sketch revolves around card-playing and the comic expressions and exchanges the game generates; these pick up considerably when Big Sweet, a central figure in *Mules and Men,* enters the scene. Sexual rivalry between Ella

Ward and Planchita over Muttsy inspires some nasty signifying right out of *Mules and Men.* A sample: "I'll carry her down just like good gas goes up. Turn me aloose! I'll make her run through a week in two hours." The big set piece is a long description of what the cards mean, beginning with "Ace means the first time that I met you/Deuce means there was nobody there but us two/Trey means the third party, Charlie was his name." When James Presley enters with a guitar the scene is set for some final dancing and singing as the curtain descends. There are several versions of this sketch in the folder, and it is the only part of *Cold Keener* that seems unfinished. One part indicates an alternate ending, with Ella singing an eight-stanza version of "John Henry."

Hurston also wrote a dramatic version of her famous short story, "Spunk," which bears the stamped date of 1935 in the folder, but the play seems of the period of the original story (1925). Here Spunk plays the guitar as well, and the play has many musical interludes. There are many more characters, however, and the story features a "toe-party" where the women line up barefoot behind a curtain and the men bid for them based only on the feet. Here, instead of Lena hooking up with Spunk, we have Ruby Jones. As in the story, however, Lena (here called Evalina) enters the scene on the arm of Jim, her husband. Although she and Spunk flirt, she goes home to her husband. The second act opens with a croquet party, and many comic expressions punctuate the game, such as "You have to play this game. Your talk don't help none. I done belled the buzzard, crowned the crow; got the key to the bushes and I'm bound to go." The dialogue is much more extended, and Lena's affair with Spunk has doubled meaning, for Ruby (not a character in the short story) loves Spunk, too (the other women tease her, claiming she gets as "hot as jail-house coffee everytime you see 'em")—this provides a parallel to the jilted husband Jim. The latter has a root-working father here, too. After Spunk kills Jim, we find him in a chain gang, where the men are singing. Spunk gets a letter saying Lena has found religion and has now left him, which compels him to run away to get to her. The characters discover that the story about Spunk having a wife and child in Bartow was hatched by old man Bishop. Act III again features the community at the start playing croquet. They let us know about Spunk and Lena's wedding and explain how Spunk was excused from the time he had left on the chain gang due to the pull of his white boss.

The play appears quite different from the story too in the powerful conjure scene in which Bishop puts the hex on Spunk. Six men dressed in cat robes attend a death ritual wherein Hodge sheds his skin and rides a giant black cat.

But Bishop himself is killed by a falling log, and Spunk lives on. Lena here is actually married to Spunk and expresses her devotion to him the way Janie talks of Teacake.

The Turkey and the Law (1930) basically parallels *Mule Bone*—and should put to rest the idea that Hughes had much to do with the latter play's content. The structure, however, as with the play *Spunk,* seems looser knit than that of *Mule Bone;* further, we get more folk games and comic bits than in the collaboration with Hughes, where the central plot, whatever its worth, emerges faster and more clearly. As a dramatist, Hurston's bias toward overall cultural representation often hindered the assembly of a lean dramatic story—that is, a focus on individuals.

Although I cannot go into an extended reading of the play, I will note that many of the jokes embedded in it offer oblique references to social and political problems and prospects of the day. This is in the tradition of the literature of indirection that takes its cue from the double-sided postures developed by enslaved Africans for survival and also typifies Hurston's fondness for hitting a straight lick with a crooked stick. Of course, they are also in congruence in this respect with Toomer's more somber narratives and the other great works of the Harlem Renaissance, which must have had an effect on these plays, written at the high point of that seismic literary event.

Despite the development of a virtual Zora cult, we still have a long way to go before arriving at a full appreciation of this great artist. As I noted earlier, it is truly astonishing to discover how much work on her has been based almost entirely on *Their Eyes, Dust Tracks,* a few short stories, and sometimes "Characteristics of Negro Expression." Her other published works and her many still-unpublished papers and manuscripts—and more are discovered each year—have much to reveal about this universally recognized, often praised, but increasingly maligned writer. In this respect she resembles Jean Toomer, who was known until recently only through *Cane,* and who has taken quite a few "hits" lately because of his personal ambivalence about his ethnic identities. The welcome publication of his lost essays, plays, and other pieces has forced us to a new consideration of his place in both the Harlem Renaissance and in the broader realm of diaspora and American literary expressionism and modernism. A parallel reading of Hurston and Toomer's plays shows each writer striving to create an African American theater along modernist lines, yet one that would find a way to include and valorize the race's Southern past. These plays failed to find an immediate audience, but we see their fertilizing effect on virtually every page of *Cane* and Hurston's masterworks of the thirties, abundant proof of the virtues of "acting out."

As these brief descriptions suggest, Hurston devised some inventive dramatizations of African American folk life and customs. White theatrical producers of her time, however, wanted tried and true formulas when they dared present plays with predominantly black casts; they had no interest in experimenting with Hurston's authentic modes. To be fair, though, Hurston's emphasis on group culture and interaction led her to sacrifice a focus on strongly individual central plots, the basic staple of mainstage American theater. Moreover, although she sought to provide an alternative to contemporary, often racist, stereotypes of blacks, today's audiences are likely to find even *her* versions embarrassing throwbacks to an earlier time, when African Americans themselves used forms of address and metaphor that now have been discarded. The fact that *Mule Bone* had to be edited prior to production and then failed to attract an audience offers illustration.

Hurston's fiction has taken a central place in the American literary canon, but few readers yet know much about her plays. When HarperCollins eventually brings out a collected version, as is now planned, it will soon be abundantly clear that Hurston was a playwright of power, imagination, and infectious humor. Her plots, characters, language, and poetic thematics abound with a keen sense of African American folk culture, creativity, and wisdom. In her drama, as in her fiction, she "jumped at the sun" of new forms of literary expression. As we had to do with her fiction, we will have to learn a new form of reading and dramatic production as we catch up with her streaking trajectory. As Americans of all races accelerate their flight from the urban centers, it seems likely that Hurston's fully fleshed characterizations, her plays' small-town settings, situations, and language will find a receptive audience that she never could realize during her own lifetime.

Notes

1. Much of the research in forming this essay has been derived from my prior work on Hurston, notably: *Jump at the Sun: Zora Neale Hurston's Cosmic Comedy.* Urbana: U of Illinois P, 1994; "Zora Neale Hurston, 1891–1960." *American Playwrights, 1880–1945.* Ed. William Demastes. New York: Greenwood P, 1994. 206–13; and "From Mule Bones to Funny Bones: The Plays of Zora Neale Hurston." *Southern Quarterly* 33.2–3 (1995): 65–78. Readers might consult these pieces for additional bibliographic citations.

2. The manuscripts of most of Hurston's plays, published and unpublished, reside in the James Weldon Johnson Collection, Beineke Library, Yale University, and in the collections of The Library of Congress. "The Fiery Chariot" manuscript is in the Hurston Collection of the University of Florida; one version of *Mule-Bone* is at the Moorland-Spingarn Research Center, Howard University. Letters by Hurston, Langston Hughes, and Carl Van Vechten related to *Mule Bone* are also at Yale.

3. Some readers may wonder why I am not discussing the theatrical performances of *Spunk* that were mounted in New York by George Wolfe in 1990, which have been repeated all over the country since then. In fact, these three one-act plays are adaptations by Wolfe of three of Hurston's short stories, and the actual short story she wrote entitled "Spunk" is *not* one of them. Those transformed into the three portions of the performance are, in order of presentation, "Sweat," "Story in Harlem Slang," and "The Gilded Six-Bits."

4. These newspaper reviews of *Mule Bone* were culled from the 1991 edition of the *New York Theatre Critics' Reviews:* John Beaufort, "'Mule Bone' Debuts After 60 Years," *The Christian Science Monitor* (26 Feb. 1991); Clive Barnes, "'Mule Bone' Connected to Funny Bone," *New York Post* (15 Feb. 1991); Howard Kissel, "Folk Comedy Tickles Funny 'Bone,'" *New York Daily News* (15 Feb. 1991); Frank Rich, "A Difficult Birth for 'Mule Bone,'" *New York Times* (15 Feb. 1991): Doug Watt, "Second Thoughts on First Nights," *New York Daily News* (22 Feb. 1991); Edwin Wilson, "Fireworks," *Wall Street Journal* (27 Feb. 1991); Linda Winer, "A Precious Peek at a Lively Legend," *New York Newsday* (15 Feb. 1991).

Works Cited

Hemenway, Robert E. *Zora Neale Hurston: A Literary Biography.* Urbana: U of Illinois P, 1977.

Hill, Lynda. "Staging Hurston's Life and Work." *Acting Out: Feminist Performances.* Ed. Lynda Hart and Peggy Phelan. Ann Arbor: U of Michigan P, 1993. 295–313.

Newson, Adele S. "Fiery Chariot." *Zora Neale Hurston Forum* 1.1 (1986): 32–37.

3

These Four: Hellman's Roots Are Showing

Theresa R. Mooney

Born in New Orleans, Louisiana, on June 20, 1905, Lillian Hellman spent her childhood as a Southerner. Long after leaving her birthplace, she maintained ties to the South. Few critics today, however, identify her as a regional writer. Nor did she consider herself one, though she conceded, during a 1977 visit home, "I suppose I see myself as Southern. Your roots are made very early. Mine are here in New Orleans" (qtd. in Isaacson 1). Applying broad definitions such as the one set forth in John M. Bradbury's *Renaissance in the South* (1963), we might classify Hellman as a Southern dramatist by virtue of her birth, her having lived in the region during her formative years, and her having set four of her eight original plays here.[1] Extrapolating from the more complex definition asserted in *The Female Tradition in Southern Literature*, we might designate her as a Southern writer because these plays "examine the nature of the Southern family and community and the South's expectations . . . for womanhood and manhood" (Manning 52). Furthermore, the earliest reviewers of her Hubbard family plays—*The Little Foxes* and *Another Part of the Forest*—tagged them as Southern dramas.[2] Only in retrospect, years after the original run of each play, did increasing numbers of critics view them as social or political parables.[3] Then, after Hellman's memoirs appeared, greater numbers of critics reinterpreted her four Deep South dramas as feminist in theme.[4]

Beyond her disavowals of regionalism and beyond the reclassification of her set-in-the-South plays as social or political or feminist is an equally strong factor leading critics to overlook Hellman as a Southern dramatist. I would argue that the gradually diminishing centrality of region as dramatic setting causes many to discount the influence of the South upon Hellman's writing. The South as setting is paramount in *The Little Foxes* (1939) and in *Another Part of the Forest* (1946); far more than historical backdrop, the region and its economic realities drive the actions of each play's lead characters. The Gulf Coast setting in *The Autumn Garden* (1951) though is merely relevant, while the New Orleans of *Toys in the Attic* (1960) is mostly incidental. Paralleling this shift in the primacy of region in these plays is Hellman's decreasing reliance upon her own family history and upon researched facts about the South. Her multiple drafts leading to the staged versions of these dramas suggest that she came to rely upon her regional roots less and less.

However, I would also argue that Hellman's roots firmly anchor each of her four Southern dramas. As their multiple drafts demonstrate, the people and history of her birthplace furnished Hellman with the factual bases for *The Little Foxes, Another Part of the Forest, The Autumn Garden,* and *Toys in the Attic.* Even when the South plays a lesser role in her later works, it still influences their creation. Hellman's roots inform these four plays which can rightly be designated Southern dramas, even if their creator rejects the label of "Southern playwright."

Biographers do not typically categorize Hellman as a regional dramatist, but all note her birth and early years in New Orleans. Most mention her mother Julia Newhouse's Alabama origins and the family traits that influenced her creation of characters in *The Little Foxes* and *Another Part of the Forest.* Most also elaborate on these influences in whichever chapters they devote to analysis of the plays. With little exception, such commentaries are brief, averaging two or three pages for biographical facts and, at most, triple that length in each analytical chapter. One result of such treatment is that labels other than "Southern playwright" get more readily applied to Hellman. But a closer tracing of biographical resonances, of Hellman's notebooks for the plays, and of the multiple drafts of the dramas confirms her Southernness and enriches our understanding of each play.[5]

The Little Foxes, Hellman's 1939 drama set "in a small town in the deep South" (*TCP* 135),[6] recounts the post–Civil War tale of the avaricious Hubbard family. Viewed by its earliest critics as a struggle of Old South against New, it is the drama for which Lillian Hellman drew most fully from her own experiences in the South and from her memories of her mother's family. In addition, she also relied upon extensive reading about the region. The physical presence of the South, the feeling of the Southern setting, appears strongest in this first of her two Hubbard plays. Her engagement with sense of place, her continuing interest in the region, reverberate in this drama; in preparing to write it, she jotted down ideas for names, characters, setting, and plot, pencilling them into a spiral composition book (Ms A3b, 1937/1938*).[7] She also read contemporary treatises on the history, economy, and culture of the South and of America; from her reading and from her pencilled writer's book, she recorded 115 pages of typed notes covering the New South period of 1880 to 1900 (Ms A3a, 1937/1938*).

Sources from which Hellman culled these notes are varied, ranging from a 1930 collection of Negro songs to turn-of-the-century travel books and even to Southern fiction.[8] These sources generate a portrait of a South more concerned with national industrial wealth and the region's role in this prosperity than with Southern agriculture or heritage. And this epitomizes precisely the South Hellman sought to understand and render in its historical reality as she drafted her play. Nineteen of these typed pages detail aspects of the postbellum South, including data and tables of statistics from Philip Bruce's *The Rise of the New South* (1905) and Howard Odum's *An American Epoch* (1930). This factual base points toward the regeneration of the Southern economy within a national context; transplanted into *The Little Foxes,* it lends authority to the Hubbard family's plans to prosper by aligning themselves with a Chicago industrialist. Also, Hellman's choice of information from Odum, one of the most prominent of the Chapel Hill Regionalists, suggests her interest in the South's economic role. The copious notes, the effort to create a historically true portrait of the South, demonstrate not only her preoccupation with authenticity but also her ongoing interest in her regional roots.

Beyond this authenticity gained from historical data, Hellman sought to generate artistic realism. Mingling family lore with regional and national history, she simultaneously creates her vulpine antagonists while revealing her interest in the South and in her own identity as a Southerner. Purportedly, she chose the region for her setting "because it fitted the period I wanted for dramatic purposes and because it is part of the world whose atmosphere I am personally familiar with as a Southerner" (qtd. in Beebe 79). In *Foxes,* characters and setting are inextricably linked; the setting and its changing economy propel the characters' actions. Without the Southern setting as its historic and artistic reality, the play could not exist.

In *The Little Foxes,* Hellman focuses on the region's shift from agriculture to industry. Spouting New South Gradyisms,[9] Ben Hubbard pretends loyalty to the region. In the initial typed script (A3c, 1938*), Ben tries to impress his prospective partner Marshall by avowing "loyalties to the land of the south" while welcoming the prosperity the Northerner offers: "We see very well what this factory will bring . . . it's been our dream, every good southerner's dream, to use the cotton on our own ground" (A3c, Act 3). But Ben's loyalty is actually to himself, his proclamation disingenuous. By having him make these remarks hypocritically, the playwright hints at her own disapproval of the Progressivist rationale. Three drafts later, Ben's New South remarks become transformed into a speech which eventually appears in very much the same form in Hellman's published text. Addressing his remarks to Regina rather than Marshall, Ben proclaims, "The century's turning, the world is open. Open for people like you and me. After all, this is just the beginning. There are hundreds of Hubbards sitting in rooms like this throughout the country . . . and they'll own this country someday" (A3f, 1938*). Here, Ben's earlier two-faced comments about bringing prosperity to the South become a bald-faced confidence that he can exploit the possibilities of industrialization. The spirit of Ben's remarks changes, but Hellman's disapproval remains; what is earlier her censure of New South Progressivism assumes a larger context in which she castigates unscrupulous opportunism. Through Ben's character, then, the playwright comments not only upon the South's changing economy but also upon America's. To that extent, this first of her Southern plays might easily be labeled "political." Yet, to that same extent, the play shows us Hellman as "the first American playwright to make productive use of the mores of the changing South in the theater" (Goodman 138). Through her notebook and drafts, as they illustrate changes in the region, Hellman reveals her continued fascination with the South.

Her concern with the South's changing economy also propels her characterization of Regina in *The Little Foxes.* Because the Hubbard fortune has been passed from father to sons, Regina is forced to rely on her own cunning and her husband's earnings to survive. Though an upper-middle-class Southerner, Regina turns to blackmail in order to control her financial destiny. The manipulativeness she displays in each draft of the play points to the desperation felt by some postbellum Southerners at the turn of the century. Enjoying a portion of the national prosperity was the goal of Regionalists like Grady and Odum, whose research appears in Hellman's A3a notebook (1937/1938*). Latching on to what she considers her rightful share of this prosperity is Regina's single-minded objective in this play.

In its earliest typed script (1938*), the play opens with Regina's husband Horace arriving home from an extended hospital stay and with Regina arguing about his alleged womanizing. She puts Horace on the defensive, as a prelude to forcing him to invest in Marshall's proposed deal. But Horace refuses participation in the venture. Reacting vindictively to his refusal, Regina banishes him first to their stifled and hot third-floor sewing room and later to a squalid cabin in the family's former slave quarters (A3c). Subsequent drafts of the play tone down Regina's tyranny over Horace, but her iron-willed determination and her icy calculation remain. In subsequent drafts, the playwright's focus remains upon the hatching of the deal and upon how the Hubbard characters react to its possibilities; through these foxes, Hellman explores how some Southerners acted in response to the changing economy at the turn of the century. And Regina's cold-blooded manipulation, like her brother Ben's hypocrisy, implies Hellman's condemnation of New South Progressivism. The playwright reveals, through Regina's reaction to her own financial circumstances and to the changing economy of the South, the responsibility the region and its people bore for the fall and decay of the South's older, agriculture-based economy.

Hellman examines this responsibility again in her 1946 play, *Another Part of the Forest,* which portrays the Hubbards as they are in 1880, twenty years prior to the period in which *The Little Foxes* is set. In *Forest,* the younger Regina, Ben, and Oscar are evolving into loveless, greedy, power-hungry "foxes." The playwright, who dedicated this work to her analyst, Gregory Zilboorg, illustrates the psychological bases of the trio's vulpine behavior. But economic and social conditions in the postbellum South are formative factors as well.

Details of these conditions appear abundantly in Hellman's A3a notebook (1937/1938*). Adapted into the various drafts of *Forest,* these details turn her focus less upon the external or national forces that influenced the region and more upon how local failures and practices led to the decay of the Old South. Revealed through the lesser characters John Bagtry (with his nostalgia for the Confederacy) and his cousin Birdie (with her ineffectual attempt to preserve her family's cotton plantation), and through the patriarch Marcus Hubbard (with his false assimilation of Old South "culture"), the theme of regional decay unfolds. In turn, the machinations of Regina and Ben underscore this theme; their drive to power and their lack of love destroy already strained family relationships. This erosion of personal relationships is emblematic of the erosion of the postbellum South's economy and culture. Drawing from sections of notebook A3a which include information about King Cotton, Hellman has Ben Hubbard proclaim, in her earliest draft of *Forest,* "Northern money's coming down. Not for cane and cotton—that's all over with" (Ms A6b, 1945*). Ben's remark in draft two, "Starving people will be glad to work and starving cotton land will be easy to buy" (Ms A6c, 1945*), underscores the decline of the region's agricultural economy. These remarks were omitted or shortened in the playwright's numerous subsequent drafts, but her published manuscript subtly links Ben's forward-looking attitude with his indictment of Southernness: "I been telling you, Papa, for ten years. Things are opening up. . . . But ever since the war you been too busy getting cultured, or getting Southern" (401-02). Ben's indictment takes fullest force in draft four, when he tells Regina,

> We live in a part of the country that thinks the world is over. It is for them. . . . That's what happened to Papa: he came out of the piney woods, laughed at the noble fools, made money on 'em, settled back and began to think he was a Southerner. . . . Papa's southern now, and that's what ruined him. (Ms A6e, Act 3, 1945*)

Through remarks like these, Hellman makes Marcus's self-delusion symptomatic of the region's shattered illusions and of its failure to recover economically.

Decline, economic and otherwise, figures thematically as important from the very opening of *Forest*. Bowden, the drama's setting, seems typical of many a small Southern town of 1880, its economy devastated by the Civil War and defeat having damaged its sense of purpose as a community. The town holds little promise for its residents. Ironically, its economic decline engenders the financial success of Marcus Hubbard.

A thriving merchant and a self-made man, Marcus appears capable of rudimentary musical composition and has taught himself Latin, French, and Greek. He prides himself upon being refined and well-educated, but unwittingly, he devalues himself because he measures his store of knowledge as he reckons his mercantile goods. Essentially, his adoption of Old South values is merely a pseudo-culture, an illusion of refinement. With his mercantile-mindedness and his ambition to thrive, Marcus builds his success upon the ruin of the town's former aristocrats and planters. During the war, he sided neither with the Union nor the Confederacy, adhering to his own cause of accumulating wealth. Shrewd and unfeeling enough to profit from others' deprivation, Marcus made his fortune then by "bringing in salt and making poor, dying people give up everything for it" (372). In his efforts to wring profit from his dealings, Marcus shows his kinship with a source recorded in Hellman's A3a notebook (1937/1938*), the money-grubbing Handback of T. S. Stribling's 1932 novel, *The Store*.[10] Marcus is as habituated to cheating as the merchant Handback, who routinely short-weights black customers and overcharges tenant farmers. So preoccupied with his own benefit, Marcus seems remorseless over the deaths of the twenty-seven Confederate soldiers to whom he unwittingly led Union troops during the war in the course of a salt run. And in 1880, fifteen years later, Marcus still adheres to the profiteer's gospel as he guards the secret behind these deaths.

In his own drive to power, Marcus's son Ben appears the most clear-eyed, the character most free of illusions. Free, for instance, of any illusion of love, Ben triumphs over his father and his siblings by play's end. In the process, he spotlights Regina and Marcus's illicit feelings for each other, thwarts Oscar's plans to marry a prostitute, spoils Regina's dream to escape to Chicago, discovers his father's secret wartime deed, and blackmails Marcus into surrendering control of the family fortune. Having constantly failed to win his father's approval or love throughout his young adulthood, Ben settles for uncovering hidden feelings and truths and for extracting Marcus's wealth. But the price Ben pays for his hollow victory is the loss of what little family love and loyalty existed.

Ben's mercenary victory, with its accompanying collapse of the Hubbards' already dysfunctional relationships, underscores Hellman's theme of decay. A final detail of staging reiterates this decline and offers a comment that is simultaneously psychological, Southern, and political. This staging at the close of *Forest* indicates that the overbearing father has been usurped by his power-hungry son and that the representative of the self-deluded Old South has fallen victim to his own foolishness and to the clear-eyed advance of the New South.

In the published play, this staging business involves Regina pouring Marcus a cup of coffee, ignoring his silent motion for her to sit beside him, and then deliberately sitting near Ben instead (403). In the earliest draft of the play that includes this business, Regina jilts Marcus merely by sitting away from him (A6b, 1945*). This rebuff is softened in a later draft in which Regina initially ignores Marcus as he tries to sit near her and then moves over so that he can sit beside her (A6e, 1945*). A still later draft is even subtler in suggesting the decline of loyalty and love; this version simply says, "Marcus is now slightly outside the circle formed by the other three," Oscar, Regina, and Ben (A6I, 1945*).

Eventually, though, Lillian Hellman emphasizes this rejection of Old South culture. In draft ten of the play, Regina snubs Marcus by taking a chair near Ben (A6j, 1945*). In three subsequent drafts, Marcus is left to sit alone, while his children eat and read at a table away from him (A6k, A6l, A6n, 1945*); he is excluded and ignored by them, as they go about their accustomed activities without regard for his distress. This blindness to others' feelings, this rejection of loyalty, this fall of the family emphasizes Hellman's view that the New South "circle" left no place for the older virtues of civility and hospitality. Her final bit of staging in *Forest* reminds us that this decay is due not only to the rise of the aggressive new order but also to the self-destructive flaws of the old. So the pseudo-genteel Marcus is left outside his children's sphere at the play's end, stripped of his wealth, power, and illusions.

In 1951, Hellman revisited the theme of decay and the role of illusions in her third Southern drama. Abandoning the Hubbards, she examined a group of faded Southerners gathered for late summer vacation at a Gulf Coast resort located about one hundred miles from New Orleans. In *The Autumn Garden*, the distinctively Southern physical setting created for these characters complements the drama's psychological mind-set. The warm, humid, lazy little community in which the Tuckerman family resort is located accentuates the ennui, routine, and decay that beset the characters. This psychological setting appears central to the drama's impact; the physical setting is simply relevant. As Nancy Tischler observes, in comparing this play with Tennessee Williams's contemporaneous *Summer and Smoke*, Hellman's drama is not "about" the physical, concrete South (330). Characters' actions in *Garden* are driven more by long-brewing internal tensions finally given release than by external forces or regional realities.

In *Garden*, an event does trigger these actions, but it is not what propels them. Here, no influence reigns as powerfully as the changing regional economy in the Hubbard plays. No ruthless connivers force others to bend to their will or to face buried secrets. In this drama, the characters face truths long hidden from themselves and others, but these secrets unfold more gently than the Hubbards' do. *Garden*'s revelations are prompted by Constance Tuckerman's European niece Sophie and by Nick Denery, a painter returning South after decades abroad. By choosing two outsiders (Sophie by her birth and Nick by his long absence) to initiate these revelations, Hellman hints that the decayed atmosphere of the Southern community is incapable of triggering such insights.

With unwitting intent, Sophie and Nick nudge the other characters toward their hidden truths. Because the Tuckerman resort is crowded with visitors, a downstairs sofa doubles as Sophie's bed; when the inebriated Nick passes out on it and stays there overnight, a turning point of sorts occurs. Prior to this event, each character seems mired in self-deceit. This "bed" incident initiates the stripping-away of illusion, the bringing-to-light of hidden truths. In a way, the physical setting does play a pivotal role in the drama. Although the psychological atmosphere generated by the characters themselves and the truths they come to see after Nick and Sophie's event are of greatest importance, the time and place in which these truths unfold seem also relevant. The small resort town in which the limited action of the play occurs constitutes a closed community that has not changed in decades. In this community, certain actions bear definite consequences. As the wealthy Mrs. Ellis says to Nick, "Mr. Denery, you are in Sophie's bed, in the living room of a house in a small Southern town where for a hundred and fifty years it has been impossible to take a daily bath without everybody in town knowing what hour the water went on" (524). This incident forces everyone to acknowledge the reality that, even though Nick and Sophie have not actually slept together, the community deems their actions improper. In turn, facing this fact leads other characters to confront the individual realities that each has previously been able to ignore or hide.

Save for the conventionalism of the community and the balminess of the Gulf Coast climate, the setting and characters of *The Autumn Garden* may not seem recognizably Southern. Yet the drama does show us Hellman's familiarity with the region and her continuing preoccupation with it. For this play, Hellman did not collect research, as she had for *The Little Foxes* and *Another Part of the Forest*. In *Garden,* the inner lives of the characters are more crucial than the physical setting, so regional data like the kind collected for the earlier plays seems unnecessary. In creating these inner lives, though, Hellman drew from her early experience of the close-knit Southern community and her remembrances of life in her aunts' boardinghouse.[11]

A sprinkling of remarks in the published play emphasizes the conservative nature of the South. For example, one character's question, "Haven't you lived in the South long enough to know that nothing is ever anybody's fault?" (477) points to the middle-class Southerner's mannerliness that makes him too polite to think ill of anyone, as it underscores the various characters' willingness to ignore obvious realities. Another example, an observation voiced after Nick is discovered in Sophie's bed—"Boys will be boys and in the South there's no age limit on boyishness" (529)—both refers to the region's Good Old Boy code and suggests each character's impending recognition of the childishness of dwelling in illusion.

Earlier drafts contain remarks about Tulane University and about William Faulkner. Though eventually excised, such remarks indicate the playwright's continuing concern with the role of the South, with the region's image, and with how it is perceived. Those few Southern remarks that remain in the published version of *Garden* give the regional setting a minimal relevance.

By comparison, the New Orleans setting of Hellman's final Southern play, *Toys in the Attic* (1960), comes across largely as incidental. In *Toys,* characters' inner lives and their interactions are foremost. Many of the playwright's lines of dialogue and notes on characters in numerous drafts of the drama confirm that she modeled the Berniers siblings and their in-laws after members of her own family. Many also indicate she was concerned with making her setting specifically Southern. However, in creating twenty-three drafts, she sifted out much of the tell-tale dialogue and notes; in her published play, these family and Southern connections are subtler.

Although Hellman claimed that the drama was set in New Orleans "for no particular reason" (qtd. in Gelb 35), her early life there does inform the drama. The published play gives no date for the actions occurring within it, while the filmed version is set in the early 1960s. But, significantly, preliminary drafts of the play (Mss A11b/1959*; A11c/Sept. 9, 1959; A11d.1959*) specify 1912, a pivotal date in Hellman's childhood. It was the first year she was no longer simply a Southerner; from 1912 through 1917, her family alternated living six months in New Orleans with six months in New York.[12] Hellman's determination of 1912 as the time of the drama and her inclusion of certain autobiographical details in her early drafts of *Toys* point to her continued engagement with her roots. Throughout multiple drafts of the play, the Berniers sisters are portrayed as two spinsters dependent upon their younger brother to provide meaning in their lives; their love for him is the mainspring of their existence. They maintain their mortgaged family home so he will have a place to return to whenever he wishes. They willingly hand over their hard-earned savings to rescue him from successive financial quandaries. They indefinitely postpone a trip to Europe because they have depleted their own funds in order to supplement his. In their self-sacrifice, Carrie and Anna Berniers fit Ned Crossman's *Garden* definition of true Southern women: "With us every well-born lady sacrifices her life for something: a man, a house, sometimes a gardenia bush" (481–82). The care and devotion of Jenny and Hannah Hellman for their brother Max is lovingly recounted in the playwright's memoirs. Their concern for him is also apparent in their letters to their niece.[13] The sisters' willingness to sacrifice for Max continued until his death in 1949; elderly and in failing health themselves, they insistently journeyed from New Orleans to White Plains, New York, to visit him in 1947, after he was committed to a sanatorium. Because Max complained often about being institutionalized, his sisters planned to have him released into their care. They contemplated "rescuing" their baby brother, even though Jenny, nearly eighty at the time, could barely care for herself (Box 124: Folder 7). In *Toys,* the Hellman sisters' self-sacrifice is echoed by Anna and Carrie Berniers.

Other hints of the playwright's personal connectedness to *Toys* appear in

Julian Berniers's loss of his shoe factory in Chicago and in his failed real estate deal in New Orleans. Money for the factory comes to Julian through his wife Lily's ample dowry, as well as from his sisters' meager earnings. In real life, Max Hellman's backing for his share of the Hellman Shoe Store at 829 Canal Street in New Orleans most likely came from his wife Julia's family. Julian seems, at the start of *Toys,* unconcerned about his business loss because he plans to launch a potentially more profitable venture. But his land deal is thwarted, leaving him, by play's end, in financial distress. Similarly, Max's privation dramatically altered his family's lives. Instead of remaining lifelong Southerners, they became semi-itinerant, shuffling between his sisters' household in New Orleans and the Newhouse family in New York; after losing his store, Max became a traveling salesman. Recounted in Hellman's memoirs and interviews, Max's loss and subsequent bankruptcy are more widely known than his failed real estate venture. His financial setback and his family's forced itinerancy may have been a result, as well, of his unsuccessful land speculation.

City records indicate that Max signed a two-year lease on a residence at 1829 Valence from October 1, 1909, to September 30, 1911, at a monthly rent of thirty-five dollars ("Lease"). City directories show Valence Street as Max's home address until 1911; after that date, he is no longer listed as a resident of New Orleans. In the 1909 city directory (Soards 494), Max was also listed as president of Hellman Shoe Co., Ltd., as he had been since 1905. By 1910, though, directories contain no listing for his shoe business. Sometime between 1909 and 1911, Max suffered a severe financial setback; whether the loss of his business caused him to forfeit some land he was purchasing or vice versa is unclear, though. A deed registered May 27, 1908, reports his April 1 purchase of six lots in square 398, an area of the city that was then relatively undeveloped. Paying a deposit of $410 and agreeing to pay $80 per month, Max bought the parcel for $4,100 ("Sale," April 1, 1908). The deed's stipulation that no residence costing less than $3,000 could be built on the property suggests that developers intended the area to become an upper-middle-class suburb. Clearly, Max had an opportunity to benefit from buying the parcel and then selling it in lots to individual homeowners. But he lost his opportunity. By May 15, 1911, Max no longer held this land. His lots and twelve others in the same square were sold by their owners. Whether Max profitably sold his land or lost it because of tax liens or nonpayment of his monthly note is not recorded. In any case, his land speculation did not make him wealthy enough to remain in New Orleans. Max Hellman's property loss resonates in Julian Berniers's failed land deal.

A number of remarks and details emphasize the play's New Orleans setting.

For instance, while Carrie Berniers's frequent visits to the cemetery serve the dramatic purpose of stressing the bleakness of her life, they also add local color; visiting burial sites with aboveground tombs is significantly peculiar to New Orleans, a city below sea level. And Julian's proclamation, "Anybody asked me what I missed most in Chicago, I'd have said a bayou, a bowl of crayfish, a good gun for a flight of wild ducks coming over" (721), portrays the state of Louisiana (The Bayou State), the city's love of indigenous ingredients for its cuisine, and the region's hunting tradition (Louisiana as Sportsman's Paradise). In earlier drafts of the drama, Julian's mention of "crayfish" is complemented by his sisters' references to a distinctively local food, the oyster loaf. First mentioned in the initial typed script of *Toys* (Ms A11a, 1959*), these food references remain in later drafts but get crossed out in the bound rehearsal script, where a better-known dish, jambalaya, is substituted (Ms A11s, Jan. 11, 1960). The playwright's eventual excision of the references to oyster loaf and of remarks like "If you don't want a doctor, then hold still . . . Southern dirt in cuts is dangerous" (Ms A11s, Jan. 11, 1960) makes the New Orleans setting less pronounced. In fact, compared to the impact that setting wields in the Hubbard plays or even in *The Autumn Garden,* setting in the published text of *Toys in the Attic* seems almost parenthetical.

All the same, though the importance of setting or place gradually diminishes in Lillian Hellman's Southern plays, each drama bears traces of the playwright's regional roots. The personal links and the cultural and historical connections revealed in notes for and drafts of *The Little Foxes, Another Part of the Forest, The Autumn Garden,* and *Toys in the Attic* confirm Hellman's continued interest in the region and in her own identity as a Southerner. Whether the regional connections are central or incidental, they infuse each drama. By tracing and recognizing these connections, we can confirm Lillian Hellman's regional "rootedness." Although the South seems to assume lesser and lesser importance as she moves from *Foxes* to *Toys,* her questioning of her own identity as a Southerner resonates in all four dramas.

Notes

1. Definitions of Southern fiction abound, but few critics agree upon characteristics of Southern drama. Sense of place, deemed a "lesser angel" by Eudora Welty, is repeatedly taken up as a definitive Southern trait by observers like John Shelton Reed and Louis D. Rubin, Jr. Sense of place is utterly integral to Hellman's Hubbard plays.

2. For typical early reviews labeling the plays Southern see, for *TLF,* Mantle (1939); Ross (1939); and Watts (1939); and, for *APF,* Atkinson (1946); Garland (1946); and Morehouse (1946). Returning to his notion of "Southern decay" in his 1960 *NY Post* review of *Toys in the Attic,* Richard Watts compares Hellman with Tennessee Williams, deeming her drama "more devious, complex and subtle" in its portrayal of decadence (48).

3. See, for example, Morris Freedman's 1971 remarks on *TLF,* as well as Timothy Wiles's comments on Hellman's "political" plays.

4. See, for instance, Sharon Friedman's "Feminism as Theme in Twentieth-Century American Women's Drama," and chapter four of Sally Burke's *American Feminist Playwrights.*

5. Cataloguer Manfred Triesch's annotations discuss the Hellman materials archived at University of Texas, Austin, as of 1966. After the playwright's death in 1984, UT received 136 permapak boxes and five oversized boxes of additional materials, as well as thirty scrapbooks; however, at Hellman's stipulation, these were not made available to researchers until after the death of her authorized biographer in 1995. These additional materials are currently being catalogued by UT's Humanities Research Center.

6. See *The Collected Plays* (*TCP*). All pages cited for Hellman's published dramas are from this 1972 volume.

7. Dates appearing with an asterisk are estimated; most of Hellman's unpublished notebooks and manuscripts are not dated (n.d.). I have estimated dates by consulting the archived materials, Hellman's letters, her interviews and memoirs, and Manfred Triesch's catalog.

8. Of particular interest are Will N. Harben's *Mam' Linda* (New York: Harper, 1907) for its discussion of "this big race question" and T. S. Stribling's *The Store* (New York: Doubleday, 1932) for its realistic portrayal of the tenancy system that kept poor blacks and whites perpetually indebted to the merchants who supplied them with credit and goods.

9. Progressivists like Henry Grady welcomed industrialism as a means of helping the agricultural South become more like (and as wealthy as) the rest of America. See, especially, pages 23–42 of Grady's *The New South.*

10. Most of the notebook passages from Stribling's 1932 book detail the unfair treatment of tenant farmers and distressed landowners at the hands of storekeepers.

11. The boardinghouse described in Hellman's interviews and memoirs is likely the Victorian at 4631 Prytania Street in uptown New Orleans, where Hannah and Jenny Hellman lived from 1912 to 1917. See Pat Sims's "Looking for Lillian Hellman" in the Sept. 27, 1978, issue of the weekly *Gambit,* pages 18–19, for information about several of the addresses where the sisters resided.

12. As early as 1941, Hellman told the tale of her father's having declared bankruptcy after losing his Canal Street shoe store when his partner stole the store's funds and disappeared (See Margaret Case Harriman's "Profiles: Miss Lily of New Orleans," *The New Yorker* [8 Nov. 1941] 23). However, city records do not confirm this bankruptcy.

13. Correspondence between Lillian Hellman and her aunts, particularly letters dated March 5, 1947 (LH to JH/HH); May 26, 1947 (LH to JH/HH); June 1947 (LH to JH/HH); Jan. 13, 1948 (LH to HH); Dec. 16, 1948 (LH to HH), and July 18, 1949 (HH to E. Stern, LH's secretary), indicates that Max's sisters were uncomfortable with his being institutionalized and that they sought to convince their niece to have Max released so they could bring him to New Orleans (Box 124, folders 4, 5, 7 and 12 of Hellman archives at the University of Texas's Humanities Research Center).

Works Cited

Atkinson, Brooks. "Eating the Earth: Lillian Hellman Tracks Down More 'Foxes.'" *New York Times* 1 Dec. 1946: sec. 2, 1.

Beebe, Lucius. "Miss Hellman Talks of Her Latest Play, *The Little Foxes.*" *New York Herald Tribune* 12 Mar. 1939: 79.

Bradbury, John M. *Renaissance in the South: A Critical History of the Literature, 1920–1960.* Chapel Hill: U of North Carolina P, 1963.

Bruce, Philip Alexander. *The Rise of the New South.* Philadelphia: G. Barrie & Sons, 1905.

Burke, Sally. *American Feminist Playwrights: A Critical History.* New York: Twayne, 1996.

Freedman, Morris. *American Drama in Social Context.* Carbondale: Southern Illinois UP, 1971.

Friedman, Sharon. "Feminism as Theme in Twentieth-Century American Women's Drama." *American Studies* 25.1 (1984): 69–89.

Garland, Robert. "At Fulton—*Another Part of the Forest.*" *New York Journal-American* 21 Nov. 1946: 18.

Gelb, Arthur. "Lillian Hellman Has Play Ready." *New York Times* 9 Nov. 1959: 35.

Goodman, Charlotte. "The Fox's Cubs: Lillian Hellman, Arthur Miller, and Tennessee Williams." *Modern American Drama: The Female Canon.* Ed. June Schlueter. Rutherford, NJ: Fairleigh Dickinson UP, 1990. 130–42.

Grady, Henry W. *The New South.* New York: Maynard, 1904.

Hellman, Lillian. *Another Part of the Forest* Mss A6a (Research Notes), A6b (First Typed Script) through A6n (Various Drafts). The Lillian Hellman archives at University of Texas (UT) Harry Ransom Humanities Research Center (HRC).

——. *The Autumn Garden* Manuscripts A8a, A8b, A8c, A8f, A8i, A8j. LH archives at UT's HRC.

——. *Box 124.* Archives at UT's HRC.

——. *The Collected Plays.* Boston: Little, Brown, 1972.

——. *The Little Foxes.* Manuscripts A3a (Typed Research Notes), A3b (Handwritten Notebook), A3c (First Typed Script), A3d (Second Draft), A3e, A3f, A3g, A3h, A3i, and A3j. LH archives at UT's HRC.

——. *Pentimento.* New York: Signet/NAL, 1973.

————. *Toys in the Attic.* Dir. George Roy Hill. Perf. Dean Martin, Geraldine Page, and Yvette Mimieux. MGM/United Artists, 1963.

————. *Toys in the Attic.* Manuscripts A11a (First Typed Script, A11b through A11s). LH Archives at UT's HRC.

————. *An Unfinished Woman.* New York: Bantam, 1974.

Isaacson, Walter. "Two Old Friends Come Home for a Visit." *New Orleans States-Item* 26 Nov. 1977, *Lagniappe* sec.: 1, 3.

"Lease: W. H. Phillpott to M. B. Hellman." *City of New Orleans Conveyance Office Book (COB)* 417, folio 74.

Manning, Carol, ed. *The Female Tradition in Southern Literature.* Urbana: U of Illinois P, 1993.

Mantle, Burns. "'The Little Foxes' Taut Drama of a Ruthless Southern Family." *New York Daily News* 16 Feb. 1939: 45.

Morehouse, Ward. "Hellman's *Another Part of the Forest* Is a Fascinating and Powerful Drama." *New York Sun* 21 Nov. 1946: 20.

Odum, Howard W. *An American Epoch: Southern Portraiture in the National Picture.* New York: Holt, 1930.

————. *Southern Regions of the United States.* Chapel Hill: U of North Carolina P, 1936.

Reed, John Shelton. *The Enduring South: Subcultural Persistence in Mass Society.* Chapel Hill: U of North Carolina P, 1986.

Ross, George. "Decay of the South Hellman Theme." *New York World-Telegram* 16 Feb. 1939: 24.

Rubin, Louis D., Jr. "The American South: The Continuity of Self-Definition." *The American South: Portrait of a Culture.* Ed. Louis D. Rubin, Jr. Baton Rouge: Louisiana State UP, 1980. 3–23.

"Sale." April 1, 1908. City of New Orleans Conveyance Office Book (COB) 215, folio 718–719.

Soards New Orleans Directory. New Orleans: Soards. Feb. 1905/1906/1907/1908/1909/1910/1911.

Stribling, T. S. *The Store.* New York: Doubleday, 1932.

Tischler, Nancy. "The South Center Stage: Hellman and Williams." *The American South: Portrait of a Culture.* Ed. Louis D. Rubin, Jr. Baton Rouge: Louisiana State UP, 1980. 323–33.

Triesch, Manfred. *The Lillian Hellman Collection at the University of Texas.* Austin: U of Texas P, 1966.

Watts, Richard. "Dixie." *New York Herald Tribune* 16 Feb. 1939: 14.

————. "Lillian Hellman's Striking Drama." *New York Post* 26 Feb. 1960: 48.

Welty, Eudora. "Place in Fiction." *The Eye of the Story: Selected Essays and Reviews.* New York: Random, 1978. 116–33.

Wiles, Timothy J. "Lillian Hellman's American Political Theater: The Thirties and Beyond." *Critical Essays on Lillian Hellman.* Ed. Mark W. Estrin. Boston: Hall, 1989. 90–112.

4

Carson McCullers, Lillian Smith, and the Politics of Broadway

Judith Giblin James

On the evening of November 19, 1953, Carson McCullers and Lillian Smith talked together at Smith's mountain home in Clayton, Georgia. McCullers had come to Old Screamer Mountain, the site of Smith's famous Laurel Falls Camp, to gather material for a *Holiday* magazine article on their home state. McCullers was born and reared in Columbus, Georgia, on the state's western border, and Smith, a native of Jasper, Florida, had made the northeastern Georgia camp her principal residence since 1928.[1] It was fitting that one acclaimed novelist of the region should seek out her sister novelist and critic of Southern mores as the focus for the article on contemporary Georgia.[2] But neither was fully fit for the interview. Smith was mentally drained from finishing her final draft of *The Journey* and still recovering from breast cancer surgery. McCullers, crippled by strokes suffered in 1947, still reeled mentally and physically from the alcoholic mania into which her marriage had dissolved. Only months before, this distress had caused her to flee her home in France, fearing her husband was trying to kill her. That night in Clayton, Georgia, a phone call announced the suicide of Reeves McCullers in Paris.

Two days later McCullers left the mountain. Never united in such intimate circumstances again, both women pursued their careers in the next decade with diminished strength. Smith revised her memoir of the Southern mind, *Killers of the Dream,* and published two other important works, the anti-segregationist tract *Now Is the Time* and the novel *One Hour,* before her death from cancer on September 28, 1966. McCullers, increasingly debilitated physically and psychologically, produced *The Square Root of Wonderful,* a play, and the novel *Clock without Hands*—both critical failures—before she died on September 29, 1967, one year and one day after Smith.

The parallel stories of their final years are less instructive than a more vital connection that may have instinctively brought them together that night on Old Screamer. Both women adapted best-selling novels for the Broadway stage and, in the process, battled producers, directors, advisers, and collaborators for control of their artistic visions. McCullers triumphed over the politics of New York theater; Smith barely survived. Their experiences constitute mutually illuminating episodes in the history of Southern women playwrights. This comparative account of the plays McCullers and Smith made from their novels argues for the value and interest of the adaptations and suggests a method of studying them. Furthermore, it expands discussion of the important place region, race, and gender occupy in the careers of these distinguished writers.

I

Strange Fruit, Smith's novel about miscegenation and its tragic consequences in a small Georgia town, stirred controversy from the start. Within three months after its publication in February 1944, it was barred from the U.S. mails for lewdness, banned in Boston as obscene, and suppressed by "gentlemen's agreement" in other cities, all the while remaining on national best-seller lists (Loveland 71–72).[3] That spring Smith agreed to adapt *Strange Fruit* for the stage. Following tryouts in Montreal, Toronto, Philadelphia, and Boston, the play opened on Broadway on November 29, 1945, only to close on January 19, 1946. Contemporary accounts blame the early closing on competition from another play about interracial love, which opened two months earlier and more auspiciously, and on the inadequacy of Smith's adaptation. Smith, however, blamed the male establishment, from politically motivated stagehands who bungled scene changes, to her producer and director, who insisted on a conventional production instead of the experimental staging she had envisioned. Smith's disappointment and anger persisted the rest of her life, though she never vented her feelings publicly.

McCullers's story has a more satisfactory outcome, though it was equally traumatic, and more personally damaging, as it unfolded. Her lyrical yet disturbing account of growing up female in a Southern town was published in 1946, on the heels of Smith's defeat. McCullers's highly successful adaptation of *The Member of the Wedding* ran for over five hundred performances on Broadway between January 5, 1950, and March 17, 1951, winning for her—among other honors—the New York Drama Critics' Circle Award as the best play of the 1949–50 season and the Gold Medal of the Theatre Club, Inc., as the best playwright of 1950. Such establishment accolades must have seemed especially sweet to the novice playwright, who believed enough in her own female-centered vision of Frankie Addams's coming of age to fight a two-year battle to dissolve her collaboration with a "script doctor" who had turned her story into a family drama focused on Frankie's father.

Having grown up in the small-town South, far from metropolitan centers, Lillian Smith and Carson McCullers had little experience with professional theater before their debuts as playwrights. Although McCullers's first writing efforts were plays staged for family and neighbors, she had not studied drama in any formal way and probably had seen only three plays in her adult life before trying, at the age of twenty-nine, to adapt *The Member of the Wedding* for Broadway. Smith had the opportunity but lacked the money to attend New York theater while a student at Teachers College of Columbia University in 1927–28. As director of Laurel Falls Camp, however, she wrote and produced numerous plays and pageants with her young campers, several of which appeared in condensed versions in *South Today,* the journal she founded and edited with Paula Snelling from 1936 to 1946.[4] Still, she did not consider herself fully equipped to adapt *Strange Fruit* and doubtless would not have begun the project without being able to rely on the knowledge of Esther Smith, her younger sister, who taught drama and directed plays at Western Maryland College. McCullers was likewise shepherded through the initial phases of adaptation by someone more experienced in dramaturgy, the renowned playwright Tennessee Williams, who first suggested that *The Member of the Wedding* should be brought to the stage.

Both women were better prepared for their debuts as best-selling novelists. *The Member of the Wedding* was, in fact, the pinnacle of an already celebrated career that had begun with the instantaneous publishing success of *The Heart Is a Lonely Hunter* in 1940, when McCullers was barely twenty-three years old. She earned plaudits for two additional works—the novel *Reflections in a Golden Eye* (1941) and the novella *The Ballad of the Sad Café* (1943)—before returning to the exploration of female adolescence in *The Member of the Wedding* that she had begun in *Heart.* Her finest work, *The Member of the Wedding* proved the most difficult to craft. Begun in 1939 as "The Bride and Her Brother" and set aside for intervening projects, the novel required, in some sections, as many as twenty drafts in the seven years before its publication in 1946 (Evans 100).

The foreground of *Strange Fruit* is remarkably similar to that of *The Member of the Wedding,* even though Lillian Smith, unlike McCullers, had never published an earlier book. Like McCullers, however, she had completed two novels and several shorter works before turning her attention to the Southern tragedy she intended as an indictment of segregation and bigotry in all its forms. Smith began *Strange Fruit* in 1936, working on it intermittently but persistently through the next seven years, sometimes devoting six months or more to a single chapter or episode. Ten publishers rejected the manuscript before an editor from Reynal & Hitchcock asked to see it. An acceptance followed immediately, with the provision that Smith change the original title, "Jordan Is So Chilly." She substituted "Strange Fruit," a phrase she had used twice in print, in 1941 and 1943, to refer to the effects of segregation on "the mind and heart and spirit" of the South (qtd. in Gladney 71). At her editor's insistence, the book's copyright page attributes the title to Lewis Allen's song of that name made popular by Billie Holiday, in which "strange fruit" refers to the victims of lynching, hanging from trees (Loveland 66–68). The implied shift in emphasis to racial violence from the more subtle psychological consequences of segregation on both white and black Southerners (and the effects of intolerance generally) frustrated Smith in producing both the narrative and dramatic versions of the story.

II

Strange Fruit is a provocative psycho-social study of virtually every stratum of race and class in Maxwell, Georgia. Its white protagonist, Tracy Deen, cannot withstand the cultural imperatives that convince him his pregnant lover, Nonnie Anderson, is a "nigger"—the "none," the non-entity implicit in her nickname, Non. Swayed by his mother, Alma Deen, and a visiting evangelist, Preacher Dunwoodie, to conform to the implacable dichotomies of white/black and male/female, Tracy confesses his salvation, announces his engagement to a white woman, and borrows $300, partly to give as conscience money to Nonnie and partly to pay his servant, Henry McIntosh, to marry her and give the child a name. Nonnie's brother slays Tracy for this betrayal. Henry, who has bragged publicly about his $100 bonus to marry Nonnie, is blamed for the murder and lynched—taken from jail, hanged, and burned at the town's baseball field by poor whites, small landowners, and minor officials, including the school superintendent. At the end, a white mill owner and the town's black doctor pronounce the bitter obsequies over race relations in the South.

Although the novel's concern with race hatred proves powerful, the theme of forbidden love often threatens to exceed it. Nonnie and Tracy's affair has an important parallel in the relationship of Tracy's sister, Laura, and the schoolteacher Jane Hardy. Laura's eastern education makes her a misfit in her hometown, as does her secret love for Jane. When Laura's mother discovers a hidden clay sculpture of a female torso and a letter which proves Jane Hardy posed for it, she immediately acts to sever their bond, attacking Jane as "unnatural." Alma tells Laura, "They're like vultures—women like that. . . . They do—terrible things to young girls" (207). Like Tracy, whose persistent (Oedipal) limp marks his psychological crippling, Laura is withered by her mother's fear and disgust: "You wouldn't want your relationship with Jane when Mother finished with it," she thinks. "You wouldn't want—anything" (211).

The dramas of race hatred and forbidden love merge, of course, in the larger conception of Smith's theme—the grave deformity to humankind caused by intolerance for the Other, however that category is constituted. A sizable novel, *Strange Fruit* touches on the lives of more than 150 characters in more than 300 pages. It develops a complex philosophy of social and psychological determinism through subtle and adroitly managed narrative techniques—particularly the use of close third-person narration to produce an effectively controlled stream of consciousness for the principal characters. Its scope and intricacy make it an especially challenging work to adapt for the theater. Smith said she approached the project with "great humility," aware that she lacked sufficient knowledge of stagecraft. "But," she said, "I knew what I wanted to say and I doubted that any other playwright could find easy access to my feelings and experiences, all of which I believed the play needed for its full realization" (Smith, "Lillian Smith Answers" 2).[5] Her decision to turn playwright came at the invitation of New York attorney Arthur S. Friend, long associated with the theater as a financial backer and representative of actors, and José Ferrer, the talented actor then riding the crest of audience acclaim as Iago to Paul Robeson's Othello. No earlier experiences had equipped Friend and Ferrer to produce and direct a project of this magnitude, but both eagerly sought the rights to Smith's sensational novel. The inexperience of all three parties was largely to blame for the difficulties that dogged the production from Smith's first draft in the summer of 1944 to the play's premature closing in January 1946.

Analysis of the dramatic version of *Strange Fruit* is impeded by Smith's desire that this disappointing phase of her career remain obscure and by the slender surviving evidence from the process of adaptation. The only complete manuscripts accessible to researchers are three mimeographed copies prepared for the cast by Hart Stenographic Bureau: one inscribed "George Greenberg, Stage Manager," in the New York Public Library at Lincoln Center;[6] a copy belonging to cast member Esther Rawls in the Wesleyan College library; and Esther Smith's copy in the Lillian Smith Papers at the University of Georgia's Hargrett Library. The Hargrett collection also holds two carbon typescripts with minor variations from the mimeographed scripts.

The playing version reportedly derived from the fifth draft of the script that Smith began in the summer of 1944 (Ferrer 6). That original version, written after the summer's activities at Laurel Falls Camp, cannot be satisfactorily reconstructed from surviving documents; however, it and the intervening versions can be partially described from autobiographical materials Smith prepared but never published and from newspaper accounts of seven weeks of tryouts before the New York opening. The most important source of information about the scripts, early and late, is Smith's sister, collaborator, and literary executor, Esther Smith, who took a two-year leave of absence from college teaching to see the play through its Broadway run at her sister's side, even performing in a minor role.[7]

The evidence suggests that Smith stripped her complex plot bare for the original version by focusing on the crippling effects of white supremacy on the white residents of Maxwell, Georgia. Prominent characters who embody or are victimized by prejudices based in class, gender, and sexuality were eliminated. The most sensational episodes of racism—the lynching of Henry McIntosh and the fierce final confrontation between Dr. Sam and the white mill owner, Tom Harris—were not to be staged. Even so, the cast was large and the scenes numerous, but Smith hoped to achieve the crisp pacing of the novel by using skeletal sets, more suggestive than realistic. She envisioned scene changes made by shifting the action from one part of the stage to another, blacking out one scene and spotlighting the next on an otherwise dark stage without curtains.[8] The set also apparently would have allowed for staging on three different levels, perhaps corresponding to the social and moral stratification inscribed in the geography of the novel: Nonnie and Tracy's meetings take place across a picket fence that liminally divides white town, stretching away to the right, from colored town, on the left.

When Smith showed her collaborators the completed script in fall 1944, she met firm disapproval. They criticized the experimental staging as well as Smith's omission of the lynching and the final confrontation between Harris and Dr. Sam. She contemplated breaking the contract, but José Ferrer, in a 2:00 A.M. phone call from San Francisco, begged her to reconsider, promising that he would work with her on revisions and that the lynching need not be dramatized. Ferrer "cajoled, flattered, talked sense, injected humor and imagination, and finally won me over against my hunches and my deep intuitions," Smith recalled ("Autobiographical Narrative").

With regard to technical decisions, Smith justifiably resented the coercion she felt from Friend and Ferrer. In other respects, the success of *Strange Fruit* as a play was compromised from the start, for, although the plot is inherently dramatic, its characters are not. Despite the talents of Jane White, daughter of NAACP leader Walter White, in the role of Nonnie Anderson and Melchor Ferrer in the role of Tracy Deen, the central characters are largely-inarticulate victims of forces they hardly understand. Tracy lacks moral courage, and Nonnie's "pliant spirit" (44), though admirable on one plane, is ultimately a curse. To transcend intolerance, Nonnie must become a sleepwalker. More than one critic rightly complained of the play's "weak hero and . . . fatalistic heroine" (Pollock). In deciding to be faithful to her original conception of character, Smith deserves responsibility for this dimension of the play's failure. In the absence of strong central characters, audiences responded to those most vividly drawn—Preacher Dunwoodie and Alma Deen, for example—sometimes inappropriately, with laughter rather than outrage (Van Gogh).

At no point in the long winter and spring of 1945 did Smith waver in her belief in her conception of characters and events, but she worried that production decisions out of her control would make the play "heavy and unviable." She was particularly concerned with the listless pacing—a product both of Ferrer's direction and of sets designed by George Jenkins. The sets—some spare and suggestive and others intricately realistic, "as literal as a Belasco set," she said—were beautifully designed and often praised by critics ("Autobiographical Narrative"). The problem lay in their number. The ease of movement between scenes Smith wanted became thwarted by the conventional staging Ferrer imposed.

When *Strange Fruit* premiered in Montreal at His Majesty's Theatre on October 13, 1945, it ran four hours and required fifteen set changes for a prologue, an epilogue, and fifteen scenes in two acts.[9] For its Broadway debut at the Royale Theatre on November 29, 1945, Smith pared its running time to under three hours, cut the prologue and epilogue, and reduced the scenes to twelve, requiring eleven set changes. The cast was leaner, but, at thirty-four, still large for a straight dramatic production; the stage crew numbered thirty-six, more typical of a lavish musical.

A columnist for the *Brooklyn Eagle* complained of the cumbersome pacing: "With swiftly moving scenes a striking effect would no doubt have been achieved." Ineptness was also at fault, he said: "If at the first performance the stage crew had been on terms of greater familiarity with the scenery [the play] would have seemed more successful. Probably by now the play moves smoothly and swiftly and hangs together neatly" (Pollock). His optimism was undeserved. A review written shortly before the play closed, after sixty performances, still found "the technical difficulties of this multiple-set method are not entirely overcome in the production. There sometimes seems to be more scene-shifting than scene and the mechanics interfere with the establishment of mood" (Gilder 74).

Smith, who had battled "Protestant segregationists" in Toronto and outwitted a group of Baptist ministers who tried to censor the play in Philadelphia,[10] was completely unprepared for the sabotage she attributed to union stagehands. It began opening night: "[A]t every hushed moment they deliberately dropped something big backstage," she recalled. "The actors saw them do it; saw them deliberately do it; they slowed down in changing scenes, they made horrible noises, they did all they could to ruin that play" ("Autobiographical Narrative"). Their hostility, she believed, was motivated by communist sympathies, not only directed against her own anti-communist stance in essays and broadcasts but also intended to bolster *Deep Are the Roots,* the competing play about interracial love that, owing to the ideological allegiances of its authors, Arnaud d'Usseau and James Gow, was, as Smith saw it, unfairly promoted by the liberal press and stage unions.[11]

Moreover, she believed that the extreme liberal bent of Broadway politics in this period supported *Deep Are the Roots* and jeopardized *Strange Fruit* because of a gender bias in Marxist iconography. Smith put it more directly, saying of her own play, "The girl should have been white and the boy black for of course that was (and is) the Commie line" ("Autobiographical Narrative"). She no doubt referred to the tendency of socialist fiction and art to portray the proletariat as masculine—downtrodden, but innately strong—and the bourgeoisie as feminine—effete and emasculated. *Deep Are the Roots* starred Barbara Bel Geddes as a Mississippi woman who falls in love with her cook's son, a returning soldier.

Smith continued to work to salvage her play, tightening and "improving it night after night," all the while dispirited by negative reviews, low attendance, Ferrer's neglect, and her conviction that what was needed was "to cut out half the cast and two-thirds of the stagehands" ("Autobiographical Narrative"). Money from her own profits helped keep the play open for its final three weeks. After it closed she refused to negotiate with a producer who wished to mount a touring production, and years later she rejected a motion picture contract, citing her disinclination to entrust *Strange Fruit* again to an untried producer ("Questions about the Motion Picture").

When Smith recalled the ordeal of adapting and producing *Strange Fruit* on Broadway from the distance of twenty years, she wrote of it as a painful but valuable experience. The process taught her to trust herself and her artistic intuition. She realized only in hindsight that the fame of her novel would have provided leverage enough in 1944 to insist on her own vision of *Strange Fruit* as a play. To have done so, she concluded, would have saved a year's harmful delay and allowed *Strange Fruit* to open before *Deep Are the Roots* and, perhaps more importantly, before the atom bomb and the end of World War II temporarily closed out audience interest in "American sins and troubles" ("Autobiographical Narrative").

III

Carson McCullers's experience on Broadway four years later was enormously more successful than Smith's, but the struggle which preceded success was greater and more anguished. In most respects, the dramatization of *The Member of the Wedding* should have been easier than the dramatization of *Strange Fruit.* McCullers started with a smaller, trimmer novel, barely one hundred pages to Smith's three hundred. She started with only a half dozen important characters, confining her narrative principally to a trio of characters in a single location, requiring only a single stage set, the kitchen of the Addams household. Smith's novel, on the other hand, encompassed an entire town; Maxwell, Georgia, in many respects, is its main character. Smith's two principal personalities, Nonnie and Tracy, cannot understand or effectively express their plight. McCullers's characters—even when limited by immaturity and inexperience—are eloquent. *Strange Fruit* is a novel heavy with dramatic action—forbidden love, racial strife, two murders—but, because of its interior-focused narrative, it lacks dramatic characterization. *The Member of the Wedding* contains little dramatic action, and what exists in the novel—Frankie Addams's journeys about town and her near rape by a drunken soldier—is absent from the play. But the novel's characters are highly dramatic, vivid and fully animated, even if they, like Smith's characters, are changed more by circumstance than by the exercise of individual will.

The Member of the Wedding concerns the events of three hot days in August, during which Frankie Addams becomes enamored of her brother's wedding, experiences the euphoria of her imagined merging with the bride and groom, and confronts the awful loneliness and shame of failed expectations. Manuscript evidence shows that McCullers's skill as a novelist relied, to a remarkable extent, on excision. Numerous preliminary drafts contain fully developed lines of imagery or characterization that were later pared away or left only in traces. One of the most pervasive patterns of the early drafts is the importance given to race. In one version McCullers emphasizes Frankie's affinity with the black inhabitants of Sugarville. Frankie thinks, "There are so many things just like a nigger about me. I like the jokes that tickle colored people. I would rather eat fried pork chops than any other mortal food. I love sad tricky nigger tunes. . . . And I love colored words and colored voices."[12]

The early typescripts show that McCullers originally planned a more elaborate role for black characters in her novel, including a more detailed depiction of the household of Berenice Sadie Brown—at one time, a truly extended family comprising four generations. The finished novel reduces Frankie's visits to Sugarville to a single consultation with Berenice's mother, the fortune teller Big Mama. On this occasion Frankie finds herself unaccountably drawn to Berenice's young foster brother, Honey Camden Brown. McCullers makes Honey Brown Frankie's dark double. His restlessness and frustration mirror Frankie's agitation during "that green and crazy summer" before she fell in love with the idea of her brother's wedding as a way of connecting herself to the world (1). Newly full of her fantasy of joining her brother and his bride on a honeymoon trip around the world, Frankie advises Honey to find a similar escape: "I don't think you will ever be happy in this town," she tells him. "I think you ought to go to Cuba. You are so light-skinned. . . . You could go there and change into a Cuban" (158–59). But Honey seeks his own brand of escape in intoxicants and is subsequently jailed for breaking into a drugstore owned by a white man who supplies him with marijuana.

In all, McCullers devotes little more than three pages to the novel's characterization of Honey Camden Brown. He is an important but decidedly minor character. In adapting the novel for Broadway, McCullers significantly expanded and altered his role; he appears prominently in all three acts of the play. His circumstances and his fate continue to echo Frankie's, but, additionally, the enlarged portrait of Honey Brown stands by itself as a criticism of Southern society and goes a long way toward reinstating racial themes that McCullers trimmed from the developing novel. This altered characterization of Honey Brown constitutes one of the chief differences between the novel and the play and one of the distinguishing features of developing versions of the script.

That the play was written and produced at all is something of a miracle in literary history. A mistaken attempt at collaboration mired the play in lengthy arbitration before McCullers could reclaim it and reassert her own vision of Frankie's story. Before it reached Broadway in January 1950, McCullers had suffered two crippling strokes and periods of hospitalization for emotional as well as physical illnesses. The stunning success of the stage version perhaps only partially rewarded McCullers's courage in seeing the adaptation through to production.

The first-time playwright gave her script to Ann Watkins, her agent for the novels, and left for France in November 1946 with her husband. Having found no producer interested in the script as it was, Watkins urged McCullers to accept the Theatre Guild's offer to produce it if the script could be revised with the help of an experienced collaborator. In what she came to call a "lapse into insanity," McCullers signed a contract with Greer Johnson, whom Watkins recommended (qtd. in Carr, "Novelist" 40). While McCullers remained in Paris, Johnson reworked her script, disastrously.

In December 1947, McCullers, seriously ill, was flown to New York and hospitalized for a month at the Neurological Institute of Columbia Presbyterian Hospital. Despair over the extent of her paralysis led her to attempt suicide shortly after her release, and she was once again hospitalized, this time at Payne Whitney Psychiatric Clinic. During this second recuperation, McCullers determined to take back control of her script. After eight weeks' work, much of it by dictation, she had completed a revision that she considered entirely her own.

Having severed her ties to Ann Watkins and, so she assumed, to Greer Johnson, McCullers turned to Tennessee Williams's agent, Audrey Wood. Before Wood had located a producer, Johnson sued McCullers for $50,000, the amount he claimed he would lose if their joint version were not produced. On November 8, 1948, the American Arbitration Association upheld Johnson's right to profit from the production of a joint version as McCullers had agreed in the contract negotiated by Ann Watkins in April 1947. The judgment continued that contract in effect until November 1949, or until the Theatre Guild chose to drop its option to produce a drama based on McCullers's novel.[13] According to the arbitration decree, Johnson would share forty percent of the profits from any Theatre Guild production, even if McCullers were solely responsible for the final script.[14]

McCullers was distressed considerably by the mandated sharing of profits and the ability of the Theater Guild to tie up the play for a full year before deciding whether to exercise its option, even though the judgment did allow for the possibility of her retaining artistic control over the version produced. Such artistic control constituted a sizable victory. A comparison of separate scripts deposited in the Library of Congress to secure copyright, one in the names of McCullers and Johnson, the other solely in McCullers's name,[15] demonstrates her wisdom in resisting and then attempting to dissolve the association with Johnson, whose distinctive handiwork was the masculinization of the story.

The novel's Royal Addams is a minor figure in Frankie's world, a remote parent to his motherless child. With the coming of her adolescence, he has turned Frankie over to the care of Berenice and gently separated himself from her physically: "Who is this great big long-legged twelve-year-old blunderbuss who still wants to sleep with her old Papa," he asks (29). His own loneliness and isolation are merely hinted at in the shaking hands and clouded head that suggest recurrent hangovers to the reader but go unidentified by Frankie. Johnson's principal contribution to the collaborative script was to place Addams at the center of the action, to enlarge his character and his role in Frankie's life, and to make his comments on the events a touchstone for the adult perspective that Berenice carries almost exclusively in the novel and in McCullers's script. In contrast to Addams's indistinct past in other versions, Johnson gives him a political career, a history of religious affiliations, and a pathetically cynical and sarcastic daughter who bears scant resemblance to the sympathetic girl McCullers created.

The John Henry of Johnson's version is a strangely delinquent youngster with a history of starting secret fires. The whimsical drawings with which he decorates the kitchen walls in the novel become in Johnson's script war scenes, both more lurid and more gender-specific. Furthermore, he is made to complain persistently from Act One of the headache that will eventually signal his fatal meningitis, a disease whose effect in the novel depends on its swift and surprising appearance. Barney McKean, the neighborhood boy whose budding sexual interests Frankie pronounces repellent and "nasty" in the novel, becomes in Johnson's hands a positive symbol of masculine energy and rebellion: he is "only thirteen, and he's got a motorcycle and already left home seven times," Frankie proclaims approvingly (1.1.17). Johnson, moreover, attempts a happy ending, with Addams thanking Berenice for the wisdom she has imparted to Frankie, and a remarkably complacent Honey Brown escorting Berenice offstage. By contrast McCullers's script leaves Berenice alone at the end, her foster brother and John Henry dead, and Frankie now seemingly oblivious to the events of the painful summer.

Fortunately for McCullers, the Theatre Guild declined its option on the collaborative script, and Audrey Wood was able to sell production rights to McCullers's independent script to Robert Whitehead and his associates, Oliver Rea and Stanley Martineau. Harold Clurman agreed to direct the play, though he was skeptical about its chances: "It had no regard for theatrical conventions, little plot, no big climaxes or sweeping movements—in short, it was not Broadway material. . . . The play was to be my fiftieth production and probably one of my biggest failures," he predicted (qtd. in Carr, "Novelist" 42). Clurman was astoundingly wrong, for McCullers had managed—largely by returning to her novel and preserving its dynamics and subtleties—to write a play that "held an audience spellbound" more through character and mood than through action (Coleman 86). Her success lay in trusting the deeply felt intuitions that Lillian Smith regretted setting aside—in that, in luck, and in the inordinate skill that allowed her to make a few brilliant compromises in translating the delicately modulated novel to the stage.

The enlarged significance of Honey Brown in McCullers's stage version is one of those compromises. Like the others, it arises from the fact that the novel's limited third-person point of view, focused through the perceptions and mental cadences of twelve-year-old Frankie Addams, cannot be duplicated on stage. As McCullers described the difficulty, "The play has to be direct. The inner monologue has to become the spoken word. It has to be more naked emotionally, too" (qtd. in Carr, *Lonely* 341). One notably negative consequence of the need to embody the novel's fragile perceptions in concrete form occurs in the portrayal of Jarvis Addams and his bride-to-be. In the novel they appear as abstractions, a composite faceless radiance that bears no more connection to physical reality than does Frankie's fantasy of uniting with them as a "member of the wedding." To bring them on stage in the first act and the third, to move the wedding from Frankie's enchanted Winter Hill to the Addamses' front parlor, just off stage from the kitchen that serves as the only set for the play, makes Frankie's essentially spiritual and idealized relationship to their wedding difficult to suggest.

Similarly, the restriction to a single set prevents the portrayal of Frankie's day as F. Jasmine, when in her fantasy of belonging and entitlement she roams about the town, visits Big Mama in Sugarville, and narrowly escapes the sexual attack of the redheaded soldier—events which occupy a large part of the second section of the novel. The attempted rape, an important event thematically, was cut from the over-long script during its pre-Broadway run in Philadelphia. In the novel, Frankie's failure to understand—much less anticipate—the soldier's attack is an important sign of her sexual ambivalence and unwillingness to accept the limited female role her culture and her developing adolescent body seem to require.

To the extent that the novel encourages its readers to applaud Frankie's resistance to the gender traps laid for her, the more poignant is her apparent capitulation at the end when—symbolically discarding her childhood boyishness with the death of John Henry—she becomes a giddy girl preparing tea sandwiches in anticipation of the visit of her new friend, Mary Littlejohn. She has become a parody of the feminine role: "The hard edge of her mind is gone, and all that is left is froth" (Westling 131). This is no happy ending. Frankie—now calling herself Frances, the more feminine form of her name—is as trapped and compromised by her new status as is Berenice, who settles for a diminished happiness in agreeing to marry T. T. Williams, a man she has heretofore rejected because he doesn't make her "shiver."

Because the play does less to emphasize Frankie's resistance to adult sexuality and prescribed gender roles—that is, because it alters her idealized relationship to the wedding couple and omits her encounters with the soldier—McCullers found another way to show that Frankie is more trapped and confined at the end than she was at the beginning. By amplifying the tragedy of racial prejudice in the characterization of Honey Brown, McCullers intensifies an appreciation of Frankie's own thwarted struggle against society's expectations. Specifically, McCullers rewrites Honey Brown as a surly misfit in open rebellion against white demands for subservience. Whereas in the novel he is merely too sensitive to live docilely in Sugarville, in the play he aggressively resists conformity—rebelling when Frankie's father insists Honey call him "Sir" and condemning his black friend, T. T. Williams, for complying: "T. T. said Sir enough for a whole crowd of niggers," Honey charges. "But for folks that calls me nigger, I got a real good nigger razor" (2.68).[16]

In the novel, Honey and Frankie share an affinity that is both artistic and spiritual. In the play, their connection is intensified in a final, highly charged confrontation. The two meet on the night of parallel attempts to escape their circumstances. Frankie has run away from the humiliation of her behavior at her brother's wedding. She has roamed the town, her suitcase in one hand, her father's pistol in the other: "I vowed I was going to shoot myself," she tells Berenice. "I said I was going to count three and on three pull the trigger. I counted one—two—but I didn't count three—because at the last minute, I changed my mind" (3.2.108). Returning home disconsolate at 4:00 A.M., Frankie encounters Honey, who has this night pulled a razor on a white man and left him for dead. He is exhilarated by his crime: "I know all my days have been leading up to this minute," he says. "No more 'boy this—boy that'—no bowing, no scraping. For the first time, I'm free and it makes me happy" (3.2.109). The play's last scene reveals that Honey has been captured and jailed and that he has hanged himself in his cell in a final act of defiance. By the addition of Honey Brown's suicide, McCullers implies that Frankie, who could not count to three and pull the trigger, has, in her capitulation to a feminine identity, committed a kind of suicide. The self destroyed in both instances is the impassioned, creative self whose difference society fears and punishes, especially when embodied in a woman or a black man.

IV

The stage version of *The Member of the Wedding,* though it represents, perhaps, McCullers's greatest personal triumph (and, certainly, her greatest financial success), has received little attention from academic critics (James 126–36). Smith's play, only available in print since 1998, has attracted almost none. As adaptations, they have largely failed to interest critics of either the novel or the drama. In fact, Charles S. Watson's recent history of Southern drama does not mention them. In their era, however, Carson McCullers and Lillian Smith were important names among the small handful of women playwrights on the American stage. As novelists, both women probed deeply the social and psychological forces that exact punishment for difference. As playwrights, both portrayed racial segregation as "a symbol of the barriers people erect between themselves" (Brantley 76). They faced similar conflicts with the politics and customs of Broadway in a period when social realism held sway and post-war prosperity reinvigorated commercial motives. Insiders believed that *Strange Fruit*'s provocative themes—racism, miscegenation, lynching—guaranteed box office success and that *The Member of the Wedding*'s poetic treatment of female adolescence would fail to draw audiences. They were wrong. Smith, of course, had written a novel steeped in realism, but she believed the play could convey her psychological insights only through starkly symbolic, almost balletic, staging. Despite the intellectual independence and courage that defeated powerful proponents of group-think who, in Boston, Philadelphia, and finally New York, tried to silence or censor her distinctive voice, Smith lacked the confidence to oppose a producer and director bent on profiting from the sensationalism of her sprawling novel. McCullers, on the other hand, summoned the courage to abandon those who threatened her or her art, whether husband, agent, or commercial script doctor. Ultimately, by providing a few strategic infusions of overt social conflict, McCullers kept faith with her original vision of Frankie's poignant psychic journey.

Carson McCullers's own rebellious spirit, though it may have contributed to her physical and emotional pain, gave her crystalline insight into those who suffer for their difference. She was sometimes reckless with her health but never reckless with her art. Lillian Smith's commitment to eradicating prejudice drove her career and gave force and amplitude to her writing. Even when she knew that her play's failure was imminent, she fought on until she had no more strength or resources for fighting that particular battle. The challenges of Broadway theater tested these Southern women in remarkably similar, yet ultimately contrasting ways. Their experiences as playwrights offer important insights into their individual careers, into the history of the theater, and—perhaps as well—into the affinities that drew them together as sister Georgians that night on Old Screamer Mountain.

Notes

The Josephine Abney Faculty Fellowship for Research in Women's Studies at the University of South Carolina helped fund research for this essay, as did a travel grant from the university's Research and Productive Scholarship fund.

1. Smith purchased Laurel Falls Camp in June 1928 (Loveland 16). She served as camp director each summer from 1925 until 1948 (Blackwell and Clay 11–13).

2. The article was written but never published (Carr, *Lonely* 422). Details of the incident of November 19 are drawn from Virginia Spencer Carr's interview with Smith's partner, Paula Snelling (404-06), and from Smith's letter to Joan Titus (9 May 1965) in the Lillian Smith Papers at the University of Georgia.

3. Lewdness and obscenity charges commonly alluded to the novel's inclusion of the word "fucking." Bernard DeVoto masterminded the Massachusetts test case, documenting it in his May 1944 *Harper's* "The Easy Chair" column.

4. The journal began as *Pseudopodia* in 1936; its name changed to *The North Georgia Review* in 1937, before becoming *South Today* in 1942. Most notable of the published plays are "The Girl" and "Behind the Drums."

5. The pamphlet "Lillian Smith Answers Some Questions about *Strange Fruit*" (Lillian Smith Papers 1283A, Box 40, U of Georgia) concerns the composition of the play as well as the novel. Questions about the play and the absence of boldface type distinguish this pamphlet from the one with the same title listed in Margaret Sullivan's 1971 bibliography.

6. The New York Public Library copy was used as the copy-text for the only published version of the play, in *Strange Fruit: Plays on Lynching by American Women* (1998). Production rights are not available.

7. Until her death, Esther Smith faithfully guarded her sister's reputation. She declined to be interviewed for this project but, by letter, graciously offered a general outline of the play's conception and history.

8. Information for this reconstruction, unless otherwise indicated, comes from autobiographical materials in the Lillian Smith Papers (1283A, Box 1), Hargrett Rare Book and Manuscript Library, University of Georgia, and from Esther Smith's letter to me.

9. Program from the Montreal production, in the Lillian Smith Papers, University of Georgia. See also " 'Strange Fruit' Acclaimed by Sympathetic Audience" and Herbert Whittaker's review, " 'Strange Fruit' Opens Here."

10. Both groups objected to the portrayal of the Reverend Dunwoodie. Baptist ministers in Philadelphia tried to close the show after Smith defied a Board of Theater Control order to delete portions of Dunwoodie's speeches. See "Lillian Smith Defies Order; Refuses to Cut 'Strange Fruit.' "

11. Burns Mantle's year book of the 1945–46 Broadway season implies that Smith had reason to complain of the earlier play's left-wing critical advantage: *Strange Fruit* "was, some reviewers and playgoers insisted, the better play of the two. But it had no effect on the forward sweep of 'Deep Are the Roots' . . . [which was] much more enthusiastically received by the critical fraternity" (95).

12. The quoted passage comes from section 3, page 14, of fragmentary drafts of the novel, donated by McCullers's cousin Jordan Massee to the Carson (Smith) McCullers Papers, Perkins Library, Duke University.

13. "Commercial Arbitration Tribunal Award of Arbitrator(s)" in "Documents in the Case between Greer Johnson and Carson McCullers *re* 'The Member of the Wedding,' " carbon typescript, Carson McCullers Collection, Harry Ransom Humanities Research Center, University of Texas.

14. Virginia Spencer Carr (in "Novelist") is mistaken in this: the judgment does not commit the Theatre Guild to use the joint script.

15. Preliminary drafts of the play in the Harry Ransom Humanities Research Center, University of Texas, bear notes by Reeves McCullers differentiating McCullers's work from Johnson's. The Library of Congress scripts were deposited on 9 May 1947 (McCullers and Johnson) and on 24 Sept. 1949 (McCullers). The latter includes the following unsigned statement: "The play being submitted for registration simultaneously herewith is a new and independent dramatization of the original novel and is substantially different from the dramatization made by McCullers and Johnson mentioned in the first paragraph. This version contains none of the material contributed by Greer Johnson in the previously copyrighted version and draws textually and directly from my own novel."

16. Thadious M. Davis alleges that the word "nigger" appears only in McCullers's play, not in the novel (213). Whereas Davis sees in the play "a narrowing down of an author's vision to suit preconceived racial attitudes and prevalent gender notions of the time" (206), I consider the play's amplification of racial stereotypes in the portrayal of Honey Brown a compensatory strategy to emphasize Frankie's parallel capitulation to gender stereotyping.

Works Cited

Blackwell, Louise, and Frances Clay. *Lillian Smith*. New York: Twayne, 1971.

Brantley, Will. *Feminine Sense in Southern Memoir*. Jackson: UP of Mississippi, 1993.

Carr, Virginia Spencer. "Carson McCullers: Novelist Turned Playwright." *Southern Quarterly* 25.3 (1987): 37–51.

———. *The Lonely Hunter: A Biography of Carson McCullers*. Garden City, NY: Anchor/ Doubleday, 1976.

Coleman, Robert. "Member of the Wedding Is a Stirring Hit." *New York Daily Mirror* 6 Jan. 1950: 86.

Davis, Thadious M. "Erasing the 'We of Me' and Rewriting the Racial Script: Carson McCullers's Two Member(s) of the Wedding." *Critical Essays on Carson McCullers*. Ed. Beverly Lyon Clark and Melvin J. Friedman. New York: Hall, 1996. 206–19.

DeVoto, Bernard. "The Easy Chair." *Harper's* May 1944: 525–28.

Evans, Oliver. *Carson McCullers: Her Life and Work*. London: Peter Owen, 1965.

Ferrer, José. "Re: The Production of 'Strange Fruit.'" Souvenir Program for *Strange Fruit*. New York: Ellison B. Greenstone, [1945].

Gilder, Rosamond. "Matter and Art." *Theatre Arts* Feb. 1946: 73–75.

Gladney, Margaret Rose, ed. "How Am I to Be Heard?" *Letters of Lillian Smith*. Chapel Hill: U of North Carolina P, 1993.

James, Judith Giblin. *Wunderkind: The Reputation of Carson McCullers, 1940–1990*. Literary Criticism in Perspective Series. Columbia, SC: Camden House, 1995.

"Lillian Smith Defies Order; Refuses to Cut 'Strange Fruit.'" *Philadelphia Record* 21 Nov. 1945: n.p. Clipping. Lillian Smith Papers. U of Georgia.

Loveland, Anne C. *Lillian Smith: A Southerner Confronting the South*. Baton Rouge: Louisiana State UP, 1986.

McCullers, Carson. *The Member of the Wedding*. Boston: Houghton Mifflin, 1946.

McCullers, Carson, and Greer Johnson. "'The Member of the Wedding,' A Play." Carbon typescript (DU 9406). Library of Congress. 1947.

———. "'The Member of the Wedding,' A Play in Three Acts." Typescript (DU 21653). Library of Congress. 1949.

———. *The Member of the Wedding: A Play*. New York: New Directions, 1951.

Mantle, Burns, ed. *The Best Plays of 1945–46 and the Year Book of the Drama in America*. New York: Dodd, Mead, 1946.

Pollock, Arthur. "Lillian Smith's 'Strange Fruit' Does Not Say All, but Enough." *Brooklyn Eagle* 9 Dec. 1945: 30.

Smith, Esther. Letter to Judith Giblin [James]. 29 May 1990.

Smith, Lillian. "Autobiographical Narrative." Carbon typescript. Lillian Smith Papers. U of Georgia.

———. "'Behind the Drums': With a Long Preface to a Very Short Play." *South Today* 8.1 (1944): 50–60.

———. "'The Girl': A Story of How Children Made a Play Out of Their Own Lives." *South Today* 8.1 (1944): 32–49.

————. Letter to Joan Titus. 9 May 1965. Carbon typescript. Lillian Smith Papers. U of Georgia.

————. "Lillian Smith Answers Some Questions about *Strange Fruit.*" Pamphlet. N.p., n.d. Lillian Smith Papers. U of Georgia.

————. "Personal History of *Strange Fruit.*" *Saturday Review of Literature* 17 Feb. 1945: 9–10.

————. "Questions about the Motion Picture Contract for Strange Fruit." Carbon typescript. Lillian Smith Papers. U of Georgia.

————. *Strange Fruit.* New York: Reynal & Hitchcock, 1944.

————. *Strange Fruit* (Play). *Strange Fruit: Plays on Lynching by American Women.* Ed. Kathy A. Perkins and Judith L. Stephens. Bloomington: Indiana UP, 1998. 221–97.

"'Strange Fruit' Acclaimed by Sympathetic Audience." *Herald* [Montreal] 15 Oct. 1945: 17.

Sullivan, Margaret, with a Foreword by Paula Snelling. "A Bibliography of Lillian Smith and Paula Snelling." *Bulletin of the Mississippi Valley Collection* 4.1 (1971): 1–82.

Van Gogh, Lucy. "Not a Stage Play but Admirably Staged." Toronto newspaper clipping. Lillian Smith Papers. U of Georgia.

Watson, Charles S. *The History of Southern Drama.* Lexington: UP of Kentucky, 1997.

Westling, Louise. *Sacred Groves and Ravaged Gardens: The Fiction of Eudora Welty, Carson McCullers, and Flannery O'Connor.* Athens: U of Georgia P, 1985.

Whittaker, Herbert. "'Strange Fruit' Opens Here." *Gazette* [Montreal] 15 Oct. 1945: n.p. Clipping. Lillian Smith Papers. U of Georgia.

5

The Delayed Entrance of Lily Mae Jenkins: Queer Identity, Gender Ambiguity, and Southern Ambivalence in Carson McCullers's *The Member of the Wedding*

Betty E. McKinnie
Carlos L. Dews

Despite the importance the South plays in her fiction and drama, Carson McCullers was ambivalent about her native region. Delma Eugene Presley, in "Carson McCullers and the South," and Louis Rubin, in "Carson McCullers: The Aesthetic of Pain," provide insight into the possible sources of her feelings toward the South and the impact these feelings had on her work, yet both critics fail to consider perhaps the most important reason for her desire to escape the South. Our essay, through the examination of an obscure character once proposed then removed from her first novel and only mentioned in a later novel and play, suggests that McCullers's ambivalence comes from her response to the South's homophobia and its strict demands of gendered behavior. We not only furnish a new reading of McCullers as a playwright and as an unconventional Southern woman, but we also encourage a more general reading of queer and gender identity in all of her work. This new key to reading McCullers's response to the South appears in the ghostly form of a "waifish Negro homosexual," Lily Mae Jenkins (McCullers, "Author's Outline" 140).

In 1938, Carson McCullers submitted an outline of her first novel, "The Mute" (published as *The Heart Is a Lonely Hunter*), to Houghton Mifflin as an entry in a first novel contest. The author described "The Mute" in her outline as "the story of five isolated, lonely people in their search for expression and spiritual integration with something greater than themselves. One of these five persons is a deaf mute, John Singer and it is around him that the whole book pivots" (125). McCullers describes one of the proposed secondary characters as "an abandoned, waifish Negro homosexual who haunts the Sunny Dixie show where Jake [Blount] works. He is always dancing. His mind and feelings are childish and he is totally unfit to earn his living" (140). McCullers also incorporated in the outline what other characters would say about Lily Mae, including Portia's description of Lily Mae for her father, Dr. Copeland:

> Lily Mae is right pitiful now. I don't know if you ever noticed any boys like this but he cares for mens instead of girls. When he were younger he used to be real cute. He were all the time dressing up in girls clothes and laughing. Everybody thought he were real cute then. (140–41)

In another section of "The Mute" outline, the reader learns why other characters tolerate Lily Mae. McCullers wrote, "Because of [Lily Mae's] skill in music and dancing he is a friend of Willie's. [Lily Mae] is always half starved and he hangs around Portia's kitchen constantly in the hopes of getting a meal. When Highboy and Willie are gone Portia takes some comfort in Lily Mae" (140). Portia says, "[Lily Mae] getting old and he seem different. He all the time hungry and he real pitiful. He loves to come set and talk with me in the kitchen. He dances for me and I gives him a little dinner" (141). According to the outline, after the character Willie returns home from serving a prison sentence, "Willie's story is repeated over and over in sullen monotones. Then this atmosphere begins to change. Willie sits up on the cot and begins to play his harp. Lily Mae starts dancing. As the evening progresses, the atmosphere changes to a wild artificial release of merriment" (143). A few significant details from these descriptions help explain McCullers's intended use of the character of Lily Mae in the proposed novel. As the words used to describe Lily Mae at his introduction suggest—"abandoned," "waifish," "homosexual," "unfit" (140)—he serves as an example of the isolated, shunned, and lonely character; an emblem of the fundamental isolated nature of all humans; a source of solace and commiseration for similarly isolated characters; and an inspiration for pity.

In fact, Portia and other characters, instead of accepting him fully, see Lily Mae only as a distraction from everyday life. The fact that Portia "takes some comfort" from Lily Mae signifies McCullers's depiction of this character as transcendent of rigid gender and sexual boundaries and able to provide comfort to another outsider. Portia uses Lily Mae as a distraction from her own loneliness because she identifies with his status; for example, she works as a domestic servant in a white household. Ultimately Lily Mae functions simultaneously as an insider and outsider: he represents the ambivalence with which the community deals with those outside its rigid boundaries of acceptable behavior, yet he also has value for his shamanistic, curative, or empathetic qualities.

It is perhaps incorrect to describe Carson McCullers as a dramatist, and in many ways the play *The Member of the Wedding* can be seen as an anomaly in the corpus of her work. McCullers penned only two plays and one of these, *The Member of the Wedding,* was an adaptation of her novel by the same name. Her only play written as such, *The Square Root of Wonderful,* was a dramatic and literary failure when it appeared briefly on Broadway in 1957. McCullers wrote of her lack of training in writing for the stage and her adaptation of *Member* in an introduction she wrote for the published version of *Square Root* in 1958:

> Tennessee Williams wrote me about the book and asked me if I could come and spend the summer with him on Nantucket and I accepted the invitation. During that sea-summer lit with the glow of a new friendship he suggested I do *The Member of the Wedding* as a play. I was hesitant at first, knowing nothing about the theatre. I had seen only about ten plays in my life, including high school *Hamlets* and *Vagabond Kings.* (viii)

If McCullers did not consider herself primarily a playwright, had so little experience with drama, and preferred writing prose, what might explain the strength, skillful nature, and mature drama of *Member* (adapted for the stage in 1946) and the relative weakness, immature style, and haphazard construction of *Square Root* written a decade later? The biographically over-determined nature of the character of Lily Mae Jenkins as well as the inherent struggles with McCullers's identity as a Southerner in writing of her own adolescence in the South might also provide an answer to this question.

Lily Mae Jenkins might not be known to those familiar with *The Heart Is a Lonely Hunter,* for when the novel was published in 1940 the "waifish Negro homosexual" (140) had been removed from the manuscript. Portia turns to other characters for distraction and solace, Highboy does the dancing at the telling of Willie's tale, and other characters (Jake Blount, Portia, Dr. Copeland, and Mick) fill the role of outsider. Six years after the publication of *Heart,* McCullers resurrected Lily Mae Jenkins in her novel then play *The Member of the Wedding.* Unlike the proposed appearance in "The Mute," Lily Mae does not actually appear as a character in *Member;* one of the central characters merely mentions him. Additionally, unlike his appearance in "The Mute" outline, where he serves various contradictory or ambiguous functions, Lily Mae appears to have a single purpose in *Member.*

The Member of the Wedding dramatizes the story of Frankie Addams, a lonely girl on the brink of sexual maturity, and details her search for a meaningful connection with another human being and the world outside her small Southern hometown. After Frankie Addams has revealed her plan to join her brother and his new bride after their wedding in her "we of me," a social and spiritual unit seen as a solution to her isolation and loneliness, Berenice, the family's cook and housekeeper, attempts to dissuade Frankie from leaving. In a pivotal scene in the play, Berenice attempts to instill in Frankie a reverence for what might be called naturalized monogamous heterosexuality:

BERENICE: Truly, Frankie, what makes you think they want you taggin' along with them? Two is company and three is a crowd. And that's the main thing bout a wedding. Two is company and three is a crowd.
FRANKIE: You wait and see.
BERENICE: Remember back to the time of the flood. Remember Noah and the Ark. (55)

. . . .

FRANKIE: That's all right. But you wait and see. They will take me.
BERENICE: And if they don't?
FRANKIE: If they don't, I will kill myself. (55–56)

Frankie believes that death provides the only recourse for non-acceptance of naturalized heterosexuality; committing suicide seems to be her only option, the threat of which underscores (to Berenice) the seriousness of Frankie's desire for a "we of me." Frankie's strong negative response to Berenice, her threat of suicide, and her refusal to accept exclusion from the wedding force Berenice to offer examples of deviant behavior as negative guideposts. Berenice continues:

BERENICE: . . . I have heard of many a peculiar thing. I have knew men to fall in love with girls so ugly that you wonder if their eyes is straight.
JOHN HENRY: Who?
BERENICE: I have knew women to love veritable satans and thank Jesus when they put their split hooves over the threshold. I have knew boys to take it into their heads to fall in love with other boys. You know Lily Mae Jenkins?
FRANKIE: I'm not sure. I know a lot of people.
BERENICE: Well, you either know him or you don't know him. He prisses around in a girls' blouse with one arm akimbo. Now this Lily Mae Jenkins fell in love with a man name Juney Jones. A man, mind you. And Lily Mae turned into a girl. He changed his nature and his sex and turned into a girl.

FRANKIE: What?

BERENICE: He did. To all intents and purposes . . .

FRANKIE: It's funny I can't think who you are talking about. I used to think I knew so many people.

BERENICE: Well, you don't need to know Lily Mae Jenkins. You can live without knowing him.

FRANKIE: Anyway, I don't believe you.

BERENICE: I ain't arguing with you. What was we speaking about?

FRANKIE: About peculiar things. (57)

Lily Mae functions in this scene solely as an example of the bizarre, of what society tolerates but does not fully accept. Berenice's suggestion that "you don't need to know Lily Mae Jenkins. You can live without knowing him" limits Lily Mae's function in the play to his use as a cautionary model. Berenice's use of Lily Mae robs him of his subjectivity and underscores the obviously disposable nature of the sexual transgressive. Louise Westling writes the following in her essay "Tomboys and Revolting Femininity": "Images of sexual ambivalence are carefully cultivated throughout the novel in the Negro transvestite Lily Mae Jenkins. . . . Always such hermaphroditic or androgynous references are placed in a negative frame, for the novel's entire movement is toward Frankie's ultimate submission to the inexorable demand that she accept her sex as female" (127). Later in the same scene Berenice returns to the lesson she attempts to teach Frankie, saying: "But what I'm warning is this. If you start out falling in love with some unheard-of thing like that, what is going to happen to you? If you take a mania like this, it won't be the last time and of that you can be sure. So what will become of you? Will you be trying to break into weddings the rest of your days?" (80).

Berenice considers Frankie's "falling in love with a wedding" even more queer than she views Lily Mae's changed nature. Berenice seems to associate what Frankie wants to do with what Lily Mae has done because both are considered unacceptable behavior by society. Concerned for Frankie's future, Berenice issues her cautionary tale to persuade Frankie to conform, to "go along to get along." Her warning to the young girl illustrates that heterosexuality remains the norm, and resistance to perceived normalcy is futile.

Lily Mae's proposed roles in "The Mute," his subsequent removal from the work in progress, and his eventual reappearance in McCullers's play and novel, *Member,* can best be explained within the context of McCullers's own struggle with sexual/gender identity and with her ambivalent relationship with her native South. Carson McCullers's living and writing conditions during the periods in which she wrote the works where Lily Mae appears are significant. McCullers wrote the outline for her proposed first novel, "The Mute," and revised the completed manuscript (by then changed to *The Heart Is a Lonely Hunter*) while living with her husband, Reeves McCullers, in Charlotte and Fayetteville, North Carolina, between 1938 and 1940. Upon publication of the novel, Carson and Reeves moved to New York in 1940, where they soon divorced, and Carson became involved with a wide range of friends from international artistic, musical, and literary circles. During this period McCullers also received her "illumination," as she described inspiration in her autobiography, for *Member* (32).

Significantly, McCullers composed *Member* primarily in New York City and in the Yaddo arts colony of Saratoga Springs, New York, between 1940 and 1945. The adaptation of the novel into the play took place under the influence of Tennessee Williams, who, as McCullers recalled, suggested the adaptation and provided friendship and inspiration during the summer of 1946 on Nantucket Island (Carr 270–78).

Lori Kenschaft, in "Homoerotics and Human Connections: Reading Carson McCullers 'As a Lesbian,'" details this period's relevance to McCullers's growing sexual and gender self-concept:

> *The Ballad of the Sad Café* was written in the summer of 1941; *The Member of the Wedding* was an ongoing project from 1939 to 1946. In 1940 McCullers fell in love with Annemarie Clarac-Schwarzenbach, whom she later considered the greatest passion of her life. According to her biographer, McCullers's husband was already accustomed to her frequent crushes on women. That fall they separated and she moved into a group house. Her housemates included Benjamin Britten and Peter Pears, who were life-long lovers, Christopher Isherwood, and W. H. Auden, whose new lover, Chester Kallman, soon moved in. The next summer at Yaddo, McCullers's men's clothes and boyish haircut made her easily identifiable as a "mannish woman." (221)

In her essay "How I Began to Write," McCullers described her feelings about her hometown and her desire to leave for New York as early as age seventeen: "By that winter [1934–35] the family rooms, the whole town, seemed to pinch and cramp my adolescent heart. I longed for wanderings. I longed especially for New York" (*Mortgaged* 251).

The negative reaction by those around her to her androgynous nature and masculine dress proved a likely factor in her desire for escape. In her biography of McCullers, *The Lonely Hunter,* Virginia Spencer Carr explains McCullers's adolescent experience with this cultural anxiety: "When Carson was younger, some of the girls gathered in little clumps of femininity and threw rocks at her when she walked nearby, snickering loud asides and tossing within hearing distance such descriptive labels as 'weird,' 'freakish-looking,' and 'queer'" (29–30).

McCullers articulated her desire to leave the South by including a similar yearning for escape in her characters Frankie Addams and Mick Kelly. As Oliver Evans writes of the autobiographical nature of Mick and Frankie: "Certainly the resemblances between Lula Carson Smith and Mick Kelly are too obvious to be ignored: both are tall for their age, both are tomboys, and the fathers of both are small-town jewelers. The resemblances between Lula Carson Smith and Frankie Addams are stronger still" (18). And as Presley has observed, "For both Mick and Frankie, leaving home would have been a means of escaping the inevitable trap" (105).

Carr reveals the ambivalence McCullers felt about the South: "Her work demanded that she go back from time to time, just as she had told Eleanor Clark at Yaddo a few years earlier that she must periodically return to the South to renew her 'sense of horror'" (313). Indeed, in an interview with *Esquire* magazine McCullers once remarked, "People ask me why I don't go back to the South more often. But the South is a very emotional experience for me, fraught with all the memories of my childhood. When I go back South I always get into arguments, so that a visit to Columbus is a stirring up of love and antagonism" (qtd. in Presley 109).

Negative reaction to characters in her second novel, *Reflections in a Golden Eye,* would confirm any fears McCullers had about the reception of Lily Mae had he remained in "The Mute." In her unfinished autobiography, *Illumination and Night Glare,* McCullers recalls the reaction she faced during a visit to her hometown after the publication of *Reflections:* "'Reflections In A Golden Eye' was just published, and this, with the attendant publicity made quite a stir in town and especially at Ft. Benning, the Army Post nearby. . . . The Ku Klux Klan even called me and said, 'we are the Klan and we don't like nigger lovers or fairies. Tonight will be your night'" (31).

If such a reaction confirmed her anxiety when contemplating the South's reaction to her work, McCullers experienced reinforcement of her positive associations with life in the North. Living with a group that became her personal "we of me" and working in a setting that fostered her political and social progressiveness, McCullers began to fully comprehend the intolerance of the South. As Presley writes, "In Brooklyn, the young Mrs. McCullers found what, in the simple logic of *The Heart Is a Lonely Hunter,* could have saved Mick Kelly: a place where she could relish being different, a sympathetic community in which she could find uncritical acceptance" (103); or as McCullers herself wrote in the essay "Brooklyn Is My Neighbourhood," "That is one of the things I love most about Brooklyn. Everyone is not expected to be exactly like everyone else" (220).

By the time McCullers published *Member,* she also had experienced an acceptance of her lesbianism or bisexuality. Having moved to New York, she discovered a new society that allowed her to pursue any type of relationship she desired. Finding a community that embraced homosexuality helped McCullers reexamine her notions about the South's rigidity and repressiveness. Upon reviewing the South's attitude toward sexual transgression, McCullers perhaps realized the flaws in her thinking about the South and saw her attempts to effect lasting social change there as futile.

McCullers's developing ideas about the racism and intolerance of the South would later be articulated in her final novel, *Clock Without Hands.* According to Virginia Spencer Carr, "The South which Carson depicted in *Clock Without Hands,* as in her earlier works, was sadly lacking in the dimensions of justice and humanity. It was a South she had left but still viewed with the ambivalent feelings of affection and rancor" (493). Presley misunderstands McCullers's reaction to the South Carr describes as an indication of McCullers's lack of knowledge of the South: "In *Clock Without Hands* Mrs. McCullers attempted to go back home, but the South as she described it never existed, and it does not exist in this fiction" (108). However, given her negative experiences with racism and, perhaps most importantly, homophobia, the South that never existed in McCullers's work was a just and accepting South.

In an attempt to come to terms with her isolation as a sexual transgressive in the South, McCullers created characters through whom she could illustrate her frustration. According to Oliver Evans, "The . . . reason Mrs. McCullers has suffered unfavorable criticism is her choice of characters and situations. It must be admitted that her characters are not always the kind one is likely to encounter in ordinary experience, and that the situations in which she places them are frequently uncommon, even implausible" (127). By creating characters who do not seem familiar to us, McCullers creates an effective isolation for these individuals which replicates her own experience as a progressive Southerner in the repressive South.

Despite their significant contribution of detail and biographical background to a consideration of McCullers's relationship with the South and the impact of that relationship on her work, Presley and Rubin fail to consider the reasons McCullers might have had to want to escape her native region. By failing to understand the influence of the South's homophobia on McCullers, Presley appears to blame her for her escape and suggests the unbearably painful life of a queer woman in the South should be credited with at least providing artistic inspiration: "The fact that she was a Southerner was a great burden she struggled to displace very early in her career. Significantly, out of the struggle emerged some literature of the first order. But once she abandoned the landscape of her agony, she wrote works which lack distinction. Her early success and her ultimate failure, I maintain, can be attributed in large measure to this pattern of struggle in her relationship to the South" (99).

Presley also seems to blame McCullers for her continued distrust of the South without recognizing the realities of the South: "Carson McCullers' relationship to the land of her youth reminds us that she engaged in something other than a lover's quarrel with the South. A quarrel between lovers implies that both parties have mutual understanding, mutual respect, as it were" (105). Presley's idea that McCullers's "chief difficulties as a writer stemmed from her disregard of her own past" might be better understood in reverse. McCullers did not abandon the South; the South disregarded her. A flight from a homophobic and misogynistic society seems justifiable for McCullers and many of her fellow queer Southerners: Tennessee Williams and Truman Capote, for example, to name only two of her friends and fellow expatriate Southerners.

In "Carson McCullers The Aesthetic of Pain," Louis D. Rubin posits this explanation for McCullers's desire to move to New York:

New York was the place of art, of culture, of fulfillment, where the dreams of the lonely provincial could come true. . . . The particular vision of Carson McCullers, the capacity for recognizing and portraying and sympathetically identifying with pain and loneliness, could arise only out of a social situation in which the patterns and forms and expectations of conduct and attitude are very firmly and formidably present, so that the inability or failure to function within those patterns seems crucial. . . . If there is a strong set of expectations, and one is unable to fulfill them and yet be oneself, then one searches out for kindred sufferers, in order to feel less lonely through assurance of their pain as well. (113, 119)

For McCullers and her characters, however, this private distance is one of necessity because of the South's response to difference. The vague "one reason or other" offers an unfortunate eliding of the very significance of the South's intransigent homophobia and racism.

Although very little is known of the process by which McCullers transformed her outline of "The Mute" into the novel *Heart,* at least two plausible explanations exist for her removal of Lily Mae Jenkins. McCullers perhaps removed Lily Mae from the published version of the novel because she believed the South would not tolerate a story of sexual transgression both in the telling of the story of the transgression (by McCullers in the act of writing the novel) and in the record of the transgressive (in the depicted life of Lily Mae Jenkins). Perhaps McCullers believed Lily Mae would be unacceptable to towns such as her native Columbus, Georgia, or that a character like Lily Mae Jenkins, with his multiple social roles, was unimaginable in a place like Columbus.

McCullers's original conception of Lily Mae Jenkins in the South and her removal of him from her first novel and subsequent return to him for her play *Member* are articulations of her ambivalence toward the South and the region's response to gender ambiguity and sexual transgression. With little experience away from her native South and perhaps an inability to imagine a place for Lily Mae in the South, or in her novel, McCullers felt compelled to remove him. Lily Mae's absence might then be simply the editorial removal of a character the author could not imagine in the setting of the work (perhaps not unlike McCullers's inability to imagine her own future in the South). Lily Mae's removal from the novel allows McCullers to spare her character from searching for a resolution to the paradox of Southern queer identity, a paradox fraught with its concomitant ambivalences—and with which McCullers found herself struggling. McCullers's extraction of Lily Mae from the novel was a generous gesture. By removing Lily Mae, McCullers spared him the painful death of spiritual and personal starvation which would have been his fate in the South McCullers knew all too well.

Returning once again to McCullers's introduction to the published edition of her failed play *The Square Root of Wonderful,* one can perhaps see McCullers herself providing answers to the lingering questions as to the source of the power of the adolescent dilemma dramatized in *Member,* for which Lily Mae Jenkins serves as a simulacrum:

> When people ask why I write for the theatre I can only counter with another question. Why does anyone write at all? I suppose a writer writes out of some inward compulsion to transform his own experience (much of it is unconscious) into the universal and symbolical. The themes the artist chooses are always deeply personal. I suppose my central theme is the theme of spiritual isolation. Certainly I have always felt alone. In addition to being lonely, a writer is also amorphous. A writer soon discovers he has no single identity but lives the lives of all the people he creates and his weathers are independent of the actual day around him. I live with the people I create and it has always made my essential loneliness less keen. (viii)

Perhaps the above pronouncement provides not only a clue to the questions regarding Lily Mae Jenkins's characterization in her novel and play but also to the questions about McCullers as a dramatist. Perhaps as a recapitulation of her own childhood drama, *Member* was the only story that McCullers could successfully dramatize. McCullers might well be said to have been dramatizing her own adolescent struggles with gender and sexuality and calling upon unresolved psychic (unconscious) material in her adaptation of *Member* rather than merely dramatizing her novel for the stage. Lily Mae could then be read as one of the characters McCullers created to "live with" in order to feel her loneliness less keenly. However, this role for Lily Mae does not consider McCullers's use of Lily Mae as a critique of the South and does not help explain her wavering use of Lily Mae.

When McCullers reintroduces Lily Mae Jenkins in *Member* and mercifully leaves him out of sight, she uses him only to reflect negatively on the South and its lack of imagination in providing a place for such a character. Had he remained in *Heart,* Lily Mae would have served as a mirror placed in front of McCullers's face, reflecting a too-painful image of her own suffering. Instead, McCullers removed him from the novel and recalled him in *The Member of the Wedding* to serve as an all-too-honest reflection of the South and its intolerant nature, a South McCullers knew in an all-too-real way as an intolerant place where her work for change was futile.

Works Cited

Carr, Virginia Spencer. *The Lonely Hunter: A Biography of Carson McCullers.* Garden City, NY: Doubleday, 1975.

Evans, Oliver. "The Case of Carson McCullers." *Critical Essays on Carson McCullers.* Ed. Beverly L. Clark and Melvin J. Friedman. New York: Hall, 1996. 123–28.

Kenschaft, Lori J. "Homoerotics and Human Connections: Reading Carson McCullers 'As a Lesbian.'" *Critical Essays on Carson McCullers.* Ed. Beverly L. Clark and Melvin J. Friedman. New York: Hall, 1996. 220–33.

McCullers, Carson. "Author's Outline of 'The Mute' (*The Heart Is a Lonely Hunter*)." *The Mortgaged Heart.* Ed. Margarita G. Smith. Boston: Houghton, 1971. 124–49.

———. "Brooklyn Is My Neighbourhood." *The Mortgaged Heart.* Ed. Margarita G. Smith. Boston: Houghton, 1971. 216–20.

———. *Clock Without Hands.* Boston: Houghton-Riverside, 1953.

———. *The Heart Is a Lonely Hunter.* New York: Modern Library, 1993.

———. "How I Began to Write." *The Mortgaged Heart.* Ed. Margarita G. Smith. Boston: Houghton, 1971. 249–51.

———. *Illumination and Night Glare: The Unfinished Autobiography of Carson McCullers.* Ed. Carlos L. Dews. Madison: U of Wisconsin P, 1999.

———. *The Member of the Wedding* (Play). New York: New Directions, 1951.

———. *The Member of the Wedding.* Boston: Houghton, 1973.

———. *Reflections in a Golden Eye.* Cambridge: Riverside, 1941.

———. *The Square Root of Wonderful.* Introduction. Dunwoody, GA: Berg, 1971. vii-x.

Presley, Delma Eugene. "Carson McCullers and the South." 1974. *Critical Essays on Carson McCullers.* Ed. Beverly Lyon Clark and Melvin J. Friedman. New York: Hall, 1996. 99–110.

Rubin, Louis D., Jr. "Carson McCullers: The Aesthetic of Pain." 1977. *Critical Essays on Carson McCullers.* Ed. Beverly Lyon Clark and Melvin J. Friedman. New York: Hall, 1996. 111–23.

Westling, Louise. "Tomboys and Revolting Femininity." *Sacred Groves and Ravaged Gardens: The Fiction of Eudora Welty, Carson McCullers, and Flannery O'Connor.* Athens: U of Georgia P, 1985. 110–32.

6

"Controversy Only Means Disagreement": Alice Childress's Activist Drama

Donna Lisker

If asked to name important figures of the Civil Rights movement, most Americans would think first of Dr. Martin Luther King, Jr. His eloquent words and memorable voice still echo in the minds of many Americans; his speeches are taught in schools, his life celebrated with a national holiday, and the site of his violent death memorialized as the National Civil Rights Museum. If pressed for more names beyond that of King, the average American might think of politicians—Robert Kennedy, for example—who championed the cause. Or one might cite "ordinary" citizens—Rosa Parks, Fannie Lou Hamer, the thousands who sat down at lunch counters and marched in the South— those whose heroism and dedication brought about remarkable social change. All of these answers would prove accurate, but they would also be incomplete, for few Americans would think to cite the artists: the playwrights and novelists and musicians whose creative expression provided inspiration and insight to the movement's participants and onlookers alike. Yet one finds it difficult imagining the Civil Rights movement without the artists, without Nina Simone, Ralph Ellison, Richard Wright, Paul Robeson, or Lorraine Hansberry. Like Martin Luther King's, their voices and words linger, giving sound and language and personal narratives to the movement.

Unfortunately, creative expression such as theirs is sometimes seen apart from social movements, for the causes they promoted and the political situations in which they were engaged provide necessary context to their work. Many artists fear this association with politics; nothing condemns a novel or play faster than a critic pronouncing it "preachy" or "didactic." If a playwright is going to plead a cause, he or she should at least have the grace to do so subtly. But some issues, such as civil rights, do not respond well to a subtle treatment. In the heart of the Civil Rights movement in the 1940s, '50s, and '60s, many African American writers felt a need to be explicitly political by representing the reality of their lives, showing the indignities, the injustice, and the endurance of their people. Depicting their realities in painful detail might help others understand the need for increased civil rights. Realism proved an appropriate genre for this purpose, with its ability to provide, in the words of Susan Stanford Friedman, "a kind of thick description of human subjectivities shaping and shaped by the material, psychological, and spiritual conditions of a given space and time" (54). Although realism seemed a popular choice among African American writers of that era (like Hansberry and Ellison), it has since been much challenged, particularly in feminist theater criticism, as an inappropriate form for plays that advocate major social change.[1] But the powerful impact of realist plays of the Civil Rights era suggests that this issue needs revisiting. Was realism an effective form for advancing the Civil Rights movement? How did it operate in the context of specific plays and their reception? To answer these questions, I would like to look at the life and work of an African American playwright and civil rights advocate little known outside theater circles: South Carolina native Alice Childress.

Alice Childress's long career—which spanned more than fifty years and included *Florence* (1949), *Trouble in Mind* (for which she won an Obie Award in 1955), *Wedding Band* (1966), and *Wine in the Wilderness* (1969)—provides many opportunities for analysis, and anything shorter than a book-length treatment will necessarily examine only a fraction of her work.[2] All of Childress's plays focus on race, and all of them make an unmistakable argument for social change. The playwright uses her double perspective as a Southerner living in the North to challenge not only the obvious target, the Jim Crow system in the South, but also to address a dicier issue, the hypocrisy of Northern integration. Childress also tackles interracial marriage, the objectification of women, and race and gender stereotyping in her plays, always using a finely crafted realist form to best suit her subject matter. Perhaps because she chose realism at a time when it was going out of vogue (supplanted by more experimental forms), or perhaps because of the controversy of her message, Childress never attained the popularity and critical attention she deserved. Still, she refused to retreat into safety, telling a 1994 interviewer that "controversy only means disagreement" (Bryer 64). As is evident in realist plays such as *Florence* and *Trouble in Mind*— as well as in the biographical details of her life—disagreement did not frighten Childress. She was happy to have her plays far off-Broadway so long as they sparked dialogue about race and gender issues.

Alice Childress was born October 12, 1916, in Charleston, South Carolina. Though her family moved to Harlem in 1925, Childress always retained a sense of her family's Southern history. As she writes in "A Candle in a Gale Wind," "events from the distant past, things which took place before I was born, have influence over the content, form, and commitment of my work" (III). The playwright's great-grandmother Ani was enslaved, freed one year after the Emancipation Proclamation, and abandoned at the age of thirteen by her owner in the center of Charleston. Ani was taken in by a white woman, Anna Campbell, and later had a daughter, Eliza, by Anna Campbell's son. Eliza eventually "married a mill-hand slave descendant and they raised seven children in abject poverty" ("Candle" 112). Eliza also raised her granddaughter Alice, but not with frequent tales of their Southern past. Childress admits that "I had to wring such stories out of her. She was not fond of remembering her mother's account of slavery and the mockery of so-called freedom" ("Candle" 112). Childress, who never finished high school, credits Eliza with shaping her into a writer. Eliza encouraged her granddaughter to write down important thoughts and ideas and, as Trudier Harris writes, "instilled a sense of value in Childress —value of herself as a human being and of her thoughts" (xii). Childress read voraciously, supporting herself through a variety of odd jobs, including work as a domestic (which later influenced her collection *Like One of the Family,* told from the viewpoint of a domestic worker). She wrote and acted on the side, originating the role of Blanche in the American Negro Theater's 1944 production of *Anna Lucasta.* Childress took this role to Broadway and received a Tony nomination for it.

That was to be Childress's only trip to Broadway; she never made it there as a playwright. Although no one can say for certain why, the fact that Childress's plays were so political and so explicit about the failures of race and gender relations may have made them a hard sell to Broadway producers in the 1950s and '60s. Broadway was (and is) a forum targeted primarily at middle- and upper-middle-class whites, not exactly the liberal vanguard in the 1950s. Childress relates that she was sometimes told, "we like your writing, but this is too political," even though, she points out, "we're living in the middle of politics everyday!" (Bryer 58). Childress's genre choice—realism—may also have limited her access to Broadway. The theater was undergoing a transformation in the 1950s; Samuel Beckett translated *Waiting for Godot* into English in 1954, and in the wake of that event realism, the dominant form of the first half of the century, suddenly seemed quaint and outdated to many. Experimental theater became the rage; playwrights wanted to break through the fourth wall, involve the audience, disrupt linear time and generally upset theatrical conventions. Certainly experimental forms can and have been used to powerful effect in plays about race (Ntozake Shange's work springs to mind), but these experimental forms did not suit Childress's purpose. She was interested in writing "about those who come in second, or not at all—the four hundred and ninety-nine and the intricate and magnificent patterns of a loser's life" ("Candle" 112). Her emphasis on ordinary people—ordinary women in particular—led her to realism. That form's wealth of mundane detail, its ability to accommodate complex psychological characterization and character development, proved ideal for Childress's purpose: to agitate for social change by shining a bright light on the contours of American racism.

As the Civil Rights movement dovetailed with the second wave of the feminist movement, scholars and critics began to debate the viability of realism as a form. Given the social change desired by both movements, some critics wondered if realism seemed too traditional, too conventional to effect that change.[3] If the goal of realism is mimesis—reflecting reality as it is—then realist plays will necessarily reflect a racist and sexist world. But does that reflection have to be an endorsement of the status quo, or can it be a criticism? What if the viewpoint shifts so that those on the margins of society occupy center stage, defining themselves and their concerns rather than being defined by inaccurate stereotypes? Such a shift helps a predominantly white, middle-class audience to understand and to sympathize with people whose lives may be foreign to them. A 1950s white woman watching a Childress play in New York, for example, may have only encountered African American women as domestic servants in her kitchen. Childress puts that viewer into a new position, asking her to recognize the complexity and difficulty of black women's lives, thus forcing her to question what her own contributions have been to racial oppression.

This shift in perspective, brought about in the hearts and minds of individual audience members by Childress's work, seems but a small event on a small scale. Only those who see Childress's plays, and then only those in the audience who are open to reevaluating their perspectives, will benefit from the viewing. Critics of realism are justified in complaining that realist drama does not alter the status quo. I would argue, however, that more experimental forms of drama do not alter it either; the social order is unlikely to be overthrown on the strength of a play, whether realist or not. Only direct social action, like that of civil rights and of feminist activists, accomplishes major change in societal norms. To maintain that a play does not alter the status quo, however, is not necessarily to say that it supports it. Realist plays such as Childress's offer important criticism of contemporary racial politics by giving voice to the objectified and by deconstructing simplistic and dismissive racial and gender stereotypes. Childress grounds her viewer in reality—then changes the rules by highlighting the margins instead of the center.

Another complaint lodged against realism suggests that its form is too linear, that its build toward climax followed by closure forces a reinstatement of the dominant order. All loose ends need to be tied up, this argument goes, and that usually means that the disruptive forces have to be silenced. But why can't the ending of a realist play challenge the dominant order? Childress cites a famous example—Nora slamming the door at the end of Henrik Ibsen's *A Doll's House* (Bryer 66). In that case, the disruptive forces that cause Nora to question her "happy" marriage and home triumph, propelling her out of her house and into the unknown. The ending of Childress's own *Trouble in Mind* (as we shall soon see) leaves the audience completely without resolution, as the protagonist Wiletta takes a moral stand that will certainly cost her a badly needed job. Realism has been put to conventional uses many times; it is easy to come up with a long list of realist plays that are racist, sexist, and supportive of the status quo. But it does not have to be this way. Alice Childress, much like her colleagues in the Civil Rights movement and the abolition movement before that, does liberationist work with her realist, race-conscious plays. As Childress herself put it, "I write what I see, hear, and feel. I think that is the only realism that some fear" (Bryer 67).

Childress's first play, *Florence,* was written for the American Negro Theater in Harlem in 1949, before the major events of the Civil Rights movement had unfolded. As a realist play, *Florence* reflects the unequal and strained racial politics of its time, but also criticizes the segregation of people by race and the assumptions that even well-meaning whites make about people of color. The play is a relatively simple encounter between Mrs. Whitney (called Mama) and Mrs. Carter in a Southern train station. Both women are headed north to New York, Mama to see her daughter Florence, an aspiring actress, and Mrs. Carter to return home after a visit to her brother. The women are similar in age but otherwise very different: Mrs. Carter is a Northern white, Mama a Southern black; Mrs. Carter is wealthy, Mama is using the rent money to fund her trip; Mrs. Carter is educated, Mama is not. During the course of the play, the "enlightened" Mrs. Carter tries to win Mama's trust, only to prove herself as racist in her assumptions and her beliefs as the overt racists of the South. In *Florence,* Childress uses the conventions of realism—set, character, modes of speech—to draw an unsettling portrait of the Jim Crow South that has equally disturbing implications for the (supposedly) less prejudiced North.

When the house lights go down and the curtain rises, the audience faces a divided set. Childress takes pains in her stage directions to accurately reproduce the Jim Crow experience: "The room is divided into two sections by a low railing . . . Over the doorway stage right is a sign 'Colored,' over the doorway stage left is another sign 'White.' Stage right are two doors . . . one marked 'Colored men' . . . the other 'Colored women.' Stage left two other doorways are 'White ladies' and 'White gentlemen.' There are two benches . . . one on each side" (34). Audience members looking at the stage see two sides of the room that are mirror-images, but with subtle differences. The white passengers are called ladies and gentlemen; the black passengers, men and women. Although the interiors of these bathrooms are never seen, it is reasonable to suppose the accommodations for white passengers are superior to the accommodations for black passengers. In fact, we learn from the porter that the "Colored women" restroom is out of order. The porter, when he comes in, mops only the white side of the room. Except for a few moments of confrontation, Mrs. Carter and Mama stay on their respective sides of the waiting room, literally divided by a railing and figuratively divided by much more.

Childress's set puts Southern Jim Crow laws under a microscope. Audience members looking at the duplication of effort (two doors instead of one, four bathrooms instead of two) can see, perhaps for the first time, the artificiality of the barriers. By accurately and realistically reproducing a segregated waiting room, Childress confronts her audiences with segregation and forces them to examine their own feelings about race and their government's response to it. In practical terms, building everything in duplicate certainly costs more; in human terms, it creates obstacles to understanding. Childress draws attention to the literal barrier dividing the room by having characters briefly cross it: Mama's daughter Marge goes to the empty white side and comments, "Don't feel a damn bit different over here than it does on our side" (36). In figurative terms, though, the white side is very different: its inhabitants have privileges and freedoms not available to the inhabitants of the other side in 1950. Marge, for example, reminds Mama that she cannot go to the dining car on the segregated train; later, Mama and the porter discuss the mean ticket-seller who tries to obstruct blacks from traveling on the trains altogether.

The two principal characters somewhat unwillingly confront racial segregation, only to realize the size and significance of the gap between them. Mrs. Carter makes a big show of telling Mama not to call her "mam" ("it's so southern" [39]), but does not reveal her first name nor ask Mama for either her first or last name. Making conversation, she tells Mama about her brother Jeff, who has just published a novel "about your people" (40). The novel's mixed-race heroine, Zelma, is "almost white," but drowns herself because she cannot handle the "deep shame" of being black (40). Mama, who had gotten caught up in Mrs. Carter's telling of the story, becomes furious when she hears the end and challenges Mrs. Carter with "that ain't so! Not one bit it ain't!" (41). Mama tries to explain to Mrs. Carter, through examples, that mixed-race people do not perceive their color as shameful, but Mrs. Carter just cannot understand. She believes that since whiteness is "superior," all blacks must necessarily hate their color and wish to be white. Mrs. Carter mistakes the social construction of white superiority for the "natural" order of things. According to Samuel Hay, Mrs. Carter gives signs of liberalism, allowing Mama to momentarily overcome her mistrust. Mrs. Carter's underlying beliefs prove racist, however, and Mama returns to her original mistrust (118).

Childress uses Mama to appeal to the audience as a spokesperson for racial equality. Childress argues (through Mama's misunderstandings with Mrs. Carter) that even well-intentioned Northern whites who want to bridge the color line are so conditioned by racist beliefs that they cannot see people of color in non-stereotypical and equal terms. After the disagreement over Jeff's novel, Mrs. Carter tells Mama, "you know I try but it's really difficult to understand you people. However . . . I keep trying" (42). Mrs. Carter does not perceive herself as racist; she tells Mama she gave a thousand dollars to a black college and boasts, "I've . . . eaten with Negroes" (42). Mama knows better, and tries to keep her distance from this woman; Mrs. Carter may not understand Mama, but Mama understands Mrs. Carter. Mama is drawn in again, however, when Mrs. Carter asks about Florence. Mama is headed to New York to bring Florence home, even though she knows Florence wants to stay in New York and succeed as an actress. Mrs. Carter reveals that she herself is an actress; Mama tentatively asks her to help Florence. Mrs. Carter agrees, only to reveal that she has a different idea of help:

MRS. CARTER (*Gives her the address*): Tell your dear girl to call this number about a week from now.
MAMA: Yes, ma'am.
MRS. CARTER: Her experience won't matter with Melba. I know she'll understand. I'll call her too.
MAMA: Thank you, mam.
MRS. CARTER: I'll just tell her . . . no heavy washing or ironing . . . just light cleaning and a little cooking . . . does she cook? (45)

Mama presumed that Mrs. Carter could see Florence as a fellow professional, a struggling colleague in need of assistance. Mrs. Carter, however, can see black women in only one role: domestic. Despite her desire to understand and help, she cannot conceive of a world of racial equality. Mrs. Carter lacks the vision that Mama has, the vision of the Civil Rights movement. Mama's reaction is to cancel her trip and to send Florence an encouraging note: "Keep trying" (47).

Mama knows full well that the odds are stacked against Florence's success. Florence has already had her share of trouble: the audience learns in an aside that her husband was killed for trying to exercise his legal right to vote. Mama therefore makes the decision not to be another discouraging voice in Florence's life. As Samuel Hay argues, Mama "recognizes the truth of her having to make a greater sacrifice if Florence is to be given a fair chance to compete" (121). Mama moves from wanting Florence to stay within her prescribed limits to wanting her to challenge and expand those limits. Childress simultaneously pays tribute to the Mamas and the Florences of the world—black women "for whom the act of living is sheer heroism" (Brown-Guillory 234)—and challenges the Mrs. Carters of the world to expand their vision. The realist framework of the play allows the playwright thoroughly to develop her two protagonists, even in so short a play. The audience understands Mrs. Carter's limitations, her blind spots, and recognizes Mama's growth as she works for a better and more equal future.

Mama and Mrs. Carter's differences can perhaps best be conceptualized in terms of segregation of discourse. Just as the public space represented on stage is divided by Jim Crow laws, the discourses of the characters are not the same. Mrs. Carter sees herself as a benevolent patron who raises up people of color with her money and her progressive support. Mama sees Mrs. Carter as part of the problem, as a patronizing woman who oppresses people of color with her assumptions and her actions. Mrs. Carter envisions Mama as overly sensitive and somewhat frightening in her anger. When Mrs. Carter hears Mama's appeal to help Florence, she can only interpret that within her own context of white privilege. In Mrs. Carter's world, black women are maids, not actresses. When Mama hears about Mrs. Carter's brother's book, she can only interpret that within her own context of discrimination against blacks. In Mama's world, black people recognize that their race is not a cause for shame but for pride, regardless of the misguided beliefs of white people. Mama and Mrs. Carter have inhabited entirely different worlds due to racial segregation, so much so that they cannot make themselves understood to one another. This is realism: the reality of a segregated world outside the theater translates to the realities of a segregated world on stage. Childress does not shrink from the unpleasant truth that "reality" includes anger, fear, misunderstanding, and a little bit of hope. Childress's realist play encourages black audience members to keep struggling for equality and asks Northern white audience members to face and conquer their prejudices and assumptions.

Six years after *Florence* (and in the midst of the major events of the Civil Rights movement), Childress continued to examine issues of segregation, stereotypes, and the possibilities of interracial dialogue. *Trouble in Mind,* her 1955 effort that won her an Obie award, utilizes a play-within-a-play format. Childress tells the story of a cast of predominantly black actors getting together to rehearse a realist play, which she calls *Chaos in Belleville,* written and directed by white men. Through the actors' sarcastic commentary on the racism and sexism of the play, Childress skillfully and humorously satirizes the race and gender stereotypes which afflict not only the fictional characters but also the actors who must play them on (and sometimes off) stage. The playwright uses realism because it permits her to show how far from reality these stereotypes are. That is, by switching between the "real" people (the characters in *Trouble in Mind*) and the supposedly realistic characters they play in *Chaos in Belleville,* she demonstrates that popular conceptions of black women and men are insulting and false. Childress takes the opportunity to comment on white theater, highlighting the limitations of the dominant (white) view of reality. She also fills in the gaps by presenting a more authentic version of the lives of struggling black actors.

The group of black actors who have assembled to rehearse *Chaos in Belleville* include Wiletta, Millie, Sheldon, and John. Wiletta and Sheldon are theater veterans; they have played every stereotypical role imaginable and claim to know how to work with "the man." Millie, younger and more glamorous, also understands what's expected of her, though she would gladly trade in her mammy roles to play an ingenue. John, just starting out and brimming with idealism, believes that his talent will conquer any racism he might encounter. There are two white actors as well: Judy, also idealistic and on her first job, and Bill, who is far more cynical. The director, Al Manners, is white. The action of the play *Trouble in Mind* is principally the rehearsal of the play *Chaos in Belleville,* with the ensuing conflicts over content, motivation, and acting style. *Chaos in Belleville,* presumably an anti-lynching play, tells the story of Job (John), a black sharecropper in the 1950s who exercises his legal right to vote and gets lynched for doing so. Job's mother, Ruby (Wiletta), inadvertently contributes to her son's fate by encouraging him to turn himself in to the white authorities, as do his father Sam (Sheldon) and family friend Petunia (Millie). The white owner of the land, Regard (Bill), and his daughter Carrie (Judy) fail to protect Job. The crux of the conflict in *Trouble in Mind* comes from Wiletta's resistance to the actions of her character and to Manners's condescending direction. Manners, a method director, wants his actors to feel and empathize with the motivations of their characters. Wiletta, who originally advises John that he should "Uncle Tom" in order to advance his career, realizes that she cannot empathize with Ruby's decision to turn her son in for voting. She confronts Manners on this issue, finally forcing him, in the play's climax, to reveal his own racism. Wiletta triumphs over Manners's condescension and superficiality, but it is a hollow triumph; she knows she will lose her job.

Trouble in Mind is a logical successor to *Florence* in that it tells the same story from another perspective. Despite the earlier play's title, the character Florence is never seen; we hear about her desire to be an actress and about her struggles, but only filtered through her family. *Trouble in Mind* looks at the theater, using this world as a microcosm for the larger society. Childress works to identify the power of race and gender stereotypes both inside and outside the theater; she demonstrates that these abstract and generalized notions of black and female identity exercise material power in the lives of individuals. Playacting the stereotypes is a matter of survival for black people and particularly black women, the difference between having a job and not having one, between surviving and not surviving. Childress demonstrates that these black actors must "perform" their race in ways that please their white employers. Wiletta, experienced in this behavior, introduces John to the subtleties of racial performance:

> WILETTA: You ever do a professional show before?
> JOHN: Yes, some off-Broadway . . . and I've taken classes.
> WILETTA: Don't let the man know that. They don't like us to go to school.
> JOHN: Oh, now.
> WILETTA: They want us to be naturals . . . you know, just born with the gift. 'Course they want you to be experienced too. Tell em' you was in the last revival of *Porgy and Bess*. (139)

Wiletta encourages John to hide his education so as not to threaten the director. In accordance with the stereotype of the "happy slave" singing on the plantation, white writers and directors ("the man") want natural, raw talent. Later, Wiletta tells John that "white folks can't stand unhappy Negroes . . . so laugh,

laugh when it ain't funny at all" (139). This behavior may eat away at John's self-esteem, but it will, Wiletta advises, help him to continue working.

This is one of many scenes that occur between the black actors without the white actors on stage. These become the truth-telling scenes, the scenes in which the black cast can drop the pretenses and be themselves. In these scenes, Childress contrasts the wit and intelligence of the black actors with the flat, shallow stereotypes they must play. The black actors must hide these finer qualities in the presence of Manners. Childress wants the audiences to cringe as they see the black actors "Uncle Tom" for the director and the white actors, recognizing (perhaps for the first time) how debasing it is. For example, when Judy first comes on stage, she asks Wiletta:

JUDY: What do you think of the play?
WILETTA: Oh, I never had anything affect me so much in all my life. It's so sad, ain't it sad?
JUDY: Oh, there's some humor.
WILETTA: I'm tellin' you, I almost busted my sides laughin'. (142)

Wiletta has already told John and the audience that the play "stinks, ain't nothin' atall" (140). She knows she cannot say this to the white cast and directors, though; she needs the work and she knows there are many others who will gladly take her place if she tells the truth. Childress carefully establishes the economic difficulties of the black actors; they are one job away from poverty and therefore cannot afford to act on their principles. Sheldon spends the play trying to find an apartment; he lives in a dilapidated rooming house, and the apartments he can afford do not accept blacks. These material difficulties are never far from the action on stage; the audience clearly understands that the black actors must accept the racism, sexism, and condescension they experience or else be out of work. Childress shows the black actors to be equal if not superior to the white actors and managers, but then depicts the painful process of their self-effacement.

Wiletta and the other black actors have years of experience in playing humiliating roles simply to keep working, as shown in the following exchange between Wiletta and Millie:

MILLIE: Last show I was in, I wouldn't even tell my relatives. All I did was shout "Lord, have mercy!" for almost two hours every night.

WILETTA: Yes, but you did it, so hush! She's played every flower in the garden. Let's see, what was your name in that TV mess?
MILLIE: Never mind.
WILETTA: Gardenia! She was Gardenia! 'Nother thing . . . she was Magnolia, Chrysanthemum was another . . .
MILLIE: And you've done the jewels . . . Crystal, Pearl, Opal! (141)

Their characters' names in *Chaos in Belleville* are, of course, Petunia and Ruby. Both are stereotypical mammy types, religious, devoted to the white family whose land they farm. They use words like "troublous" and "iffen"; Petunia says to Carrie, "bless your soul, you just one of God's golden-haired angels" (148). The language is an exaggerated form of the more realistic black English spoken by the actors. Although the lines and the play are funny, the humor comes not from the truth of the stereotypes but from their ridiculousness. But just because the stereotypes are false, it does not mean the actors can change or even avoid them. These are the stereotypes that continue to haunt black women through images like "Aunt Jemima." Millie and Wiletta have to play the stereotypes, but they clearly resist them in their own lives.

Chaos in Belleville, like *Trouble in Mind,* is intended to be a realist, issue-oriented play, meant to rouse sympathy for the plight of black people. Childress mocks the "realism" of white-authored plays like *Chaos in Belleville;* she suggests that a racist white author cannot be relied upon to write a realistic play about African Americans. Writing from an insider's perspective, she shows the rest of the story through her three-dimensional black characters. An important part of telling the rest of the story, for Childress, is placing her story in the social context of its day. Childress succeeds in raising the issue of lynching and other issues from 1955, particularly the Montgomery bus boycott. In a key scene, Manners patronizingly assumes that the actors have never seen a lynching, only to learn from Sheldon that he has. Sheldon, at the urging of the rest of the cast, movingly tells the story of seeing "a burnt, naked, thing" dragged along behind a wagon accompanied by peals of laughter from the white lynch mob. The victim, Mr. Morris, was lynched for "talking back" (166). Manners's response is typically self-centered and inadequate:

MANNERS: When I hear of barbarism . . . I feel so wretched, so guilty.
SHELDON: Don't feel that way. You wouldn't kill nobody and do 'em like that . . . would you?

MANNERS: (*Hurt by the question*). No, Sheldon.
SHELDON: That's what I know. (166)

Sheldon's momentary doubt in Manners's sincerity proves prophetic; this begins the build toward the climactic scene between Manners and Wiletta. By this point in the play, the audience understands that Sheldon and the other black actors have no reason to trust their white employers and colleagues; their life experiences have taught them otherwise. In his unadorned and unaffected account of the crime he witnessed, Sheldon delivers a far more effective anti-lynching message than the stereotypical characters of *Chaos in Belleville* ever could. Childress also includes multiple references to the boycott in Montgomery and to other milestones of the Civil Rights movement, proceeding as she wrote this play to keep those events in the front of her audience's consciousness. Her intent is to help her audiences connect the racism they see depicted on stage (to which they object) to the racism being fought in the South. Childress uses her play to provide impetus for audience support of the Civil Rights movement.

Like Mama in *Florence,* Wiletta is Childress's spokeswoman for racial and sexual equality. She belongs to the proud group of remarkable black women characters created by these (and other) black women playwrights. Wiletta evolves from a woman willing to compromise and placate "the man" to a character devoted to speaking her mind, even though it will cost her a job. As Gayle Austin notes, "Wiletta becomes a critic/artist of the play she is performing, changing from passive object to active subject in front of our eyes" (57). After four days of enduring Manners's condescension and trying to understand the play, Wiletta finally explodes, questioning "Why this boy's people turned against him? Why we sendin' him out into the teeth of a lynch mob? I'm his mother and I'm sendin' him to his death. This is a lie. . . . The writer wants the damn white man to be the hero—and I'm the villain" (169). Wiletta has measured her own reality, the reality of poverty and racism and never being able to trust white people, against the supposed realism of *Chaos in Belleville,* and found the script lacking. Although the other actors and Manners try to convince her that this play is realistic, Wiletta will not budge. Manners finally explodes:

MANNERS: The American public is not ready to see you the way you want to be seen because, one, they don't believe it, two, they don't want to believe it, and three, they're convinced they're superior. . . . Now you wise up and aim for the soft spot in that American heart, let 'em pity you, make 'em weep buckets, be helpless, make 'em feel so damned sorry for you that they'll lend a hand in easing up the pressure . . .

WILETTA: Would you send your son out to be murdered?

MANNERS: (*So wound up, he answers without thinking*) Don't compare yourself to me! What goes for my son doesn't necessarily go for yours! (170–71)

Manners unmasks his own racism, demonstrating without doubt that he has only given lip service to racial equality, and that he places greater truth in the stereotypes of the play he's directing than he would like to admit. His advice to the black actors is that they must use the stereotypes, that playing Uncle Tom and Mammy will win the white audience to their side. Wiletta (and the rest of the cast) know better. The stereotypes which grew out of slavery have never contributed to racial or sexual equality, only offered impediments to whites viewing blacks as equal, whole human beings. Wiletta confronts Manners, knowing that it will cost her this job.

Interestingly, Childress was pressured by the play's producers at the Greenwich Mews to change this ending so it would be happier and display more racial unity. Specifically, they asked her to rewrite it so that the entire cast rallied around Wiletta, and all of them—black and white—quit in protest and walked out together. Childress did not want to do this for the simple reason that she "saw nothing of this sort happening anywhere in the commercial theater . . . I haven't known of any Broadway company where they all walked out because some actress or actor felt a certain way. I totally disbelieved the ending they wanted" (Bryer 52–53). The producers sought to undermine the carefully constructed realism of the play by imposing a false sense of racial unity, allowing them to send the audience home with a neat, clean ending. Because the show was so close to opening, Childress gave in despite her misgivings, but later said, "I always hated myself for giving in and changing the ending" (Bryer 52). In subsequent productions, she removed the happy ending, leaving it ambiguous and challenging the audience to struggle with what they would do in the same situation.

Alice Childress defies the formula Manners suggests for winning sympathy for the plight of black Americans. She understands that she must attack the feeling of superiority Manners assigns to white audiences and deconstruct the damaging race and gender stereotypes. Guilt and pity may lead to temporary concessions but will rarely lead to significant changes in the social order. Once minor concessions are made out of guilt, the dominant group can then continue to defend its own superiority. The strategy Childress employs instead is to use realism to create truer representations of black women and men, instead of the stereotypical ones that so often appear in white-authored plays. Childress believes that telling the truth of black experience will encourage white audiences to recognize dominant racial and sexual norms as social constructs that cripple the potential of minorities and women.

In 1974, Childress said that "all Black writers, whether they intended to or not, have been writing about not being free. Always—from the beginning of America right up to now" (Taylor-Guthrie 9). Her plays fit that description; they testify to the need for the United States to radically revise its racial attitudes and practices. Her choice of realism grounds her audiences in the racial and sexual politics of their own times; they cannot distance themselves from the unjust world they see on the stage. The two hours of "entertainment" provided by an Alice Childress play served the same purpose as any of Martin Luther King, Jr.'s speeches: to persuade, challenge, inspire, and provoke the audience. Indeed, those who felt indifferent to the Civil Rights movement might have avoided a speech as too political and controversial, whereas a play could sneak past those defenses and get to the issues underneath. Alice Childress's name belongs on the same roll of honor as her colleagues in the Civil Rights movement; more than five years after her death in 1994, it is time to shine a light on her distinguished career and bring her to Broadway at last.[4]

Notes

1. See, for example, Sue Ellen Case's *Feminism and Theater* (New York: Routledge, 1988); Jill Dolan's *The Feminist Spectator as Critic* (Ann Arbor: U of Michigan P, 1988) and *Presence and Desire: Essays of Gender, Sexuality, and Performance* (Ann Arbor: U of Michigan P, 1993); Jeanie Forte's "Realism, Narrative, and the Feminist Playwright—A Problem of Reception," *Modern Drama* 32 (Mar. 1989) 115–27; and Patricia Schroeder's *The Feminist Possibilities of Dramatic Realism* (Madison, NJ: Fairleigh Dickinson UP, 1996).

2. There have, as yet, been few book-length treatments of Alice Childress's work. Several critical articles exist, but their number is relatively few considering the length and productivity of the playwright's career.

3. See Catherine Belsey's "Constructing the Subject: Deconstructing the Text,"

Feminist Criticism and Social Change: Sex, Class and Race in Literature and Culture. Ed. Judith Newton and Deborah Rosenfelt (New York: Methuen, 1985) 45–64. See also Toril Moi's *Sexual/Textual Politics* (London: Routledge, 1985).

4. I would like to thank Paul Dudenhefer for his close reading of an earlier version of this essay. I would also like to thank Robert L. McDonald, Linda Rohrer Paige, and the reviewers and copyeditors of this volume for their thoughtful suggestions.

Works Cited

Austin, Gayle. "Alice Childress: Black Woman Playwright as Feminist Critic." *Southern Quarterly* 25.3 (Spring 1987): 53–65.

Brown-Guillory, Elizabeth. "Black Women Playwrights: Exorcizing Myths." *Phylon* 48.3 (Fall 1987): 229–39.

Bryer, Jackson, ed. *The Playwright's Art: Conversations with Contemporary American Dramatists.* New Brunswick: Rutgers UP, 1995.

Childress, Alice. "A Candle in a Gale Wind." *Black Women Writers (1950–1980): A Critical Evaluation.* Ed. Mari Evans. New York: Anchor, 1983. 111–16.

———. "Florence." *Masses and Mainstream* 3.10 (Oct. 1950): 34–47.

———. "Trouble in Mind." *Black Theater.* Ed. Lindsay Patterson. New York: Dodd, 1971. 135–74.

Friedman, Susan Stanford. "History's Return: The Politics of Rupture and Repression in Modernism." A work in progress.

Harris, Trudier. Introduction. *Like One of the Family: Conversations from a Domestic's Life.* By Alice Childress. Boston: Beacon, 1986.

Hay, Samuel A. "Alice Childress's Dramatic Structure." *Black Women Writers (1950–1980): A Critical Evaluation.* Ed. Mari Evans. New York: Anchor, 1984. 117–28.

Taylor-Guthrie, Danielle, ed. *Conversations with Toni Morrison.* Jackson: UP of Mississippi, 1994.

7

Role-ing on the River: Actors Theatre of Louisville and the Southern Woman Playwright

Elizabeth S. Bell

Scarcely a stone's throw from the Ohio River, Actors Theatre of Louisville serves as an anchor for the historic downtown of Kentucky's largest city. Founded in 1778 by George Rogers Clark as a military stronghold and portage point on the major water route connecting Philadelphia and New Orleans, Louisville was once upon a time as famous for its open red-light district as it was for its accommodation of river trade and services. By the 1800s, Louisville was also famous for its hospitality to thespians and theater companies, including the illustrious Booth and Barrymore families.[1] While its days as a rowdy river town for the unsavory elements of society have largely ended, Louisville still maintains its theatrical heritage, serving as home to one of the most active and prosperous regional theaters in the country. Indeed, Actors Theatre's reputation for excellence and innovation spreads far beyond the banks of the Mighty Ohio River to garner international appreciation of its repertoire. In the thirty years of its existence, it has also earned a reputation as a congenial forum for women playwrights.

Actors Theatre's reputation for encouraging women playwrights arises from several sources. Playing crucial roles in this endeavor, a strong financial foundation and loyal community support provide the theater with both the means and the opportunity to be innovative, particularly in producing plays by relatively unknown women playwrights. In addition, ATL's management decisions and artistic risk-taking attract playwrights whose perspectives have been underrepresented on the American stage. In a field dominated by men until the latter quarter of the twentieth century, this combination has been particularly important to women writers. *New York Times* critic Mel Gussow, writing for *American Theatre* in 1996, makes the point that over the years, ATL has excelled in producing plays by women writers, including, specifically, Southerners Marsha Norman, Beth Henley, and the pseudonymous "Jane Martin," who over the years have succeeded in fulfilling the professional promise ATL saw in them (53).

Notable because it shows the complex interconnections of all of these factors, the theater season of 1981–82 serves as a kind of exemplar for the combination of roles that have made Actors Theatre of Louisville such a welcoming forum for women playwrights. The elements that permeate the theater gathered in intense form during that one season. In November of 1981, ATL announced that it had been awarded a $20,000 grant from the Ford Foundation to commission ten women playwrights to create one-act plays, three of which would be produced by ATL ("ATL Commissions"). That grant enabled ATL not only to spotlight women playwrights, but also to showcase the educational facet of its role in regional theater. The ten women chosen were relatively unknown voices in American theater. Four of them were Southern: Lezley Havard of Georgia, Claudia Johnson of Florida, Trish Johnson of North Carolina, and Sallie Bingham of Kentucky. By the time the project ended in August, all involved hailed it a success.

Julie Beckett Crutcher, Actors' literary manager at the time and more recently a playwright well known to Kentucky audiences, credited the women themselves for much of the success. In essence, she said in an interview with Louisville *Courier-Journal* theater critic Owen Hardy, the women playwrights brought a more cooperative and much needed approach to the theater: "Women have traditionally been underdogs within the theatrical hierarchy. It's important that their point of view be expressed. Ten women in a room create a very different atmosphere from five women and five men . . . the women were freer with each other, like an all-woman gym class" (qtd. in Hardy 6). The playwrights themselves expressed appreciation of the atmosphere created. Trish Johnson remarked that the workshop became a "quiet, private" place where egos did not clash; Laura Cunningham, a participant from New York, added, "There was certainly criticism, but it was never hurtful criticism." A third participant, Barbara Schneider, originally from Germany, observed that while there was no common theme or issue involved in the ten plays, they did share one feature: "By and large, these one-acts have better women's roles in them." Jon Jory, Actors Theatre's producing director, expressed in the same interview his support for the project and, incidentally, for women playwrights in general: "Some of the best work today is being done by women writers. Also, a lot of these writers are those we've worked with previously" (qtd. in Hardy 6). Part of what had made the project so successful was the freedom these women had to write what they chose without interference, while they still had the opportunity to communicate in a workshop situation with each other and with Jory and his staff. Indeed, the opportunity to network with other women playwrights, to discuss ideas and theatrical techniques with each other, and to have the pragmatic perspective of a producing director openly available to them created an extremely supportive atmosphere for these women and foreshadowed a role as mentor Jory would establish in his relationships with other playwrights over the years.

At the same time this project was ending, ATL was co-sponsoring, along with American Express, a theater trip for patrons who wished to fly to New York for a production at the Manhattan Theatre Club of *Talking With,* a series of monologues by the playwright known as "Jane Martin" which had premiered at Actors in the 1981–82 Sixth Humana Festival of New American Plays ("ATL Trip") and which, incidentally, introduced Martin as a playwright. Jory was directing the New York production, as he had the Louisville premiere, and most of the original cast had followed him to New York. Although this involvement with Martin's play may seem, at first glance, to be unrelated to the grant supporting women playwrights, together they form a pattern of active engagement with the work of women writers, at a time when the conventional wisdom told us that the most noteworthy playwrights were male.

While ATL does not seek on a regular basis grants geared especially for women playwrights and no longer transports their plays to New York, deciding instead to focus on the initial production, the 1981–82 theater season illustrates part of the magic formula that has worked so well over the years: The combination of philanthropic foundation, corporate, and community support; Jory's respect for the playwright and his vision of what a theater might be and accomplish; and the presence of women in artistic and managerial decision-making positions at Actors—along with the playwrights themselves—have created a fertile ground for emerging women playwrights. Each of these roles has been crucial to ATL's ability to promote the plays of women from around the nation and especially the South.

Virtually everyone associated with the theater gives much credit to Producing Director Jon Jory, who joined ATL in March of 1969. In a 1974 interview with Louisville *Courier-Journal* theater critic William Mootz, Jory summed up his perspective, born of his lifetime involvement with the theater, by pointing out how crucial effective management is for a theater. Quite literally, management decisions can determine life or death for a professional regional theater, as well as determine how innovative its repertoire can be. Under his leadership, ATL has maintained a high level of financial security, developed a multifaceted theatrical repertoire of classic and contemporary works, encouraged an array of new playwrights representing the major voices in contemporary theater, and won the three most important awards given to regional theaters: in 1979, the Margo Jones Award and the Schubert Foundation's James N. Vaughan Memorial Award and in June 1979 the Special Tony Award. Indeed, Jory's leadership is one of the features of ATL that makes its success possible.

While Jory's vision for the theater has many facets, the Humana Festival of New American Plays remains one of the most important of those, especially to women playwrights, for this festival, designed to encourage new voices in the theater and new experimentation from more established voices, has always been an open vehicle for women playwrights. Premiering two Pulitzer Prize–winning plays in its first four years, including Beth Henley's *Crimes of the Heart* (1979), while ATL also produced Marsha Norman's *'night, Mother* (1982), the festival also early won the attention of New York theater critics and producers who regularly peruse the festival's productions in search of new talent.

Based on his personal experience with sixteen of the twenty festivals through 1996, Mel Gussow in *American Theater* credits Jory with both "discovery and nurturing" of women playwrights and also women directors, all of whom have played a key role in ATL's successful repertoire (53). And indeed, with the artistic encouragement available at ATL, the lists sometimes overlap; Marsha Norman, for example, tried her hand at directing with *Semi-Precious Things* in 1980.

Nevertheless, as significant as the Humana Festival is for women playwrights, it does not exist in a vacuum. The openness to women's plays permeates the entire managerial structure of the theater. According to Literary Manager Michael Bigelow Dixon, ATL's role in fostering women playwrights is a complex balance: While Jon Jory "wants women represented in all facets of the theater program," they are not singled out for consideration and no favors are awarded to them. "The great thing about Actors is the parity it offers playwrights. We do nothing special for women playwrights. Everyone gets our best treatment, suited for them and the project" (Personal Interview). Alexander Speer, Executive Producer at Actors, attributes the prevalence of women playwrights who have had works produced at Actors to the entire array of projects the theater has sponsored, of which the Humana Festival of New American Plays is but one feature. "Our repertoire," he says, "is congenial to women playwrights and also women directors. We make no decision to look particularly at women writers; however, many of the plays we are interested in happen to be written by women" (Personal Interview).

In deciding which plays to produce, Dixon, his assistants, and Jory weigh several matters. Dixon is interested in how the script works and whether it engages the reader, for, after all, that is how the script first attracts attention. He then decides whether or not the script has what he calls "that sense of theatricality" that will elicit response from an audience. While he values a "poetic sense of language," he also wants multidimensional characters and an exploration of social issues—"a grappling with ideas, fresh and penetrating" (Personal Interview). Amy Wegener, Assistant Literary Manager, looks for plays she "hasn't seen before." When she finishes with a script, she wants to feel "completeness, that the play has a point that has been fulfilled" (Personal Interview). Jory has a slightly different focus. He must determine whether the play can be produced with ATL's facilities and resources. "The production problems are Jon's deal," Dixon laughs. Nevertheless, Dixon stresses that the decisions about which plays to produce are formed after collaborative discussions, with members of the literary staff and Jory mulling over the merits of each particular script. Once that decision has been made, the choice of director for the production represents a collaborative effort between Jory and the playwright, each having "mutual veto" power (Personal Interview).

Dixon also notes that Jon Jory has a "particular interest in Southern playwrights" (Personal Interview). This is both an artistic and a managerial concern. According to Speer, "It's a huge compliment" to be recognized as a Southern regional theater with an international reputation: "A theater needs to be both a stimulus to and a reflection of its community. Jon Jory and I agree on this" (Personal Interview). ATL's heritage and its community draw from the South, and the themes typically associated with the South—strong family ties, a proclivity for violence, women as "steel magnolias"—offer fertile ground for complex plays that explore many facets of the human experience. As a result, ATL frequently commissions playwrights, such as Southerners Jane Martin, Marsha Norman, and Elizabeth Dewberry, to write plays on topics of their own choosing. Indeed, there is no effort by ATL to shape the canon of a particular playwright. The result is a wide array of perspectives. Thus, women playwrights have extended the boundaries of so-called women's issues to create a repertoire of plays as varied as the approximately 230 women playwrights and their almost 300 plays that ATL has produced. Predictably, some of these playwrights have been irrevocably associated with ATL, and their work represents a sample of the themes and approaches ATL has welcomed over the years.

One such playwright, an acknowledged Kentuckian who writes under the pseudonym Jane Martin, is one of the most frequently produced playwrights at ATL, either male or female. Martin neither appears in public nor grants interviews. Indeed, Jory habitually provides the only public comment on Martin's intention in a script or her assessment of her own work. As Janet Gainor's essay in this volume explains, rumors abound as to Martin's identity, with one of the more persistent whispers being that "she" is Jory himself, or perhaps, Jory and an associate, such as Alexander Speer. Nevertheless, the theatrical persona of "Jane Martin" is relentlessly female, and "her" strong, provocative scripts explore the many facets of women's lives, from the bizarre to the painfully familiar.

Martin first emerged on the American stage in the 1981–82 theater season when *Talking With* premiered at the Humana Festival and later won the Best Foreign Play of the Year Award from Germany's *Theater Heute.* As the title suggests, this production exists as a series of monologues spoken by women in some degree of isolation. The monologues, related neither by character nor by theme, together create a collage of women's experiences masked by their specific circumstances but essentially readily recognizable for their revelation of the human condition. Many of the eleven women spotlighted in this production are performers of some sort—an actress bemoaning the anonymity of the audience, a housewife dressing up in the costumes of *The Wizard of Oz* as she vacuums the floor, a disillusioned rodeo rider who sees the sport she loves losing its free spirit to become a tool of corporate America, a third-generation serpent handler explaining the value of her faith and the need for a good performance, among others. As a collection, *Talking With* allows the women it portrays to define themselves, to reveal the insights or the illusions, the meaning or the pain, they find in life. As individual monologues, each creates a believable individual voice denoting a person striving for self-recognition. Herein lies the substance of Martin's first work: the playwright creates women who must negotiate between a public face and a private one. They must find themselves somewhere in the mixture of what society expects of them and what they really care about. At the same time, regardless of their circumstances, Martin writes of them with understanding and compassion. Because the writer respects the essential nature of "her" characters, we, the audience, do as well.

Martin's most critically recognized and, perhaps, most controversial play, *Keely and Du*—a 1993 Humana Festival production pitting a young woman, pregnant from a rape and wanting an abortion, against radical pro-life activists who drug, kidnap, and imprison her—won the 1994 American Theater Critics Award, was nominated for a Pulitzer Prize, and "was the most produced new work in America" (Dixcy xi). Wherever it has played, it has engaged audiences in its complexity and won the praise of theater critics. Here, Martin carries the audience through the extremities of life and death, placing one person's belief that what she does is right against another person's inherent right of freedom and free choice with her own life. The mood of this play is decidedly dark, the issues profoundly difficult to deal with. The conflict revolves around the nature of good and evil and brings the audience face-to-face with its own preconceived labels in the emotional national issue of abortion. To enhance the dramatic impact of the play, Martin's stage directions recommend no intermission and no pre-show or intermission music to alter the mood and tension the script creates.

During the course of the play, the two women—Keely, the young rape victim, and Du, the older woman who is her prison-keeper—develop a kind of bond, a "complicity" (291) as the male kidnapper later labels it. From this bond, both perspectives in the abortion rights controversy become humanized. Keely recounts the horror of rape and displays her anger at her life being discounted and trivialized for what she sees as a political statement on the part of the kidnappers. While Martin never waivers in presenting the kidnapping as the criminal and misguided act it is, Du is allowed to express a sincere compassion for the unborn baby she is trying to protect. At the same time, Du comes to recognize the trauma and pain the rape has caused Keely, and, after Keely aborts with a concealed coat hanger, Du chooses to stay with her until emergency medical help arrives, even though she knows it will result in her arrest and imprisonment and her abandonment by the other kidnappers, who flee to protect themselves. Keely, too, recognizes the bond they share, for even though she can't quite forgive what Du and the others have done, she visits Du regularly in prison and cares for her. Yet at play's end, realistically neither woman can explain why she made the choices she did. Again, the strength of this play, as with most of Martin's work, is that it allows women to speak, to reveal the issues at the center of their hearts.

Throughout the two decades of her productivity, Martin's emergence and place in the theater world owe a great deal to Jory and ATL's active sponsoring. Ensuring the playwright's privacy and anonymity, Jory provides a public voice for Martin, perhaps in order that the messages of her private voice, conceived and revealed in the sensitivity and complexity of the plays performed under the name Jane Martin, may be maintained. While Martin's experience differs in the extent to which Jory and ATL have fostered her career—indeed, as some have claimed, *constructed* her achievement—it does not ultimately differ in kind from the experience of other playwrights given their start at ATL.

In a 1996 interview with W. Dale Brown, Elizabeth Dewberry tells of her own experience as a commissioned writer for ATL. Sending them a play she had written while just beginning to learn how to use dialogue in a dramatic form, she received in return a telephone call from Jory who "gave [her] a crash course in playwrighting" (qtd. in Brown 112). As a result of that telephone call, Dewberry realized that her original conception was not working, so she began an entirely new play, which became *Flesh and Blood,* produced by ATL for the Twentieth Humana Festival in 1995–96. Literary Manager Michael Dixon recalls the events surrounding that play: "It was amazing. Jon told her about what to do. Thirty days later she sent us a completely different play. Jon does a great 45-minute seminar on the phone" (Personal Interview). *Flesh and Blood* explores a theme in women's scripts introduced early in the Humana Festival saga: the complex interrelations of women in a family. Henley's *Crimes of the Heart* and Norman's *'night, Mother,* as well as, more recently, Regina Taylor's *Jennine's Diary* (1993), all develop various elements of this relationship.

Marsha Norman, too, has spoken in several published interviews and a Kentucky Educational Television production about the mentoring she received at ATL. After spending several years in a variety of jobs, including writing for a children's publication in Louisville and *Louisville Today,* Norman was offered the opportunity by Jory to interview people in Louisville about the then explosive issues of desegregation and school busing. This opportunity would form the raw material for a collaborative play Jory, Norman, and several others would write about the controversy. When Norman expressed her lack of interest in the project, Jory offered to let her write about any subject that interested her. The result is *Getting Out,* her first produced play, premiering in the ATL 1977–78 season.

The play, as raw in its language and as confined in its visual spaces as it is brutal in the situation in which its protagonist finds herself, chronicles the attempt of Arlene, just released from prison, to lead a law-abiding life, even though those who knew her as a child found her violent and unreachable. To add to her difficult adjustment, she remains both uneducated and unskilled and carries with her the stigma of prison. Central to the development of the play, Norman's creative use of the stage space itself provides two time frames for action—one, the present day with the adult Arlene, and the other, the past with the rebellious child Arlie providing a visual correlative of Arlene's memory of herself. The play revolves around Arlene's confrontation with the realities of life outside of prison and the audience's realization that, given her lack of employable skills, the lack of support she receives from her mother, and the temptations around her that beckon her back to her previous criminal life, Arlene finds herself in a prison of another sort. While Norman in no way trivializes the hardship Arlene faces, she provides for her a ray of hope in the form of Ruby, the upstairs neighbor, who is herself an ex-con and who has decided that she will not return to the life that led to her prison experience. The bond that just begins as the play ends suggests that Arlene will have an ally in her quest for a straight life. Theater critic John Simon, writing for the *Hudson Review*, called *Getting Out* "an astonishing first play," adding the qualifier that it deals with a kind of violence and a way of life with which the thirty-one-year-old Norman had had very little contact (81).[2]

ATL also indirectly influenced Norman to write *'night, Mother*, her 1983 Pulitzer Prize–winning play about a young woman preparing her mother for her suicide in a real-time, tension-filled confrontation taking place over the performance time of the play. In a 1993 interview with writer Elisabeth Beattie, Norman tells of several friends whose children had committed suicide and of news articles she had read about the increasing number of suicides among young people. Furthermore, she felt Brian Clark's 1974 play, *Whose Life Is It, Anyway?*, failed to create a meaningful forum for discussing suicide (294). She felt the issue demanded some kind of exploration from her, so she set about writing her own play. Norman insists the play is about two women—mother and daughter—who have "a deep, long, complicated relationship of great, intense love" (294), so the confrontation between them really matters.[3]

The play, however, is problematic for audiences, for the relationship between Jessie and her mother provides ample opportunity to interpret it in a vastly different light. If read one way, Jessie's deliberate and carefully orchestrated movements prior to her suicide, which she glibly tries to justify to her mother, take on a more sinister connotation. They suggest a final attempt by Jessie to chastise her mother for not providing her with a reason to live. Several times during the play, she complains that her life in her mother's house is not sufficient. She realizes that after her marriage failed, she chose an unsatisfying life, just as her child chose a life she does not approve. The various lists Jessie has made and the chores she has completed, including choosing what her brother should buy her mother for holidays in the future, while perhaps an expression of love, also function as grim reminders, ongoing for several holidays, of the daughter who committed suicide. Regardless of its interpretation, however, in Jessie and her mother, Norman's play provides two voices, two perspectives, neither one of which is entirely blameless nor entirely culpable in Jessie's suicide. This complex layering of motives and meanings is a hallmark of Norman's most enduring work.

Norman's more recent contributions to ATL have been lighter in tone. Commissioned in 1992 by Jory under a grant from the Kentucky Colonels to write something celebrating the state's bicentennial, Norman created *D. Boone,* a time-traveling exploration into the nature of heroes and human beings. Her protagonist, a staff member at a small historical museum modeled on Louisville's Filson Club, finds contemporary life uncongenial and longs for the pioneer days of Daniel Boone. She discovers a time portal in the museum which transports her back to Daniel Boone's settlement, where she becomes involved in various escapades. Of course, both the museum director and a newly hired cleaning man, who becomes by play's end her love interest, follow her through the portal.

While clearly not on the level established by her more serious plays, *D. Boone* marks a new trend for Norman's writing. In a 1992 interview with William Mootz, she described the play as a comedy from start to finish ("Pride"). Norman gives much of the credit to director Gloria Muzio, who decided to emphasize the humor of the play with comedic actors. In the same interview with Mootz, Norman describes how fulfilling entertaining an audience can be and how much she finds it a welcome change from her more serious and pain-filled plays ("Pride"). ATL and Jon Jory have been receptive to Norman as she explores new voices and new visions. In the interview with Beattie, Norman acknowledges the value of that bond and of her enduring friendship and professional relationship with Jory (296).

Another Kentucky native, Naomi Wallace, has just begun what appears to be a positive relationship with ATL. To date, two of her plays have been produced during the Humana Festival, *One Flea Spare* in 1996 and *Trestle at Pope Lick Creek* in 1998. The first originally premiered at the Bush Theater in London and carries an ostensibly British flavor. Set in London during the plague year of 1665, the play explores the relationship of four people quarantined together under guard. The play was well received in Louisville, as *Courier-Journal* critic Judith Egerton articulates ("*Trestle* Spans"). It received mixed and unenthusiastic reviews from other parts of the country, however. Much of the criticism focused on Wallace's penchant for creating social-issue commentaries rather than character-driven dramas.[4]

Scarcely known in this country, Wallace's works clearly fare better in England, where the playwright now lives. During an interview with Louisville theater critic William Mootz, Dominic Dromgoole, who directed *One Flea Spare* at both the Bush and ATL, characterized the discrepancy between Wallace's British following and her American audience as a matter of American demand to be entertained in the theater. This is not one of Wallace's priorities, for according to Dromgoole, she prefers to cause her audience to think, to be concerned (qtd. in Mootz, "Play Time"). Then, too, Wallace appears clearly more of a social activist than many playwrights, which is evident in all her plays, regardless of the subject matter or ostensible theme. An indictment of some element of society underlies them all. And this may be part of her problem with American reception, as *Boston Globe*'s Ed Siegal has observed ("Slaughter City"). Wallace seems not to worry about such judgments, for she continues to write her gutsy, disturbing plays.

Jon Jory and ATL don't seem to be concerned either. As a result of their production of *One Flea Spare,* ATL commissioned Wallace to write a second play, which became *The Trestle at Pope Lick Creek.* In many ways, this play is more representative of the body of Wallace's work, for it—as do her other major plays—draws on her Kentucky heritage.[5] The plot, suggested in the title, is chilling in its surface simplicity. Set in the 1930s, this play deals with a teenaged couple who challenge each other to outrun a train on the narrow trestle over the Pope Lick Creek of the play's title. Based on a real location, it allows Wallace to combine familiar surroundings with a story that belies its surface simplicity with unexpected forays into both societal and personal concerns. As she points out in an interview with Judith Egerton, the two are irrevocably connected for Wallace ("Writer NW").

Adrian Hall, the founder of Trinity Repertory Company in Providence, who directed *Trestle,* pointing out the depth, poetry, and pain embodied in Wallace's writing, rates her as a major new voice in American theater. He believes Jon Jory deserves praise and credit for bringing this new talent to American audiences (Egerton, "Writer NW"). And that credit should be extended to include the myriad of playwrights Jory and ATL have introduced to the theater world.

The list of playwrights who have been produced at ATL contains many of the major names writing for theater today, as well as many names less well known. ATL's health, innovation, daring, and success over three decades have provided audiences around the world with substantive plays, some of which would not have been produced were it not for the attention and trust of that fertile atmosphere. In part, the vision of one man combined with the efforts of a dedicated and talented organization; in part, the support of a theater-going community generating financial security for the contemporary troupe of thespians in its midst; in part, the forum for talented, daring, and articulate playwrights from around the world; and in part, the logical result of a regional culture steeped in a deep, rich storytelling tradition, ATL presides on the river as an internationally acclaimed theater fulfilling a much-needed role.

Notes

1. For information on Louisville's founding and early history, I am indebted to James M. Prichard, Research Room Supervisor, Kentucky Department of Libraries and Archives. From him, I first heard of some of the antics of the theatrical Booth and Barrymore families as they visited Louisville. For more information on these two families, Prichard recommends James Kotsilibas-Davis, *Great Times, Good Times: The Odyssey of Maurice Barrymore* (Garden City: Doubleday, 1977) and Gene Smith, *American Gothic: The Story of America's Legendary Theatrical Family—Junius, Edwin, and John Wilkes Booth* (New York: Simon & Schuster, 1992).

2. From the very beginning, Norman's plays have received diverse readings from critics. *Getting Out* is no exception. In a review published in *New York* in 1978, John Simon calls the play honest and humane (152). Timothy Murray, on the other hand, considers it a paternalistic exploration of societal power structures. He sees the play as allowing the audience, as well as Norman, to absolve themselves of the abuses that society and authority figures hand out to the powerless. While agreeing with Murray to the extent that she, too, sees the play as presenting limited frames of action for women, feminist critic Patricia R. Schroeder also finds that the play moves toward a developing sense of individual responsibility and the support of the women with similar concerns. To her, its value as a play is in its dramatizing of the situations that limit women. Nevertheless, many feminists have also read Norman's plays as a co-option to male-dominated theater hierarchies, a charge that gained new life with Norman's *'night, Mother.* See also William Demastes, "Jessie and Thelma Revisited" (*Modern Drama* 36 [1993]); Jill Dolan, "Feminism and the Canon" (*The Feminist Spectator as Critic* [1988]); and for a more general discussion, Jeanie Forte, "Realism, Narrative, and the Feminist Playwright—Problem of Reception" (rpt. in Keyssar).

3. This emphasis on the relationship between the characters may well have been something Norman internalized from Jon Jory. In the interview with W. Dale Brown, Dewberry suggests that part of the original problem with the play she submitted to ATL (which occasioned Jory's telephoned advice to her) was that the characters were strangers who had met at an airport. "[T]he characters didn't know or care about each other, so there wasn't conflict between characters. . . . That doesn't work very well on the stage, because they become five unrelated monologues almost" (113). The implication is that Jory's advice was to make the characters' actions matter to each other.

4. See reviews by Laurie Stone, Robert L. Daniels, and Clive Barnes.

5. Wallace's other major plays include *Slaughter City* (1996), about the Fischer Packing Co. strike in Louisville; *In the Heart of America* (1995), about a Kentucky soldier's reaction to the Gulf War; and the screenplay for *Lawn Dogs* (1997), set and filmed in an affluent suburb of Louisville.

Works Cited

"ATL Commissions Women to Write Plays." Louisville *Courier-Journal* 31 Jan. 1982: H5.

"ATL Offers New York Trip." Louisville *Courier-Journal* 22 Aug. 1982: H6.

Barnes, Clive. Rev. of *One Flea Spare,* by Naomi Wallace. *New York Post* Online. 24 July 1998 <http://nypostonline.com/reviews/theater/flea.htm>.

Beattie, Elisabeth, ed. *Conversations with Kentucky Writers.* Lexington: UP of Kentucky, 1996.

Brown, W. Dale. *Of Fiction and Faith: Twelve American Writers Talk about Their Vision and Work.* Grand Rapids, MI: Eerdmans, 1997.

Daniels, Robert L. Rev. of *One Flea Spare,* by Naomi Wallace. *Variety* 17 Mar. 1997: 63.

Dewberry, Elizabeth. "500 Words A Day." *Of Fiction and Faith: Twelve American Writers Talk about Their Vision and Work.* Brown 97–114.

Dixcy, Marcia. Introduction. *Jane Martin: Collected Plays 1980–1995.* New York: Smith and Kraus, 1995. vii–xii.

Dixon, Michael Bigelow. ATL Literary Manager. Personal Interview, 22 July 1998.

Egerton, Judith. "*Trestle* Spans Humana Festival as Most Original and Memorable Production." Rev. of *The Trestle at Pope Lick Creek,* by Naomi Wallace. Louisville *Courier-Journal* 28 Mar. 1998, Arts I1. Full-text. *Newsbank Newsfile Collection.* Online. Newsbank, Inc. 23 July 1998.

———. "Wallace Play Echoes with Meaning." Rev. of *The Trestle at Pope Lick Creek,* by Naomi Wallace. Louisville *Courier-Journal* 15 Mar. 1998: News B3. Full-text. *Newsbank Newsfile Collection.* Online. Newsbank, Inc. 23 July 1998.

———. "Writer Naomi Wallace Draws on Her Kentucky Home." Louisville *Courier-Journal* 8 March 1998: Arts I1. Full-text. *Newsbank Newsfile Collection.* Online. Newsbank, Inc. 23 July 1998.

Gussow, Mel. "The Play Tells the Tale." *American Theatre* 13.6 (1996) 52–54. Full-text. *Info Trac Search Bank: Expanded Academic Index.* Online. Information Access. 15 July 1998.

Hardy, Owen. "Women Writers at ATL Project Find Support and New Insight." Louisville *Courier-Journal* 22 Aug. 1982: 1, H6.

Keyssar, Helene, ed. *Feminist Theater and Theory.* New York: St. Martin's, 1996.

Martin, Jane. *Keely and Du. Jane Martin: The Complete Plays, 1980–1995.* New York: Smith and Kraus, 1995. 253–300.

Mootz, William. Rev. of *D. Boone,* by Marsha Norman. Louisville *Courier-Journal* 28 Feb. 1992: Metro C2. Full-text. *Newsbank Newsfile Collection.* Online. Newsbank, Inc., 23 July 1998.

———. "From Rags to Artistic Riches." Louisville *Courier-Journal* 26 May 1974. 1, H11.

———. "Play Time: Newcomer and Veteran Kick Off ATL's Humana Festival." Rev. of *One Flea Spare,* by Naomi Wallace. Louisville *Courier-Journal* 25 May 1996: Arts I1. Full-text. *Newsbank Newsfile Collection.* Online. Newsbank, Inc. 23 July 1998.

———. "Pride in Heritage: Two Humana Festival Playwrights Explore Their Cultural

Ties." Louisville *Courier-Journal* 16 Feb. 1992. I1. Full-text. *Newsbank Newsfile Collection.* Online. Newsbank. 23 July 1998.

Murray, Timothy. "Patriarchal Panopticism, Or The Seduction of a Bad Joke: *Getting Out* in Theory." *Theater Journal* 35 (1983): 376–88.

Norman, Marsha. Interview. *Conversations with Kentucky Writers.* Ed. L. Elisabeth Beattie. Lexington: UP of Kentucky, 1996. 282–97.

Schroeder, Patricia R. "Locked Behind the Proscenium: Feminist Strategies in *Getting Out* and *My Sister in the House.*" Keyssar 155–67.

Siegal, Ed. "*Slaughter City:* Politics Bloody and Unbowed." Rev. of *Slaughter City,* by Naomi Wallace. *Boston Globe* 2 Apr. 1996. 24 July 1998. http//www.fas.harvard.edu/ ~art/globe7.html.

Simon, John. "Free, Bright, and 31." *New York* 13 Nov. 1978: 152.

———. "Theater Chronicle: Kopit, Norman, and Shepard." *Hudson Review* 32 (1979): 77–88.

Speer, Alexander. ATL Executive Director. Personal Interview. 23 July 1998.

Stone, Laurie. Rev. of *One Flea Spare,* by Naomi Wallace. *The Nation* 19 May 1997: 34–36. Full-text. *Info Trac Search Bank: Expanded Academic Index.* Online. Information Access. 24 July 1998.

Wegener, Amy. ATL Assistant Literary Manager. Personal Interview. 22 July 1998.

8

Precursor and Protégé: Lillian Hellman and Marsha Norman

Sally Burke

In October 1974, Israel Horowitz told of a conversation with Samuel Beckett during which Beckett expressed admiration for a line in Horowitz's new play, a line about something having occurred "in the space of a closing window." Excited, Horowitz began to discuss the scene; then came the flash in which he realized—and said—"Oh, hell, I got it from you." To which Beckett replied, "That's alright. Mine was a door, and I got it from Dante" (Horowitz "Address"). Apparently such an admission from the younger male artist and such amiability on the elder's part are rare. Rarer still, at least until recently, were such exchanges between older and younger female playwrights, women having had far less access to the stage and to publishing their dramas than did their male counterparts, and thus fewer opportunities to establish a women's canon. Gender discrepancies in opportunity still predominate, but as the precursor-protégé relationship between Lillian Hellman and Marsha Norman illustrates, female artists in such relationships seem more akin to Beckett and Horowitz and less like the males described by Harold Bloom who wish to annihilate their predecessors.

When Bloom articulated the "anxiety of influence" as an Oedipal battle between a "strong Poet" and his "precursor," feminist critics realized that this male struggle did not apply to the woman writer, nor, as Sandra Gilbert and Susan Gubar point out, could "Bloom's male-oriented theory of the 'anxiety of influence' . . . be simply reversed or inverted in order to account for the situation of the woman writer" whose "precursors [were] almost exclusively male, and therefore significantly different from her" (48). The younger male poet, feeling overwhelmed and threatened by the originality of his poet predecessors, responds with a poem of his own as defense, or as Bloom said, "The meaning of a poem can only be another poem" (94). The female writer, meanwhile, undergoes an "Anxiety of Authorship—a radical fear that she cannot create, that because she can never become a 'precursor,' the act of writing will isolate and destroy her" (Gilbert and Gubar 49). Like Gilbert and Gubar, Joan Feit Diehl, Lillian Faderman, Louise Bernikow, and Annette Kolodny remark the inadequacy of Bloom's model for the woman writer. Kolodny, for example, points to the lack of a woman's canon—or to the failure of women's writing to become canonical —as meaning that "again and again, each woman who took up the pen had to confront anew her bleak premonition that both as writers and as readers, women too easily became isolated islands of symbolic significance, available only to, and decipherable only to, one another" (54).

The absence of women, as readers and writers, from Bloom's theory underscores the need to explore the woman's tradition. In *Sister's Choice: Tradition and Change in American Women's Writing,* Elaine Showalter presents a crucial question: "Does a 'muted' culture have a literature of its own, or must it always revise the conventions of the dominant [culture]?" (6). Using as analogy the quilt whose pattern name—Sister's Choice—provides her title, Showalter suggests that rather than the revising and repetition which have been the bases of men's writing, "piecing and patchwork" provide "[b]oth theme and form" in women's writing and have "become metaphors for a Female Aesthetic, for sisterhood, and for a poetics of feminist survival" (146). In sum, these critics all suggest that to overcome the "anxiety of authorship," the "woman writer must actively [seek] a female precursor who . . . proves by example that a revolt against patriarchal literary authority is possible" (Gilbert and Gubar 49).

Marsha Norman, as she has acknowledged in numerous interviews and essays, found her precursor in Lillian Hellman. Norman began reading Hellman's plays in high school; more than twenty years later, in the summer of 1983, she met the frail, nearly blind Hellman who was attended by nurses around the clock. A year later, Hellman was dead. In the introduction to her transcription of their conversation that day, "Articles of Faith: A Conversation with Lillian Hellman," Norman wrote: "Quite simply, I owe her a great debt" (10); in the conversation itself, she told Hellman, "I was a kid who didn't really know it was possible to write for a living. I grew up in a religious fundamentalist family in Kentucky and my mother hoped I would work for the airlines for a few years and then marry a doctor. But all through high school there were teachers who put your plays in my hands" (11). The ensuing conversation touches upon the subjects of love, faith, and morality, and ends with Norman reminding Hellman of a statement in the introduction to Chekhov's letters in which the elder writer noted that "all great art requires a kind of spiritual violence" (15). Norman, stating her "desire to protect" the older playwright and, one assumes, to refrain from doing "her privacy" any violence (10), makes no further comment about the impact the meeting had upon her. Later, in writing of this meeting for the *New York Times,* Norman acknowledges that Hellman's "voice was the one that carried all the way to Kentucky, where I lived"; she adds, "Writers like Lillian Hellman, who are willing to share their lives as well as their work make it possible for those who come after them to survive." Calling herself Hellman's "admirer and debtor," ("Lillian Hellman's Gift" H7), Norman also describes Hellman as "[t]his wonderful, looming model, this great, vibrant, feisty, swearing lady who had managed to make a life in [the theater]" (Harriot 156).

Most obviously, of course, Hellman and Norman share a Southern heritage. Born in New Orleans, Hellman spent the first six years of her life there. Even after moving to New York, the family returned to New Orleans each year for six months, which they spent with Hellman's two unmarried aunts. In *An Unfinished Woman,* Hellman writes of being bored by school; she preferred to retreat to a perch in a tree from which she observed the world below and read what she chose (20–21). Norman, a native of Louisville, Kentucky, also reports being solitary as a child. Forbidden to play with the neighborhood children whom her mother considered inferior, Norman, like her precursor, spent much time reading. She remained in the South for college, becoming a scholarship student at Agnes Scott College, a Presbyterian liberal arts institution for women in Decatur, Georgia. After earning her bachelor's degree in philosophy, she took a master's degree in education at the University of Louisville.

In *Pentimento,* Hellman reveals her lasting tie to the South, stating that "there's nothing like the look of Southern land, or there's no way for me to get over thinking so. It's home for me still" (94). Like Hellman, who sets dramas in Washington, D.C.; Bowden, Alabama; a Louisiana town on the Gulf of Mexico; and New Orleans, Norman utilizes her native South in her settings. *Getting Out* takes place in both a women's prison in Alabama and Arlene's apartment in Louisville. While the playwright specifies no city as the setting of *Third and Oak,* there once was a laundromat in Louisville at the location named in the title. Norman also confesses that, in preparing to write *Loving Daniel Boone,* she "sat down and made a list of the things [she] loved best about Kentucky. It was a silly list including things like Mammoth Cave, Shaker Lemon pie, spoonbread, country ham, the Paris Pike, and the whole town of Harrodsburg" (*Loving* 332). At times this protégé departs markedly from her precursor. For example, in *The Autumn Garden,* Hellman utilizes the specifically Southern Gothic locale of the Tuckerman house on the Gulf of Mexico to pursue the universality inherent in the wasted life of Constance Tuckerman, who devotes her life to memories of loving Nick Denery and thus remains unmarried, and that of General Benjamin Griggs, who discovers that he has "frittered [him]self away" (542). Norman tracks the same issue by locating 'night, Mother in "a relatively new house built way out on a country road" (3). The locale in which Jessie determines to make the wasted life of the "somebody [she] lost . . . [her] own self" (76) count for something remains unspecified. Indeed, in the notes on the characters, set, and setting preceding the drama's text, Norman insists that the set "should simply indicate that [Jessie and Thelma] are very specific real people who happen to live in a particular part of the country" (3). She also rules out "[h]eavy accents" (3). Yet, to those familiar with the Norman canon, Southern threads are visible in this drama, also.

A deep-seated connection to the South also manifests itself in both play-wrights as they carry on the Southern tradition of creating grotesque charac-ters. Of course, non-Southern writers have also created eccentric personages, but when one contemplates the gallery of grotesques created by Edgar Allan Poe, William Faulkner, Flannery O'Connor, Carson McCullers, and Tennessee Williams, for example, one almost wishes to grant copyright on such characters to Southern writers. Hellman's "pig-face cute" (360) Laurette Sincee in *Another Part of the Forest* makes the pig-calling noise "Squee" (365), speaks of being taught to love music by an uncle who "had a little drum" (365), leading Marcus Hubbard to remark, "Sincee's uncle played Mozart on a little drum. Have you ever heard of that, Miss Bagtry?" (365). Laurette also admits that her "business" is "fancy whoring" (361). Rose Griggs of Hellman's *The Autumn Garden,* who wears clothes "that [are] much too young for her" (465), speaks in non sequi-turs, and has only a slight grip on reality, typifies the faded Southern belle. One might say of her what Jacob H. Adler does of Tennessee Williams's Alma Wine-miller, that is, Rose is "beyond question southern" in such traits as "the living of life as though it were a work of fiction, [and her] insulation from the world" (352). Among Norman's grotesques are the offstage Josie Barrett of *Traveler in the Dark,* the good-hearted "joke" (163) who, Sam fears, might ruin Mavis's funeral with a misguided attempt at singing (163), and Agnes Fletcher, Mama's friend in 'night, Mother, who has a "house full of birds" (40), "wears . . . [sev-eral] whistles around her neck" (40), and has "burned down every house she ever lived in. Eight fires, and she's due for a new one any day now" (38). Clearly, both playwrights mine the vein of the Southern grotesque.

Interestingly—but perhaps not surprising, considering the patriarchal heri-tage of these Southern women—strong, successful men influenced the careers of both playwrights, especially in the subject matter of each woman's first play. Hellman's lover, Dashiel Hammett, creator of the *Thin Man* mystery series, suggested to her that the chapter "Closed Doors; or The Great Drumsheugh Case" in William Roughead's *Bad Companions* would make a good drama (Wright 73). Moved from Scotland to the fictional Lancet, Massachusetts, the story became *The Children's Hour.* In 1971, Norman met Jon Jory, artistic director of the Actors Theatre of Louisville, and began her long affiliation with that institution, serving as its playwright-in-residence in 1978–79 and, over the ensuing years, contributing many dramas to its annual Humana Festival of New American Plays. (Louisville was an early center of drama in the South, where, as William S. Ward reports in *A Literary History of Kentucky,* "as early as 1808 there had been amateur performances and by 1814 a 'season' of plays" [108]). Initially, Jory suggested that Norman write a docudrama about busing, which had just begun affecting Louisville (Stone 57). When she decided against it, he recommended she write about a time when she was "physically frightened" (Norman, "Introduction" 2). Recalling a teenager she had observed while serving as a hospital volunteer, Norman created Arlie/Arlene, the dual protagonist of *Getting Out.*

Hammett also suggested that Hellman center a drama around a male protagonist, telling her, "There's this man. Other people, people who say they love him, want him to make good, be rich. So he does it for them and finds they don't like him that way, so he fucks it up, and comes out worse than before. Think about it" (*Pentimento* 206). Hellman reports that after writing an act and a half she discovered, "I can write about men, but I can't write a play that centers on a man. I've got to tear it up, make it about the women around him, his sisters, his bride, her mother and—" (*Pentimento* 206). She transmuted Hammett's idea into *Toys in the Attic,* a drama set in Hellman's native New Orleans that centers on the middle-aged and unmarried Berniers sisters, Anna and Carrie, who dote on their brother, Julian, and attempt to exercise control over his business life and his marriage.

Unlike her precursor, Norman created several male protagonists, among them the adolescent Archie Tucker in *The Holdup,* Shooter in *Third and Oak: The Pool Hall,*[1] and Sam of *Traveler in the Dark;* however, she does portray her male protagonists as strongly influenced by the women around them. Lily, the ex-whore turned innkeeper of *The Holdup,* initiates Archie sexually (150), encourages his dream of becoming an aviator (150), and pronounces a blessing upon him: "Goodness and mercy . . . follow you all the days of your life" (156). Sam, overwhelmed as a child by the Imaginary, grows up to become a staunch disciple of the Symbolic and a world-famous surgeon. In declaring his allegiance to the rule of phallogocentrism, Sam must flee both parents. He finds his preacher father's theology, which includes a vision of Sam's dead mother in heaven "singing and flying around" (172), as much a fairy tale as the story of Sleeping Beauty read to him by his mother, who would greet him after school each day with "milk . . . and a pile of things she'd found in the ground . . . like dragons' teeth, witches' fingers and fallen stars" (171). Norman locates Sam's mirror stage of development in the shiny crystals held within the geodes he once collected. Figuratively seeing himself, Sam rejects the feminine principle located both in his mother's fairy tales and nursery rhymes and in his father's Bible. He insists, "I don't, in fact, believe in anything. It has taken me my whole life, Dad, but I have finally arrived. I am free of faith" (192) Yet, contrary to his claim, Sam cannot live without faith, here portrayed by his allegorically named wife Glory. Initially Sam thinks he wishes to leave her; by the end of the drama they reconcile and he makes a leap of faith, acknowledging in the words of his mother's nursery rhyme that though he "knows not what you are," the brightly twinkling little star truly does "[g]uide the traveler in the dark" (204). Thus, though her protagonist proclaims allegiance to the male symbolic, Norman depicts him finally as relying on the female imaginative.

As late as 1984, the younger playwright had never seen any Hellman play performed. In fact, she showed a preference for Hellman's memoirs, calling them "the most compelling [story] she wrote" ("Lillian Hellman's Gift" H1); Norman also told Esther Harriot that she based her admiration for Hellman more on her predecessor's craft and sense of style than on her subjects (156). Still, Norman, wittingly or unwittingly, does piecing and patchwork in her precursor's fabric bag, as she adopts, adapts, and further develops Hellman's subjects and, in some instances, even echoes her language.

Like Hellman's work, many of Norman's plays center on the family, delving into the forces that unite as well as those that divide. The family drama, a staple of the American stage, is far from being the exclusive province of Southern playwrights. Yet, viewed through the prism of Southern drama, Richard Poirier's claim that the South fosters "intense familial . . . relationships" (x) compels agreement. Both Hellman and Norman scrutinize the parent-child relationship. Hellman's cold, withdrawn, or failed mothers such as Regina Hubbard Giddens in *The Little Foxes* and Lavinia Hubbard in *Another Part of the Forest* resurface in Norman's dramas. A thrall to greed to such an extent that avarice might be said to be her identity in *The Little Foxes,* Regina Giddens distances herself from her daughter. Norman repeats this distancing in *Getting Out,* where it arises from a willed blindness. When she visits her newly paroled daughter, Mrs. Holsclaw clearly resists Arlene's embrace; Arlene "*moves as if to hug her. Mother stands still* [and] *Arlene backs off"* (15). Furthermore, she ignores Arlene's initial *"request"* (22) to be invited to Sunday dinner and, after they argue about Bennie, the guard who has driven Arlene home, Mrs. Holsclaw, variously described in the stage directions as *"cold, fierce,* [and] *furious"* (26), rages, "You're hinting at coming to my house for pot roast just like nothin ever happened, an all the time you're hidin a goddam guard under your bed" (26). When Arlene asks whether she'll visit again, her mother responds, "You ain't got no need for me" (27). As she moves to leave, Arlene rushes toward her, only to be repelled by the words, "Don't you touch me" (27). She exits, leaving Arlene *"stunned and hurt"* (27), and echoing her line: "No! Don't you touch Mama, Arlie" (27). With this scene of estrangement, the mother disappears from the drama. While Arlene may be stunned by the rejection, the audience is not. The earlier flashback which details the aftermath of Arlie's being raped by her father explains Mrs. Holsclaw's attitude—for to embrace her daughter she would have to open her eyes to the sexual violence her husband inflicted upon Arlie and see what was truly hiding in her own bed all those years ago.

Incest in drama is as ancient as Sophocles' *Oedipus Rex* and as current as Paula Vogel's 1998 Pulitzer Prize–winner *How I Learned to Drive.* In her introduction to *Southern Quarterly's* special issue on Southern women playwrights, Milly S. Barranger notes that these women have brought to the Southern theater "enactment of such taboos as incest" (7). She adds: "Southern writers know that human beings are fallible; they are, therefore, more tolerant as observers and recorders of human foibles. Out of this understanding that human beings are not perfectible comes a tolerance for the unusual, the bizarre, even the perverse. Hence the playwright's depiction of suicide, miscegenation, violence, incestuous relations, grotesque characters and whole families takes place within a local literary tradition one hundred and fifty years old" (8).

Exploring one of these taboo subjects in *Getting Out,* Norman illustrates the effect of incest on mother-daughter as well as father-daughter relationships. Here, too, Hellman's influence seems to pertain. In *The Little Foxes,* Oscar points out to Ben and Regina that "our grandmother and grandfather were first cousins" (151). In the later *Another Part of the Forest,* the closeness between Regina Hubbard and her father, Marcus, carries the scent of his incestuous desire, a desire which Regina seeks to manipulate to gain her own ends. The father and daughter call each other "darling" (333) and "honey" (334), and Marcus indulges his daughter's appetite for sumptuous clothing, allowing her to spend three hundred dollars for one fur piece alone. (Hellman sets her drama in 1880; in 1893, "$700 was a comfortable, if modest annual income" ["Late

Nineteenth Century" 8]). Regina's brother, Ben, extrapolating from Marcus's desire to have Regina to himself, forecasts an evening fifty years in the future when: "Papa'll still be living, and he'll interrupt us, the way he does even now; he'll call from upstairs to have you come and put him to bed. And you'll get up to go, wondering how the years went by—(*Sharply*) Because, as you say, he's most devoted to you, and he's going to keep you right here with him, all his long life" (341).

Ben also points out the fact that "Papa didn't just get mad about you and Horace Giddens. Papa got mad about you and any man, or any place that ain't near him" (342); later Ben underscores the anticipated vehemence of Marcus's reaction to Regina's plan to marry John Bagtry by saying, "I'm taking a vacation the day he finds out about your marriage plans" (358). Indeed, Marcus exhibits jealous anger when he discovers that Regina has invited John to the Hubbard home (368); later, when he learns of her affair, he rages, "How could you let him touch you? When did it happen? How could you—*Answer me*" (379). As he breaks down, Regina continues to manipulate his desire:

REGINA: *(softly, comes to him)*. All right, Papa. That's all true and I know it. And I'm in love with him, and I want to marry him. *(He puts his hands over his face)* Now don't take on so. It just won't do. You let me go away, as we planned. I'll get married. After a while we'll come home and we'll live right here—

MARCUS: *Are you crazy?* Do you think I'd stay in this house with you and—

REGINA: Otherwise, I'll go away. I say I will, and you know I will. I'm not frightened to go. But if I go that way I won't ever see you again. And you don't want that. My way we can be together. You'll get used to it and John won't worry us. There'll always be you and me—*(Puts her hand on his shoulder)* You must have known I'd marry someday, Papa. Why, I've never seen you cry before. It'll be just like going for a little visit, and before you know it I'll be home again, and it will all be over. You know? Maybe next year, or the year after, you and I'll make that trip to Greece, just the two of us. *(Smiles)* Now it's all settled. Kiss me good night, darling. (379)

Meanwhile, Regina's mother, Lavinia Hubbard, consumed by her own desire to atone for what she sees as the sin of marrying Marcus, has no time for her daughter and seems not to notice the abnormal relationship between her daughter and her husband. Finally, in her last original drama, *Toys in the Attic,*

Hellman returns to the topic of incest. Anna Berniers tells her sister Carrie that soon their brother Julian will become aware of Carrie's desire for him: "You lusted and it showed. He doesn't know he saw it, but he did see it, and someday he'll know what he saw. *(With great violence)* You know the way that happens? You understand something, and don't know that you do, and forget about it. But one night years ago I woke up and knew what I had seen in you, had always seen. It will happen that way with him. It has begun" (737).

In Norman's *Getting Out,* predecessor Hellman's intimations of incest grow into the repeated incestuous rapes of Arlie, who denies the assaults with the words, "Daddy didn't do nuthin [sic] to me" (16). Mrs. Holsclaw, to preserve her marriage, wishes to accept the lie and, like some real-life incest victims, Arlie further obliges by protecting the criminal perpetrator, claiming, "Was . . . *(Quickly)* my bike. My bike hurt me. The seat bumped me" (15), thus enabling her mother to ignore the child's bleeding body.

Arlie's later behavior also mirrors that of real-life incest victims; she runs away to join her pimp lover, Carl, and works as a prostitute, a not infrequent occurrence, as Ellen Westerlund points out in *Women's Sexuality after Childhood Incest* (13). As Judith Lewis Herman notes in *Father-Daughter Incest,* the fall into prostitution, whether the daughter literally becomes a prostitute or not, occurs along with the incest, for: "The father, in effect, forces the daughter to pay with her body for affection and care which should be freely given. In doing so, he destroys the protective bond between parent and child and initiates his daughter into prostitution. This is the reality of incest from the point of view of the victim" (4).

Most tellingly, in prison, Arlene rejects, then symbolically slays, her younger self Arlie, the child within who suffered the sexual assaults. By doing so, Arlene exhibits the behavior that Ellen Bass and Laura Davis report in survivors of childhood incest in *The Courage to Heal,* "Many survivors have a difficult time with the concept of the child within. . . . Too often women blame her, hate her, or ignore her completely. Survivors hate themselves for having been small, for having needed affection, for having 'let themselves' be abused" (111). Victims, add Bass and Davis, "feel split, caught in a real schism. There is the 'you' that's out in the 'real' world, and then there's the child inside who is still a frightened victim" (111). In *Getting Out,* Norman's dual protagonist, prior to her partial reintegration at the drama's end, offers a stunning portrait of a psyche split by incestuous rape and experiencing all of the emotions of hate, fear, and revenge prompted by her father's violation of her.

As noted above, in *Another Part of the Forest,* Hellman's twenty-year-old

Regina is quite conscious of and thus able both to manipulate and deflect her father's desires. Marcus willingly indulges his daughter's appetite for expensive clothes as the price of her company—and his fantasies. Mr. Holsclaw is never seen onstage, but Norman makes it clear that he bribes the vulnerable, prepubescent Arlie to remain silent about his attacks on her, the price he pays being the few "crumpled dollars" Arlie tells the school principal she has earned by "[d]oin things . . . [f]or my daddy" (18).

The onstage relationship between Hellman's Regina and Marcus Hubbard also reverberates in Norman's later drama 'night, Mother, in the deigetic relationship between Jessie and her father. Just as Marcus prefers Regina's company to that of his wife, Lavinia, Mr. Cates would rather spend his time in nonverbal communication or quiet whispering with his daughter than in uncomfortable silence with his wife. The silent and near silent modes of communication between father and daughter effectively shut the mother out of the relationship. As Thelma remarks,

> Agnes gets more talk out of her birds than I got from the two of you. He could've had that GONE FISHING sign around his neck in that chair. I saw him stare off at the water. I saw him look at the weather rolling in. I got where I could practically see the boat myself. But you, you knew what he was thinking about and you're going to tell me.
> JESSIE: I don't know, Mama! His life, I guess. His corn. His boots. Us. Things. You know.
> MAMA No. I don't know, Jessie! You had those quiet little conversations after supper every night. What were you whispering about?
> JESSIE: We weren't whispering, you were just across the room.
> MAMA: What did you talk about?
> JESSIE: We talked about why black socks are warmer than blue socks. Is that something to go tell Mother? You were just jealous because I'd rather talk to him than wash the dishes with you.
> MAMA: I was jealous because you'd rather talk to him than anything!
> (47–48)

Norman further illuminates the closeness of father and daughter through Jessie's epilepsy, a disease not often inherited. Mama tells Jessie, "I think your daddy had fits, too. I think he sat in his chair and had little fits" (62); later Mama explains that both Jessie and her father experienced absence seizures, which mimic daydreaming or "thinking spells" (62) as Mama calls them: "Oh, that was some swell time, sitting here with the two of you turning off and on like light bulbs, some nights" (69). The playwright displays an obvious clinical knowledge of the disease, knowing that seizures can intensify with age (69), that both victims and their families experience shame and other emotional problems (70), and that many drugs used to treat epilepsy have undesirable side effects—Dilantin, for example, can cause the swelling of the gums that Jessie once suffered (66). Although Mama insists at one point that "[y]our daddy gave you these fits, Jessie. He passed it down to you like your green eyes and your straight hair. It's not my fault" (68), she also appears unable to discount a mother-child connection. Finally, she assumes blame—"It has to be something I did" (71)—and when Jessie insists, "It's just a sickness, not a curse," accepts culpability not for the epilepsy but for "this killing yourself" (72).

In the father-child relationship, Norman intimates subliminal sexual desire, perhaps played out in Jessie's choosing a phallic symbol of her father—his gun—as her means of committing suicide. In childhood, Jessie develops such a strong attachment to her father that she cannot later resolve it in favor of her relationship to her husband. Discussing her choice of weapon, she tells Mama, "I had Cecil's [gun] all ready in there, just in case I couldn't find this one, but I'd rather use Daddy's" (14). In the film version of *'night, Mother* (1986), on the night of her suicide, Jessie places her father's picture on her bedside nightstand, but removes it saying, "That wouldn't be right." She then puts it on her mother's bureau, but decides "That's not right, either" and places the photograph on a sideboard in the living room. Thus Norman reveals in her screenplay that the sexual overtones of the father-daughter relationship in the play remained on her mind.

Despite her daughter's obvious preference for her dead father, Thelma Cates does not turn away. In fact, unlike *Getting Out's* Mrs. Holsclaw, she wishes to embrace her daughter, but despite her desire, she cannot beguile her child into continuing to live. For although Jessie promises Thelma that she will "do whatever you want before I go" (34), ultimately Jessie rejects the embrace meant to hold her within this life. When, just prior to Jessie's suicide, Thelma grabs her daughter, Jessie "*[t]akes her hands away*" and says, "Let go of me, Mama" (87). To some extent, this scene is prefigured at the end of Hellman's *The Little Foxes* when Regina tells Alexandra that she will not make her stay. The daughter replies, "You couldn't, Mama, because I want to leave here. As I've never wanted anything in my life before" (199). Both Hellman's Alexandra and Norman's Jessie, in their moves to free themselves of their mothers, act in a manner that contradicts the Freudian theory that a woman, lacking a penis and thus not impelled by castration anxiety, experiences a lesser need to resolve her pre-Oedipal attachment to her mother.

Interestingly, surrogate mothers may succeed where biological mothers fail. In *The Little Foxes,* Hellman provides a surrogate mother for Regina's daughter Alexandra in the person of Addie, the black servant to whom Zan looks for guidance. While Regina accuses Addie of babying Zan, the dying Horace turns to Addie in seeking protection for his daughter. Here Hellman perpetuates the myth of the all-loving, self-sacrificing "Black Mammy" found in the work of many Southern writers, most notably, perhaps, in Faulkner. Horace asks Addie to take Zan away from the foxes' influence and she hesitates for only a second before responding, "Yes, sir. I promise" (184). Hellman repeats the sacrificing of the black woman's life to the needs or desires of the white woman in *Another Part of the Forest* when Lavinia assumes that the patient, motherly Coralee, her black caretaker, will accompany her on the return to Lavinia's childhood home. In *Getting Out,* Ruby, Arlene's upstairs neighbor, plays the surrogate. (Ruby's race is not designated; she could be played by an actor of any race. On the other hand, in using the name Ruby, a Southern writer like Norman may have had a black woman in mind as her mother surrogate, thus providing another echo of Hellman's dramas.)[2] After revealing how she attempted to exorcize Arlie by repeatedly stabbing herself, Arlene breaks down and falls into Ruby's lap. Ruby tells her, "You can still love people that's gone" and *"hold[s] her tenderly, rocking as with a baby"* (61). Norman underscores the surrogate mother's success through the partial reintegration of personality in the drama's final scene when Arlie and Arlene, each spotlighted,

> *(say together, both standing as Mama did, one hand on her hip)* Arlie, what you doin in there?
> ARLENE: *(Still smiling and remembering, stage dark except for one light on her face)* Aw shoot. *(Light dims on her fond smile as Arlie laughs once more).* (64)

Hellman herself seems to have found a black surrogate mother in Sophronia Mason, the woman who was "her wet nurse and her guide through childhood and the pain of early adolescence" (Poirier x). She also might have experienced a surrogate mother-daughter relationship in the time she spent with her aunts Jenny and Hannah in their New Orleans boarding house. They surely serve as the models for the Berniers sisters—one of whom bears the name Hannah in an early draft of the drama (Falk 90)—who mother their brother Julian in *Toys in the Attic.* In *The Little Foxes,* Regina's daughter Alexandra deals with her less-than-adequate biological mother by deciding to leave home. When confronted with an unfeeling mother, Deedee in Norman's *Third and Oak* chooses to become a surrogate daughter. Indeed, she literally forces the older widow, Alberta, who, according to the stage directions "*[w]ants Deedee to vanish*" (63), to pay attention to her. Norman underlines Deedee's symbolic adopting of Alberta by giving both characters the same last name, a fact that leads Deedee to exclaim, "Hey! We might be related" (64). Later, the initially reticent Alberta admits her own childlessness while also responding "Oh yes" when Deedee asks, "Didn't you want some?" (66). She then becomes Deedee's mother for the moment, instructing her about such disparate topics as bullfighting, doing laundry, and dealing with marital infidelity. When Shooter appears, he mistakes Alberta for Deedee's biological mother (71), again underscoring the connection between the two women. (Of course, his mistake also says something about the male assumption that a biological relationship accounts for every instance of an older and a younger woman associating with each other.) In contrast to Deedee's biological mother, who seems never to enjoy seeing her daughter and "do[es]n't say two words while [she's] there" (76), Alberta offers Deedee counsel and a parting kiss, and one sees that, for a moment at least, the younger woman, by becoming Alberta's surrogate daughter, has had her fantasy mother, one who is "Smart. Nice to talk to" (75).

Most Southern playwrights comment on race relations in their dramas. Hellman and Norman are no exceptions. In *Another Part of the Forest,* Hellman's Oscar defends his riding with the Klan by saying, "I'm a southerner. And when I see an old carpetbagger or upstart nigger, why, I feel like taking revenge" (343). Hellman clearly detests this bigotry and makes it a hallmark of others of her foolish or villainous characters. Ben Hubbard frequently uses the word "nigger" and Carrie Berniers professes astonishment that "Julian d[oes]n't mind" that Mrs. Warkins is "part nigger" (*Toys* 742). In *Third and Oak,* Norman presents Shooter as being a person of some prominence to Deedee, who seems thrilled to meet the disc jockey who is "the Number One Night Owl!" (70). Yet once he leaves the laundromat, she speculates that he "[c]oulda been a murderer, or a robber or a rapist" (73). When Alberta objects to the sexual innuendo that took place between the two, Deedee calls her "prejudiced" (73), adding:

DEEDEE: If that was a white DJ comin' in here, you'd still be talking to him, I bet. Seein' if he knew your "old" favorites.

ALBERTA: If you don't want to know what I think, you can stop talking to me.

DEEDEE: What you think is what's wrong with the world. People don't trust each other just because they're some other color from them.

ALBERTA: And who was it said he could be a murderer? That was you, Deedee.

Would you have said that if he'd been white? (73)

Race relations continue to be problematic. Deedee, despite what she sees as her devotion to the cause of equality, ponders accepting Shooter's invitation to the pool hall as a means of hurting her husband, Joe. She feels that finding her with Shooter "Might just serve [Joe] right though. Come in and see me drinkin' beer and playin' pool with Willie and Shooter. Joe hates black people. He says even when they're dancin' or playin' ball, they're thinkin' about killin'. Yeah, that would teach him to run out on me. A little dose of his own medicine. Watch him gag on it" (74). Alberta, resuming the role of surrogate mother, counsels her to make something productive of her anger by going home, not by attempting to use Shooter as a pawn.

Often, the biological mothers created by both playwrights try to be or to do everything for their daughters. In *Toys in the Attic,* Albertine[3] Prine arranges Lily's marriage to Julian Berniers, just as Thelma by, in Jessie's words, "flirt[ing] Cecil] out here" (57–58), arranges her daughter's marriage in *'night, Mother.* Interestingly, each mother takes part in an exchange historically transacted, as Claude Levi-Strauss pointed out, by men; however, such an exchange is no more benign in female hands. Women who are treated as chattel have little opportunity to develop a sense of worth. Even when mother love precipitates the exchange, the traffic yields bitter fruit: in Hellman's *Toys in the Attic,* Lily's fear of losing Julian results in his being savagely beaten, and in Norman's *'night, Mother,* Cecil divorces Jessie.

Hellman's and Norman's onstage mothers also make the all-too-common mistake of identifying with their daughters to the extent of viewing them as extensions of themselves. In *The Little Foxes,* Hellman's Regina promises Alexandra that she shall have "all the things I wanted. I'll make the world for you the way I wanted it to be for me" (198). Following Jessie's suicide in *'night, Mother,* Norman's Thelma cries, "Jessie, Jessie, child. . . . Forgive me . . . I thought you were mine" (89). Here the work of Nancy Chodorow offers illumination. As Chodorow notes about the mother-daughter relationship in *The Reproduction of Mothering,* "Mothers tend to experience their daughters as more like, and continuous with, themselves" (166). Linda Kintz goes so far as to suggest we read Thelma's line as "I thought you were me" (229). Mama's words certainly bear out Kintz's claim; earlier in the drama Thelma insists, "Everything you do has to do with me, Jessie. You can't do *anything*, wash your face or cut your finger without doing it to me. That's right! You might as well kill me as you, Jessie, it's the same thing" (72). However, such identification, interference, and possessiveness can lead only to problems, especially in reference to separation. Chodorow finds that, "Mother-daughter relationships in which the mother has no other adult support or meaningful work . . . produce ambivalent attachment and inability to separate in daughters" (213). The pain thus engendered is evident in *'night, Mother;* as Jessie screams, "What if I could take all the rest of it if only I didn't have you here? What if the only way I can get away from you for good is to kill myself? What if it is? I can *still* do it" (72), her suicide, read symbolically, enacts a desperation-driven breaking of the mother-daughter bond.

Chodorow also points out that "the mother-child relationship recreates an even more basic relational constellation" than that of mother-father-child, because in the former "[t]he exclusive symbiotic mother-child relationship of a mother's own infancy reappears, a relationship which all people who have been mothered want basically to recreate" (201). Through Arlene in *Getting Out*, Norman presents compelling images of the frustration of this desire. When the authorities take away the child she bears in prison, Arlene goes "crazy" (33), escapes, and kills the cab driver who attempts to assault her (30). Given an extended sentence, Arlene, longing for her infant, creates a pathetic substitute from a pillow (33). After singing to this surrogate child, she asks what he will be when he grows up, but her tone turns bitter when she remembers her own childhood. She tells the infant Joey: "Best thing you to be is stay a baby cause nobody beats up on babies or puts them . . . (*Much more quiet*) That ain't true. People is mean to babies, so you stay right here with me so nobody kin get you an make you cry an they lay one finger on you (*Hostile*) an I'll beat the screamin shit right out of em. They blow on you and I'll kill em" (33). Although Arlene later speaks of regaining custody of Joey, Mrs. Holsclaw disrupts her daughter's narrative, cutting off her protest of "But I'm his . . . " (17), thus refusing to let the daughter acknowledge her own motherhood. To Arlene's plan of Joey coming to live with her, the mother responds, "Fat chance" (17). Not only does she attempt to dash Arlene's dream, she claims that her daughter "never really got attached to [Joey] anyway" (17) and forecasts that she'd be an inadequate mother because "[k]ids need rules to go by an he'll get them over there [in his foster home]" (17), but not—she implies—from an ex-convict like Arlene.

In the later *'night, Mother,* Jessie Cates, commenting on one of her own baby pictures, repeats Arlene's claim about infancy as an idyllic stage, but without adding any bitter revelations about child abuse. Jessie's infantile desire to be taken care of by an all-powerful (m)other provides insight into the failure of her relationship with her son, Ricky, who has progressed from stealing Jessie's possessions to "start[ing] in on other people, door to door" (11). If the mother-child relationship is crucial to a child's development, Jessie's own failure to mature may be central to Ricky's anti-social behavior. Admitting that she holds no hope of getting through to her son (25), Jessie refuses to join Mama in day-dreams about Ricky getting a job, getting married, or "bring[ing] her grand-babies over" (74). But she does willingly own her influence on him: "I see it in his face. I hear it when he talks. We look out at the world and we see the same thing: Not Fair. And the only difference between us is Ricky's out there trying to get even. And he knows not to trust anybody and he got it straight from me. And he knows not to try to get work, and guess where he got that. He walks around like there's loose boards in the floor, and you know who laid that floor, I did" (60). Ultimately, Norman's parent-child relationships, like those of her predecessor, range from troubled to criminal in desire, if not in fact.

Each playwright also represents patriarchy, a hallmark of Southern culture, in the form of a controlling older brother. Hellman's Ben Hubbard cajoles, threatens, and dominates Regina in both Hubbard family dramas. In 'night, Mother, Jessie's brother, Dawson, never appears onstage, but it is he whose name is on their charge accounts, who knows the intimate details of their lives, and who manages their finances (53). Both dramatists also mention clothing to characterize certain aspects of the brother-sister relationships. To remind Ben that she is her father's favorite, Regina flaunts her expensive wardrobe. In 'night, Mother, Jessie cringes to remember that, when her mail-order bra was mis-delivered to Dawson's house, he opened the package and "saw the little rosebuds on it" (24). To Jessie, his act seems that of an all-seeing patriarch, perhaps not unrelated to the ultimate patriarch, God the Father. Yet, unlike Ben, who as-serts his control at the end of Another Part of the Forest, Dawson controls Jessie only until her final night, for the bullet she fires says "No" to Dawson as much as to life itself (75).

Finally, Hellman's influence is strikingly audible in the dialogue of 'night, Mother. In one instance, Jessie tells Mama that she might have decided to live "if there was something I really liked, like maybe if I really liked rice pudding or cornflakes for breakfast or something, that might be enough" (77). This line probably has its genesis in Hellman's first drama, The Children's Hour, in which Joe promises to take both Martha and his fiancée, Karen, to Vienna for "good coffee cake" (57). Martha, not long before she commits suicide, replies, "A big coffee cake with lots of raisins, it would be nice to like something again" (57).

A second echoic instance occurs when Thelma asserts ownership over her daughter, telling Jessie, "You are my child!" (76). Jessie responds: "I am what became of your child. I found an old baby picture of me. And it was somebody else, not me. It was somebody pink and fat who never heard of sick or lonely, somebody who cried and got fed, and reached up and got held and kicked but didn't hurt anybody, and slept whenever she wanted to, just by closing her eyes. Somebody who mainly just laid there and laughed at the colors waving around over her head and . . . felt your hand pulling my quilt back up over me" (76). Here Jessie speaks of the comfort and nourishment found in being loved. In Hellman's *Toys in the Attic,* Lily tells Albertine that early in her marriage to Julian, "I was beloved, Mama, and I flourished" (719). Later, when Lily asks where she would go should Julian cease to want her, Albertine replies, "You will come home to me. *You are my child"* (748, emphasis added). Norman's echo of the earlier Hellman play is obvious and, of course, Jessie comes home to Mama when Cecil no longer wants her. (Also obvious is the childishness of these women, found in Jessie's nostalgic desire to be taken care of and Lily's childish mentality.)

Jessie's sense of estrangement from her earlier infant-self may be the product of the overprotectiveness that led Thelma to such acts as concealing Jessie's epilepsy even from her (69) and wooing Cecil for Jessie because she thought her daughter should be married (57–58). Jessie's reference to the quilt, which can function for the infant as both a comfort and a restraint, emphasizes this possibility. Mama acknowledges that had Jessie not moved in with her after divorcing Cecil, the daughter would have "[h]ad a life to lead. Had [her] own things around [her]" (27). But Jessie does move in, leading to her experiencing herself as a split consciousness: an adult woman and mother of Ricky in her own right, yet a child again in her mother's house. Unable to reconcile the two, she now appears to long for the comfortable, preconscious life of the infant. On the other hand, in *Getting Out,* Arlene's unstable identity arises from experiencing too little mother love and from her mother's failure to protect her. Later in life, she attempts to ignore the schism within by renaming herself:

MOTHER: So, you're calling yourself Arlene, now?
ARLENE: Yes.
MOTHER: Don't want your girlie name no more?
ARLENE: Somethin like that. (21)

Again, Hellman's work offers a possible key, this time to a character's inability to recognize or accept the self she has repressed. In *The Children's Hour,* just prior to committing suicide, Martha confesses to Karen, "*I have loved you the way they said*"[4] (62). She then adds:

> I don't know how. I don't know why. . . . maybe because I wanted you; maybe I wanted you all along; maybe I couldn't call it by a name; maybe it's been there ever since I first knew you—
>
> . . . .
>
> it's all mixed up. There's something in you, and you don't know it and you don't do anything about it. Suddenly a child gets bored and lies—and there you are, seeing it for the first time. . . . I didn't even *know.* (63)

Hurt, confused, unable to accept the lesbian self she only now begins to perceive, Martha shoots herself. Her choice of weapon leads back to Norman's Jessie, with a twist. Jessie claims she wants to die to preclude the possibility of losing the control that she feels she has achieved over her life. For the first time, her epilepsy is under control; she is "feeling as good as [she] ever felt in [her] life" (66). When Mama asks what is wrong with her, Jessie responds, "Not a thing. Feel fine"; she adds that she "[w]aited until [she] felt good enough, in fact" (14). Furthermore, when Mama protests that Jessie doesn't have to kill herself, Jessie illustrates her feeling of elation at gaining such self-determination by saying, "No, I don't. That's what I like about it" (27). Restrained in the past by her roles as dependent child and wife, and hampered by her illness, Jessie now exults in being able to decide what she will do, in controlling her own destiny. If she cannot change her life, cannot make it better, she can, she asserts, "stop it. Shut it down, turn it off like the radio when there's nothing on I want to listen to. It's all I really have that belongs to me and I'm going to say what happens to it. And it's going to stop. And I'm going to stop it" (36). Yet Jessie experiences a profound sense of dissociation from self, signaled in her speech about the picture of herself as an infant. Is the control she thinks she exercises a chimera? She is as alienated from herself as are the early Arlene in *Getting Out* and Hellman's Martha, and the character's response in each case, albeit symbolically in Arlene's slaying of Arlie, is death.

In suggesting that Hellman's memoirs, craft, and style influenced her more than did the elder playwright's dramatic subjects and characters, Norman overlooks the homage to Hellman evident in her own dramas. When one examines Norman's plot points, character relationships, and even her dialogue, it seems obvious that the Hellman dramas put into Norman's hands by her high school teachers impressed the fledgling playwright at least as much as did the memoirs. In a review of *'night, Mother*, Robert Brustein comments that "in the way it exhumes buried family secrets, exposes the symbiotic links among parents and children, and alternates between bitter recriminations and expressions of love, *'night, Mother* is a compressed, more economical version of *A Long Day's Journey into Night*" (67). Being male, Brustein might well think first of a male precursor, but one could easily substitute Hellman's dramas, particularly the Hubbard plays, for O'Neill's drama. For, as Showalter remarks in *Sister's Choice*:

> Surely one element which unites us and which permeates our literature and our criticism is the yearning for community and continuity, for the bonds of even an unequal sisterhood. To a striking degree, American women writers have rejected the Oedipal metaphors of murderous "originality" set out as literary paradigms in Harold Bloom's *The Anxiety of Influence;* the patricidal struggle defined by Bloom and exemplified in the careers of male American writers, has no matricidal equivalent, no echo of denial, parody, exile. Instead, Alice Walker proclaims, "each writer writes the missing parts to the other writer's story." (174)

Rather than the "anxiety of authorship" produced in earlier women writers by male precursors, an assurance of authenticity now arises when a woman writer finds her female precursor and thus her own place in the line of succession. In an article Norman identified as "a simple tribute to the power of her voice to carry down the dark road, the strength of the example she never meant to set, and the generosity she unwittingly showed to another girl, who, like Lillian Hellman, 'stepped too early into solitude'" ("Lillian Hellman's Gift" H7), the younger woman acknowledges herself as in her precursor's debt. As she told Elizabeth Stone, Norman found her place in the theater thanks to Hellman and may now repay the debt as a precursor for today's twelve-year-old girl wishing to write for the theater, to whom she says, "There is a place for you in American theater. Now come *get it!*" (59).[5]

Notes

1. "The Pool Hall" is act 2 of *Third and Oak*. The acts have been published and performed separately, but Norman notes that she "prefer[s] that the two acts be seen together. Rather like the right foot following the left" (*Third and Oak* 60).

2. When questioned about Ruby's race at Methodist College's Twelfth Southern Writers' Symposium in March 1996, Norman replied that she had not "consciously" written Ruby as a black woman, but is "thrilled when [the role] is cast that way." She added that Whoopi Goldberg once played Ruby. (I presented an earlier version of this paper at that conference.)

3. Yet another Hellman-to-Norman echo occurs in the names Albertine (*Toys in the Attic*) and Alberta (*Third and Oak*).

4. Hellman does not attribute Martha's lesbianism to inadequate mothering. She may have intuited that lesbianism, seen as sexual "inversion" in her era, had a genetic basis.

5. I thank Linda Rohrer Paige for suggesting that I look into the subjects of both surrogate daughters and the divided self, particularly as Martha represents that self in *The Children's Hour.*

Works Cited

Adler, Jacob H. "The Rose and the Fox: Notes on the Southern Drama." *South: Modern Southern Literature in Its Cultural Setting.* Ed. Louis D. Rubin, Jr., and Robert D. Jacobs. 1961. Westport: Greenwood, 1976. 349–75.

Barranger, Milly S. "Southern Playwrights: A Perspective on Women Writers." *Southern Quarterly* 25.3 (1987): 5–9.

Bass, Ellen and Laura Davis. *The Courage to Heal.* New York: Harper, 1988.

Bloom, Harold. *The Anxiety of Influence: A Theory of Poetry.* New York: Oxford UP, 1973.

Brustein, Robert. "Don't Read This Review!" *Who Needs Theatre: Dramatic Opinions.* New York: *Atlantic Monthly,* 1987. 64–67.

Chodorow, Nancy. *The Reproduction of Mothering: Psychoanalysis and the Sociology of Gender.* Berkeley: U California P, 1979.

Falk, Doris. *Lillian Hellman.* New York: Ungar, 1978.

Gilbert, Sandra M., and Susan Gubar. *The Madwoman in the Attic: The Woman Writer and the Nineteenth-Century Literary Imagination.* New Haven: Yale UP, 1984.

Harriot, Esther. "Interview with Marsha Norman." *American Voices: Five Contemporary Playwrights in Essays and Interviews.* Jefferson, NC: McFarland, 1988. 148–63.

Hellman, Lillian. *Another Part of the Forest. The Collected Plays.* Boston: Little, 1972. 325–403.

——. *The Autumn Garden. Collected Plays.* 461–545.

——. *The Children's Hour. Collected Plays.* 1–69.

——. *The Little Foxes. Collected Plays.* 131–200.

——. *Pentimento.* Boston: Little, 1973.

——. *Toys in the Attic. Collected Plays.* 681–751.

——. *An Unfinished Woman. Three.* Boston: Little, 1979. 13–305.

Herman, Judith Lewis. *Father-Daughter Incest.* Cambridge: Harvard UP, 1981.

Horowitz, Israel. "Address." Dedication of the Robert Will Theatre. U of Rhode Island, Kingston. 5 October 1974.

Kintz, Linda. *The Subject's Tragedy: Political Poetics, Feminist Theory, and Drama*. Ann Arbor: U Michigan P, 1992.

Kolodny, Annette. "A Map for Rereading." *The New Feminist Criticism*. Ed. Elaine Showalter. New York: Pantheon, 1985. 46–62.

"Late Nineteenth Century, 1865–1910." *The Heath Anthology of American Literature*. Eds. Paul Lauter et al. 3rd ed. Vol. 2. Boston: Houghton. 3–34.

Norman, Marsha. "Articles of Faith: A Conversation with Lillian Hellman." *American Theatre* May 1984: 10–15.

———. *Getting Out*. Garden City, NY: Doubleday, 1979.

———. *The Holdup. Marsha Norman: Four Plays*. New York: Theatre Communications Group, 1988. 159–204.

———. "Introduction." *Marsha Norman: Collected Plays*. Lyme, NH: Smith, 1998. 2–3.

———. "Lillian Hellman's Gift to a Young Playwright." *New York Times* 26 August 1984. H1+.

———. *Loving Daniel Boone. Marsha Norman: Collected Plays*. 331–91.

———. *'night, Mother*. New York: Hill, 1983.

———. *Third and Oak. Marsha Norman: Four Plays*. 59–103.

———. *Traveler in the Dark. Marsha Norman: Four Plays*. 161–204.

Poirier, Richard. "Introduction." *Three*. vii–xxv.

Showalter, Elaine. *Sister's Choice: Tradition and Change in American Women's Writing*. Oxford: Clarendon, 1991.

Stone, Elizabeth. "Playwright Marsha Norman: An Optimist Writes about Suicide, Confinement and Despair." *Ms.* July 1983: 56–59.

Ward, William S. *A Literary History of Kentucky*. Knoxville: U of Tennessee P, 1988.

Westerlund, Elaine. *Women's Sexuality after Childhood Incest*. New York: Norton, 1992.

Wright, William. *Lillian Hellman: The Image, the Woman*. New York: Ballantine, 1986.

9

"Un-ruling" the Woman: Comedy and the Plays of Beth Henley and Rebecca Gilman

Janet L. Gupton

To be a feminist in the American South might seem an anomaly. No doubt the South has earned its reputation well as a patriarchal society where women don't sweat—they perspire—and where the men have placed them on a pedestal so high that the women either enjoy the view or are afraid to jump. The idealization of the white Southern "lady" is not new. The following homage to the Confederate Southern lady shows how the patriarch not only has placed her on a pedestal but also has tried to sculpt her into a silent statue: "The Confederate Woman. Imagination cannot dwell too tenderly upon a theme so inspiring. Reverence cannot linger too fondly at so pure an altar. . . . It took the civilization of an Old South to produce her. . . . The Confederate woman in her silent influence, in her eternal vigil, still abides. Her gentle spirit is the priceless heritage of her daughters" (Knight 221–22). Words such as "produce," "silent," "pure," and "gentle" here emphasize how the South has constructed the concept of white womanhood to fit a conservative patriarchal notion. And, although the concept of the Southern lady has changed during the twentieth century, vestiges of the abiding, quiet, unassuming Southern lady still manifest themselves in current dramatic literature as well as in popular culture.

Despite this tight girdle placed on them, Southern women writers have wrestled free to point out the ambiguities and discontentment that the role of Southern lady engenders. Southern women playwrights also have addressed the inconsistencies that arise for Southern women who don't fit this mold. Certain playwrights, creating their own style of comedy that pokes fun at Southern traditions such as the Southern lady, skew patriarchal paradigms. These playwrights combine an interesting mixture of the gothic and the grotesque to create "unruly women" characters who affront the notion of the Southern lady. In creating their plays, these playwrights break the rules of traditional comedy and un-rule the women characters in their plays. Because traditional play analysis falls short in appreciating this rule-breaking, these plays deserve further investigation and a feminist reading strategy to discover how they exemplify the new paths that contemporary Southern women playwrights are forging in comedy.

Two contemporary playwrights, in particular, have captured this style of comedy that speaks specifically to and of Southern culture—Beth Henley and Rebecca Gilman. While Henley's plays are more widely known, Gilman's plays evidence some of the same whimsical yet sardonic elements that characterize Henley's work. Both of these playwrights are invested in analyzing certain aspects of Southern culture, and both examine some of the same issues such as family, relationships between sisters, community standards, eccentric relatives or in-laws, and relationships, in general. Their plays manifest the complexities of Southern culture and the delicate power structures that exist in the South, but do so while making us laugh and sometimes cry at the same time. This article examines Beth Henley's *Crimes of the Heart* and *The Debutante Ball* and Rebecca Gilman's "Canannie and Alice" and *The Land of Little Horses* to illustrate a reading strategy for comedy and its feminist possibilities.

Traditional approaches that view comedy as a social preservative that brings societal outcasts back within the confines of "proper" behavior overlook the power of comedy as a disruptive, transformative challenge to the status quo. While the final aim of socially preservative comedy is to reinstate the status quo, socially transformative comedy focuses on the anti-authoritarian liminal phase of the genre that turns social orders upside down. As Regina Barreca notes in *New Perspectives on Women and Comedy,* "Certain forms of comedy can invert the world not only briefly but permanently . . . [and] can effectively channel anger and rebellion" to show that the "world turned upside down . . . has no rightful position at all" (6).

Henley and Gilman's plays demonstrate how comedy creates socially transformative outcomes for Southern women. In particular, the dialectical tension between the content of the plays and the comic forms the playwrights employ necessitates a new reading strategy for women's comedies. In these four plays, the female protagonists seek to break free of traditional roles and redefine themselves in Southern society. However, the structure of traditional comedy does not meet these needs. Thus, Henley and Gilman experiment with comic form to supply their comic heroines with alternative outcomes.

Restructuring traditional comic form places Henley and Gilman in a delicate position. They must adhere to certain structures or conventions when writing so that their work is considered comedy while simultaneously attacking these very conventions in order to avoid reinforcing traditional outcomes. For example, a traditional comic play ends happily. This, in turn, often translates into the heterosexual marriage of the comic hero and heroine as the play's resolution. Comedy that does not end happily or that provides an alternative ending risks not being identified as a comedy. In challenging the traditional roles afforded women protagonists in Southern culture, Henley and Gilman modify the comic narrative structure to avoid closure and the reinforcement of the status quo, sometimes leaving their characters with a "recognition" rather than with a tidy happy ending.

Resisting Traditional Roles for Southern Women

In *Crimes of the Heart, The Debutante Ball,* "Canannie and Alice," and *The Land of Little Horses,* the female protagonists redefine their roles as Southern women and defy the stereotype of the genteel Southern lady. While thoroughly evaluating the role that the Southern lady plays in the American South's construction of itself is beyond the scope of this short article, a brief description of the social hierarchy of the Old South as well as of the traditional Southern lady within this hierarchy helps illuminate the stereotype that Henley and Gilman subvert in their comedies.

Traditionally, the South has separated itself geographically and ideologically from the rest of the United States. In particular, it idealizes notions of chivalry and a simple agrarian life-style. In colonial times the South identified its way of life as a "natural aristocracy" in which the plantation owner was a stern but fair patriarch who cared for his white and black families. The residual effects of this notion of a "natural aristocracy" resonate in how the present day South sees itself and enforces behavioral codes.

The Southern lady is the natural companion to the patriarch and the one to whom a Southern gentleman should pledge his life. In *Caste and Class in a Southern Town,* John Dollard describes a fraternity ritual in which the members march in procession and their leader stands and delivers the following toast: "To woman, lovely woman of the Southland, as pure and chaste as this sparkling water, as cold as this gleaming ice, we lift this cup, and we pledge our hearts and our lives to the protection of her virtue and her chastity" (89). The protection and containment of the Southern white woman closely aligns with the identity of the Southern white male. The Southern white man feels obligated to keep the female pure because "she represents her culture's idea of religious, moral, sexual, racial and social perfection" (Jones 9). In her work on the concept of white Southern womanhood, literary historian Anne Goodwyn Jones describes the Southern lady as one who is chaste, "embodies virtue," and is sometimes lacking "sexual interest altogether" because "it is unthinkable for her to desire sex, much less sex with a black man" (9). The white man must protect her from "the black man's presumably uncontrollable sexual desire" to keep her genes "pure white" (Jones 9). Jaquelyn Hall in her book *Revolt against Chivalry: Jesse Ames and the Women's Campaign against Lynching* identifies the Southern lady as "the most potent symbol of white male supremacy" (155) because, as Louis Westling corroborates in her work, the Southern patriarchy needs its vision of the "inviolate" Southern lady to sustain its "elaborate fiction of aristocratic civilization" (39).

In Henley and Gilman's plays, the women characters are not Southern ladies. Instead, they become unruly women—the "disorderly one[s] par excellence" (Davis 124). The unruly woman, as described by Natalie Zemon Davis in her seminal work on early modern France, makes a spectacle of herself without fear of retribution and through her acts initiates cultural and/or political disobedience. She works outside the definition of "acceptable" characteristics for a woman and turns qualities such as boldness, bawdiness, and defiance into weapons. An unruly woman making a spectacle of herself creates a "multivalent image" that "widens behavioral options for women" (131).

Mary Russo in "Female Grotesques: Carnival and Theory" expands on Davis's image of the unruly woman by incorporating Mikhail Bakhtin's theories of the grotesque body but particularizes his theories to the female body. In short, for Bakhtin the grotesque body contests notions of stability and tidiness because it cannot be contained nor can its materiality be ignored. The grotesque body celebrates the everyday biological happenings of life, such as eating, drinking, and other bodily functions, as opposed to the lofty and static ideals found in the concept of the classical, individualized, bourgeois body. The grotesque body shows the relativity not only of the body, but also of life itself. For Bakhtin, the body becomes a metaphor for the ever-changing social state and the fragile, malleable structures on which a culture constructs itself.

Russo applies Bakhtin's ideas to the female body and posits that the grotesque female body becomes an unruly public spectacle when it is too old, or too irregular, or too pregnant (214). Further, she uses the grotesque female body to challenge the ideals of female beauty and femininity and to deconstruct imaginary identities based on the idealization of a certain kind of body, an untouched, sleek, individualized body. Russo's notions of the privileged, idealized type of body mirror the body expected of a Southern lady. For Russo, femininity becomes a masquerade and those who master the game can, of their own volition, put on and take off the mask "with a vengeance" (228). The ability to "perform" femininity and recognize it as performance can empower a woman to create her own subjectivity as long as she realizes that she is performing and controls that performance. In this regard, many a Southern woman has realized and reaped benefits from performing the role of the Southern lady. Many a Southern woman also has learned to put on and take off the mask of femininity with a vengeance.

In these four plays by Henley and Gilman, the female protagonists make spectacles of themselves, and in doing so, challenge the tropes of femininity validated by traditional Southern culture and offer models of transgressive, alternative behavior. The characters' anger and rebellion at being placed within restrictive behavioral codes of femininity illustrate that the white Southern patriarchy "has no rightful position at all" (Barreca 6).

In *Crimes of the Heart,* Babe, Lenny, and Meg all exhibit unruly behavior and commit crimes against Southern culture. They perpetrate cultural and social disobedience that threatens the Southern hierarchy. Babe's crime stems from her need to defend herself from an abusive husband. When Babe has a sexual relationship with a young black man and shoots her husband after he finds the two together, her actions strike deep at the very foundation of the white man's supremacy. When Zackery Botrelle, "the richest and most powerful man in all of Hazlehurst," is shot "slap in the gut" by his wife, the town is in an uproar and all the newspapers report it (15). Babe's act of rebellion turns the town upside down and shakes the very foundation of the Southern aristocracy. She debunks the myth of the white Southern patriarch and his identity in Southern culture. As her husband, Zackery should be able to govern his wife as inviolate sexual property and protect her from the black male. Thus, Babe's transgressive behavior not only redefines her role from obedient, submissive Southern lady to unruly woman, but also challenges her husband's identity.

Meg's crime, her ability to put on the masquerade of femininity with a vengeance, grants her the right to flout notions of pure and submissive Southern femininity by being sexually uninhibited, or "cheap Christmas trash" to use Chick's words (7). She refuses to be chaste and pure, and she does not lack "sexual interest altogether" (Jones 9). Instead, she devastates her lover, Doc, leaving him in the wake of her desire to be a singer. The community criticizes Meg's behavior because she leaves the relationship. Her act of leaving is behavior normally allotted a male in a traditional narrative. When Meg abandons Doc, whose leg is seriously hurt in the hurricane that she insists they stay and experience, she literally and figuratively leaves Doc a "cripple" in the eyes of Southern society. To the community, Doc's manhood has fallen prey to female vengeance and he is the one who deserves sympathy, not Meg. Further, Meg's unruliness toward her grandfather represents a threat to the Southern hierarchy because she contests the family patriarch's authority to control the sisters' lives.

Lenny's unruliness appears less flamboyant than her sisters'. Nonetheless, by the end of the play, the audience has watched the eldest daughter learn to laugh at the absurdity of her grandfather's condition and to deny his insistence that she can't find a husband because of her "shrunken ovary." In the beginning of the play, she is convinced that she does not live up to the ideals of female beauty because of her ovary. With the help of her sisters, Lenny comes to realize that this supposed defect is how her grandfather has tried to keep her as his nurse-maid rather than allow her to pursue a relationship. As Russo would suggest, Lenny learns that the shrunken ovary does not make her any less of a woman, because the concept of an ideal woman remains imaginary. Instead of deferring to her grandfather's wishes, Lenny musters the nerve to telephone the suitor whom she initially rejects. Defying her grandfather's wishes signals a step in her social disobedience, culminating in her chasing her cousin Chick (the keeper of traditional Southern values) with a broom out of the house and up a tree by the end of the play.

In *The Debutante Ball,* Henley continues to challenge the foundations of Southern patriarchal society by "carnivalizing" a Southern tradition—the debutante ball. The main character, Teddy, appears as a young Southern woman who has returned home from college to make her debut into Southern society, an event which signifies her eligibility for marriage and her readiness to fulfill the role of Southern lady. Teddy, however, seems unsure if conforming to the dictates of a Southern debutante is either possible or desirable. As her masculine name implies, she seems ill-suited to wearing a white gown and to performing the tropes of femininity that the debutante tradition promote. Furthermore, Teddy conceals her pregnancy when she returns home for the ball.

At first, Teddy tries in vain to construct herself as a debutante. She applies make-up, puts on the dress, and practices "acting" like a lady (Henley 12). Through the course of the play, however, she fails miserably at becoming a debutante. Her debut at the ball—unfortunately, not shown on stage—becomes a fiasco. The audience learns from other characters recounting the event that Teddy's gown flies over her head when she takes a bow, toilet paper gets stuck on her shoe, and her hairpiece falls into the punch bowl. Eventually, Teddy abandons all attempts at performing femininity and becomes an unruly woman, crawling under tables and spreading cream cheese on the shoes of other guests. In short, she makes a spectacle of herself.

The act of making a spectacle frees Teddy from the tyranny of unrealistic cultural expectations. Armed with this new-found freedom, Henley's heroine also finds the confidence to reveal the truth—that she, in fact, killed her abusive father to protect her mother. Until this point, her mother, Jen, has taken the responsibility for the father's death and has used this as leverage to get Teddy to conform to the debutante way of life.

Teddy is not the only female to find freedom from social constraints in *The Debutante Ball*. Bliss, Teddy's half-sister and Jen's illegitimate daughter by an itinerant fruit picker, takes advantage of the disruptive liminal state of affairs in this Southern household to venture into a new type of relationship. Bliss, denied her own debut because of her father's disputable identity, has recently split from her husband and enters a sexual relationship with Frances, a deaf woman, who, until Bliss, also has been neglected by society and men. Bliss and Frances's lesbian relationship undoubtedly defies traditional Southern roles for women.

In *The Debutante Ball*, Henley highlights the construction of femininity and the imaginary identity of the debutante, filling her play with images of grotesque female bodies shaving underarms and legs, plucking eyebrows, and applying ridiculous amounts of cosmetics as they prepare for the ball. In her preface to the play, Henley argues that such images are imperative to her play about facades: "I wanted my characters to be seen as animals fighting to pluck and spray and shave away their true natures—adorning themselves with lies" (xii). Under Russo's theory, the highlighting of the grotesque female bodies in *The Debutante Ball* destabilizes ideals of beauty and challenges the idea of the Southern lady (or debutante) and the "natural aristocracy" that produces her.

While Henley's *The Debutante Ball* lampoons Southern "high society" and the debutante mentality, Rebecca Gilman's "Canannie and Alice" examines the consequences that two older, unruly women face in a small, rural Southern town. In "Canannie and Alice," a jealous neighbor publicizes that the two women (the title characters) are lesbians because her young (somewhat mentally challenged) son, whom she grossly mistreats, prefers their company to hers. The neighbor first seeks revenge by trying to blackmail Canannie and Alice, but when they refuse to deny the information, she tells the rest of the town. The community eventually isolates Canannie and Alice.

These protagonists' unruliness arises not only from their nontraditional relationship but also from their advanced ages. At the beginning of the play, the two women celebrate their anniversary by dancing around in their slips, drinking wine, and openly acknowledging their affection for each other. They realize the danger, however, that their relationship represents to the small community in which they live:

ALICE: To our silver anniversary.

CANANNIE: As tarnished as it may be.

ALICE: Be nice for a second, can't you?

CANANNIE: Happy Anniversary. (They look at each other for a moment, drink.) Think they'll put our picture in the paper with all the other couples?

ALICE: They'll put our pictures in the post office. (6)

Canannie and Alice defy the traditional narrative of a heterosexual marriage, creating their identities through their desire for each other and their nontraditional marriage. Further, their age and comfortableness with each other afford them the right to contest standards of femininity by discussing bowel movements and other bodily functions, not to mention their use of derogatory language such as "bitch" and "whore" (Gilman 17). Canannie and Alice flaunt the freedom and irreverence that come with the aging, grotesque female body and widen behavioral options for Southern women.

Jean Louise in Gilman's *The Land of Little Horses* uses her youth to create unruliness by refusing to accept the tropes of femininity assumed by young Southern ladies. Like Canannie and Alice, she defines herself through her own interests, rather than by desiring the company of a man. The youngest of three sisters, Jean Louise spends much of her time taking care of her eccentric Aunt Dot and, supposedly, writing a dissertation. Unlike her sisters, Jean Louise eschews men and marriage. Rather than follow the Freudian Oedipal narrative of rejecting her mother and aligning herself with a man (via marriage), she remains in the liminal stage of virginity.

In "The Matrix of War: Mothers and Heroes," Nancy Huston proposes that virgins possess a certain power from their liminality because they remain outside the social and symbolic dictates of marriage, and, thus, can participate in activities usually afforded only to men (128). Judith Wilt in "The Laughter of Maidens, The Cackle of Matriarchs: Notes on the Collision between Comedy and Feminism," corroborates Huston's position by proposing that the virgin has unique powers because she "expresses, rather than represses" ideas, thoughts, and actions, and "exposes and deflates" the superficialities and misconceptions of a world built around the traditional marriage narrative. For Wilt, the virgin remains in a liminal stage because she can find "no role in the world which totally satisfies her" (179–80).

In *The Land of Little Horses,* the virgin, Jean Louise, cannot find a role in her current situation that satisfies her, so she and her aunt run away from home to follow miniature horse racing. Upon finding out the sad existence of these horses—how they are bred to be objects of display and freaks of nature—the two women free the horses in the middle of the night. Activities such as running away from home and freeing horses generally are reserved for the male hero in traditional comedy, but because Jean Louise remains outside the social constraints of marriage and "respectability," she can commit these unruly acts. With the power of the virgin on her side, Jean Louise exposes the mistreatment of the horses, and, by releasing them, deflates the world that makes money off of them.

The women characters in Henley and Gilman's plays, through their acts of unruliness, offer models of transgressive behavior for other Southern women. Their resistance to the patriarch's definition of a Southern lady challenges the social structure on which the patriarch bases his aristocracy. Instead of having chaste and pure bodies that (em)body the ideals of a Southern lady, they have Bakhtinian flesh and blood bodies, ones which breathe, bleed, have sex, give birth, and die. Their bodies rub up against the notions of the idealized, static, and contained body of the Southern lady. The destabilization of the identity of the Southern lady sends shock waves through the rest of the South's social structure. These plays ask the question: if the Southern lady is an imaginary identity, what other imaginary identities lurk behind the Southern patriarchal paradigm?

In addition to questioning the traditional roles for Southern women, the acts of unruliness by Henley and Gilman's female protagonists occur in the company of other women. Acting together to support and validate the other's actions, Babe, Meg, and Lenny; Teddy, Bliss, and Frances; Canannie and Alice; and Jean Louise and her Aunt Dot join forces to redefine themselves, thus assuming roles not normally allotted them in the traditional Southern narrative. Traditional comic form generally reserves the status of protagonist for a single male hero. In Henley and Gilman's plays, however, the protagonist comes in the form of a "group of women."

Resisting Closure and Traditional Comic Endings

Employing a group protagonist instead of a single protagonist exemplifies one way that both Henley and Gilman play with comic form. Another way in which their plays challenge the writing of traditional comedy is the subversion of a traditional linear narrative. A linear narrative presupposes a neat cause-and-effect approach to plot. In general, women writers of comedy have chosen a much looser conception of plot. Susan Carlson in *Women and Comedy* uses the term "texture," instead of "plot," to refer to the weaving together of many discrete items (184), while Regina Barreca in *Last Laughs: Perspectives on Women and Comedy* suggests that women who write using "multiplicity and diversion" open the door for all kinds of possible outcomes (17–18). Texturing and multiplicity allow for the reframing of events and issues in the women characters' lives, possibly leading the audience to a greater understanding of the conditions in which the women characters find themselves.

Linear narratives also seem suspect to feminist writers because the resolution of a linear narrative can create closure. In comedy, an author imposes closure when a return to the status quo through a traditional ending presents itself. Such an ending creates the illusion that all transgressive and "improper" behavior of the comic heroine during the disruptive liminal phase of comedy has been brought into line with societal norms, thereby placing the world back to its "rightful" position. This type of ending fails to address the cost of such a tidy denouement. In *Crimes of the Heart, The Debutante Ball,* "Canannie and Alice" and *The Land of Little Horses,* the playwrights supply no tidy, neat and happy endings. By doing so, however, the playwrights risk acceptance of their work as comedic.

While a feminist playwright can reject a linear narrative completely, the strong desire for "story," particularly in Western drama in which audiences expect a logical sequence of events, makes certain narrative forms attractive to playwrights. Henley and Gilman both employ a narrative structure, but they often play with this structure to resist traditional outcomes. In "Changes: Thoughts on Myth, Narrative and Historical Experience," feminist film theorist Laura Mulvey proposes that feminists resist the "easy acceptance of closure" by rethinking their application of narrative to question the myths, symbols, and values of a culture (175). Mulvey proposes using narrative to reframe the issues through which the audience views the world.

In *Crimes of the Heart,* Henley begins the play at the climax of the traditional narrative. Babe has shot her husband and Henley thrusts her audience right into the anti-authoritarian, liminal phase of comedy. The improper behavior has occurred and the town talks about those crazy Magrath women. Not only has the youngest Magrath sister turned unruly, but also Meg, her even more unruly older sister (who abandoned the South), has returned home and her "appearance isn't gonna help out a bit," Chick complains (7). Henley adds even more disruptive ingredients to the mix: the events occur on Lenny's birthday; Doc, Meg's scorned lover, delivers the news that Lenny's old horse has been struck by lightning; Chick's kids eat paint; Barnette Lloyd, the new attorney in town, has a personal vendetta to settle with Zackery Botrelle; Meg and Doc go on a ride to "look out at the moon" (51); and "Old Granddaddy's had himself another stroke" (53).

By focusing on the middle, liminal phase of comedy, Henley seeks to sustain this phase and to prevent the "easy acceptance of closure" (Mulvey 175). In doing so, she addresses a large portion of the play to the anti-authoritarian events in which the Southern paradigm remains "upside down" due to the transgressive behavior of the three women. To satisfy the audience's desire for narrative, Henley allows the play to progress toward some kind of an ending; in defiance, however, of a traditional happy comedic ending, Henley leaves the three sisters in an ambiguous state of affairs, refusing to reinstate the status quo. The women's worlds have changed directions, but Henley resists giving the audience the unequivocal happy ending that characterizes traditional comic form.

Criticizing the ambiguous ending of *Crimes* and asking whether these Southern women remain dependent on the validation of men fails to consider an alternative reading strategy for comedies written by women. Henley's *Crimes*, more importantly than providing a happy ending, points up the complexities and inconsistencies these characters face within Southern culture. The culture teaches the women to validate themselves through the approval of the white male, but when such a validation does not satisfy the women, ready and suitable alternatives may not appear simultaneously.

Henley resolves *The Debutante Ball* similarly with an ambiguous ending, having Teddy achieve a recognition of sorts rather than a pat resolution. At the end of the play, she loses her child in a miscarriage (occurring on stage) but does reconcile with her mother. The final image of *The Debutante Ball* presents Teddy rubbing ointment on her mother's psoriasis-ridden body as Jen takes a bath. Teddy says: "I don't have a feeling anymore like it's never gonna get better . . . it's like I can smell the rain coming and I can feel it's gonna start to thunder. . . . Yeah, and that ole snapping turtle's gonna let loose and I'll just be standing there in the rain and the thunder and these arms will want to hold onto somebody and have their arms holding on to me" (96). While Teddy's feelings appear hopeful, Henley refuses her comic heroine concrete resolutions, allowing Teddy only the recognition that life can get better and that it can be on her own terms.

As in *Crimes of the Heart,* the many events and details about the characters' lives in *The Debutante Ball* may seem excessive or extraneous. Characters labor over their pasts and obsess over their presents. Henley's abundance of detail denies a linear narrative, but, instead, provides multiplicity. An examination of the characters' histories creates the necessary background for understanding how the female characters arrive at their current status in life.

The multiplicity of events and the diversions created by retelling the past get reinforced through other plot diversions in *The Debutante Ball* as well. In particular, Henley incorporates references and images of the grotesque female body as important plot diversions that demand a reevaluation of what a Southern debutante represents. She sets much of the play in the bathroom, a potentially liminal space, because the women constantly put on and take off their Southern identities. Henley repeatedly parades these women's grotesque bodies as material flesh and blood rather than as a fetish or object of the white patriarch's desire, and thus destabilizes the idealization of a certain type of beauty validated by the debutante tradition. By incorporating and highlighting these images into the telling of the story, she questions the myths, symbols, and values of Southern culture.

Like Henley, Gilman also resists traditional narrative closure by focusing on and sustaining the liminal disruptive phase of comedy. The disruptive phase of *The Land of Little Horses* begins when Jean Louise and Dot run away from home. While away from home, Jean Louise finds her purpose—to set free the miniature horses. In freeing these animals, she extricates herself from her past and from her mother and sisters, who believe her incapable of living on her own. Jean Louise's separation from family grants her the independence and confidence to return home by the end of the play at the heightened status of having proven herself.

Furthermore, Jean Louise obtains this heightened status without submitting to comedy's traditional happy ending of a heterosexual marriage. Ironically, Gilman includes three marital-type relationships in her play, all three fraught with unhappiness. Evelyn, the oldest of the three sisters, is getting married, but it is obvious to the other sisters and to the audience that Evelyn feels obligated to get married to avoid being alone. Hers appears to be a marriage of convenience, not of passion. Laura, the mother, confesses that her second marriage is a contractual arrangement turned sour as of late, and Jessica, the middle sister, tends to move from one relationship to another but admits her dependency on relationships with men to create her own sense of self. Instead of marriage, Jean Louise and Dot choose to live in the family house and paint the "ceilings blue" and the "walls green," if they so desire (Gilman 83), while the mother and sisters reluctantly return to the men in their lives. Jean Louise achieves a happy ending on her own terms, not because of society or her family's expectations.

In addition to resisting closure, Gilman also employs the soliloquy, which reframes the character of Jean Louise as different from the other women in the play. Gilman breaks the narrative flow on several occasions when the character of Jean Louise presents these monologues to the audience. She remains the only character in the play given soliloquies. Although the use of soliloquies obviously is not new, by limiting this technique to Jean Louise, Gilman allows the audience to gain further insight into the comic heroine's feelings.

In "Canannie and Alice," Gilman provides another ironic, dark twist to the narrative and to the concept of a "happy ending" through marriage. She mixes elements of tragedy into her play and questions the cost of a "happy ending." When the neighbor blackmails Canannie and Alice for being lesbians, they refuse to deny the allegations. The community and church ostracize them, and the women withdraw from community activities. Eventually the townspeople realize how much they miss the two and invite them back to church. Canannie returns to church, deciding to make it "hard on them [the community]" rather than fade into oblivion, while Alice seems still reluctant to return (70). Upon leaving the church, Canannie gets struck and killed by a truck. At the play's end, after losing Canannie, Alice finally agrees to marry Mr. Beevies, a long-time, ill-suited suitor.

The mixture of the happy and tragic in Gilman's play provides a "happy ending" in name only by including a marriage. Real happiness comes arguably not from Alice's union with Mr. Beevies, a potentially conventional ending, but rather from the community's recognition that casting out Canannie and Alice was both wrong and costly. Mr. Beevies evidences the community's recognition of its lesson:

> It was, well, Alice, it was that we were all mutually embarrassed wadn't it? I mean everybody was shocked, or surprised I mean. And I guess it's good ya'll didn't deny it, because it made me, well, realize some things. But then ya'll just got so quiet.
>
> We none of us handled it right. I didn't know how to call you for the longest time. How to get over that thing of well, do I say something or just chat. When maybe just chattin' is rude but maybe saying something is worse. Especially when none of us know much and would probably go puttin' our foot in our mouth. You see? Alice?
>
> Only maybe we did finally figure it out. That we missed ya'll. That was the thing. We missed ya'll a lot. And you wouldn't come to church Alice. Why wouldn't you come to church today? (72)

Mr. Beevies's confession suggests a movement by the community toward acceptance and reconciliation, but only after paying too high a price.

Alice, too, comes to recognize that the two women empowered each other when she realizes the depth of Canannie's love for her and her love for Canannie. Alice explains to Mr. Beevies: "I thought, before she went to church I thought she said something . . . well, I thought no matter what we'd always be freaks here. But why stay here? Why be in this place. (Beat.) We'd go somewhere and start having fun again. All she meant to tell me was that . . . she loved me and that . . . well . . . we shouldn't let anything stop us from . . . each other" (76). The nominally happy ending with which Gilman ends her play forces an audience to resist the "easy acceptance of closure" (Mulvey 175) by demonstrating the high price of the community's prejudice.

Because Henley and Gilman resist traditional roles for their comic Southern heroines, they also resist traditional comic narrative form and outcomes. These four plays typify both playwrights' work with a group protagonist of several women. Further, the protagonists achieve recognitions rather than orderly resolutions, which question the cost of a traditional "happy" status quo comic ending. Because the playwrights find more freedom and power for their protagonists in the liminal anti-authoritarian phase of the comedy, they sometimes leave their protagonists in that liminal stage at the end of the play, resulting in a disconcerting ambiguity for traditionalists who crave closure.

Conclusion

For many people, the reputation of the South as a patriarchal stronghold that keeps women within submissive, subservient roles rings true. Women playwrights of the South, nonetheless, have sought to illustrate the inconsistencies and undesirability of some of the social roles foisted upon them by their culture. Through their deft skills in the genre of comedy, Henley and Gilman destabilize the stereotype of the "Southern lady" and explore the anti-authoritarian aspects that can make comedy a socially transformative tool. Playwrights like Henley and Gilman, those who refuse to reinstate the status quo and make us laugh while doing so, should be acknowledged for their special use of comedy. Their work should receive a different reading strategy than that given to traditional comedy so that those who seek to employ comedy for only socially preservative outcomes and who have a vested interest in maintaining the status quo might realize that the cackle of an unruly Southern woman may be only one emotion removed from toppling the patriarchal hierarchy.

Works Cited

Barreca, Regina, ed. *Last Laughs: Perspectives on Women and Comedy.* New York: Gordon, 1988.

———. *New Perspectives on Women and Comedy.* New York: Gordon, 1992.

Carlson, Susan. *Women and Comedy.* Ann Arbor: U of Michigan P, 1991.

Davis, Natalie Zemon. *Society and Culture in Early Modern France.* Stanford: Stanford UP, 1975.

Dollard, John. *Caste and Class in a Southern Town.* Garden City, NY: Doubleday, 1957.

Gilman, Rebecca. "Canannie and Alice." Unpublished play, 1992.

———. *The Land of Little Horses.* New York: Dramatists Play Service, 1992.

Hall, Jaquelyn. *Revolt against Chivalry: Jesse Ames and the Women's Campaign against Lynching.* New York: Columbia UP, 1979.

Henley, Beth. *Crimes of the Heart.* New York: Dramatists Play Service, 1982.

———. *The Debutante Ball.* Jackson: UP of Mississippi, 1991.

Huston, Nancy. "The Matrix of War: Mothers and Heroes." *The Female Body in Western Culture.* Ed. Susan Suleiman. Cambridge: Harvard UP, 1986.

Jones, Anne Goodwyn. *Tomorrow Is Another Day: The Woman Writer in the South 1859–1936.* Baton Rouge: Louisiana State UP, 1981.

Knight, Lucien Lamar. Introduction to Mrs. Bryan Wells Collier, *Biographies of Representative Women of the South* as quoted in *The Southern Lady: From Pedestal to Politics, 1830–1930,* by Anne Firor Scott. Chicago: U of Chicago P, 1970.

Mulvey, Laura. "Changes: Thoughts on Myth, Narrative and Historical Experience." *Visual and Other Pleasures.* Bloomington: Indiana UP, 1989.

Russo, Mary. "Female Grotesques: Carnival and Theory." *Feminist Critical Studies.* Ed. Teresa de Laurentis. Bloomington: Indiana UP, 1986.

Westling, Louise. *Sacred Groves and Ravished Gardens: The Fiction of Eudora Welty, Carson McCullers, and Flannery O'Connor.* Athens: U of Georgia P, 1985.

Wilt, Judith. "The Laughter of Maidens, The Cackle of Matriarch: Notes on the Collision between Comedy and Feminism." *Gender and Literary Voice.* Ed. Janet Todd. New York: Holmes, 1980.

10

Pseudonymy and Identity Politics: Exploring "Jane Martin"

J. Ellen Gainor

I

The Actors Theatre of Louisville, Kentucky, under the Artistic Direc-torship of Jon Jory,[1] has emerged as one of the more prominent professional regional theaters in the United States, known particularly for its script develop-ment through its internationally recognized Humana Festival of New American Plays. Simultaneously, the Actors Theatre has gained considerable notoriety in the past two decades for perpetuating one of the longest-running mystery sto-ries in the American theater—the real identity of the pseudonymous play-wright "Jane Martin," the author of more than a dozen plays to date, almost all of which were first produced at Louisville and directed by Jory. Since pre-senting "her" first work in 1981, Jory and his staff have steadfastly refused to divulge any information about the identity of the playwright, other than to maintain that "she" is a Kentucky resident who wishes to protect "her" privacy and who has entrusted "her" work to the Actors Theatre.[2]

Journalists have repeatedly highlighted the Martin mystery amidst their cov-erage of the annual Humana Festival. The press, in their single-minded dedica-tion to this story, has thus, albeit unintentionally, deflected attention from a closer analysis of the works themselves, or of Martin as a Southern woman writer, or of the broader theatrical and cultural ramifications of the relationship between Martin and the Actors Theatre. This essay will touch on each of these neglected topics. Its primary concern, however, is with Jane Martin as a pseud-onymous author, and I am frankly uninterested in who Martin "really" is. Nev-ertheless, the phenomenon of Martin has real significance for literary theory, gender studies, and theater history, and these areas will be the focus of my exploration.

According to legend, the Actors Theatre sponsored an "in-house, one-act play[writing] competition" (Gussow, "Mystery" 58) in 1981. A short script entitled *Twirler,* the monologue of a fanatic female baton twirler, was submitted with no author's name attached. The piece was selected for production, and the writer was listed in the program as "Anonymous" (Mootz 1). *Twirler* was an overwhelming audience and critical favorite, as *New York Times* reviewer Mel Gussow explained: "All during the festival, as critics reached for encomia and producers reached for contracts, the author remained unknown. Guesses ran from Marsha Norman to Phyllis George Brown, wife of the Governor of Kentucky. Romulus Linney suggested that the play was "handed down from heaven by Flannery O'Connor" (Gussow, "Critic's Notebook" 24). Soon thereafter, apparently, the author supplied the pen name Jane Martin for the piece, and by the next year she had created a series of additional monologues for women that Jory put together under the title *Talking With.* . . . Jory produced and directed this work in 1982, occasioning one critic to remark wryly that the playwright "who last year preferred to be anonymous . . . has at least become pseudonymous" (Young 17).

As Gussow's depiction of the reception of *Twirler* indicates, critics and audiences alike saw in this piece the emergence of a new Southern voice in the theater, one linked to the Gothic style of O'Connor, refracted through the more recent theatrical sensibility of Norman, another of Jory's protegés. The fact that each of Martin's female figures is a misfit particularly ties her to this Southern literary tradition. While this technique makes her drama compelling —particularly for actresses looking for challenging roles—it also heightens the object status of her characters through the distancing that may occur in the process of negative audience identification. Although Martin sets *Twirler* in Ohio (*Talking* 38), its comic-grotesque sense of local color further aligns it with Southern literary traditions: "I started when I was six. Momma sawed off a broom handle, and Uncle Carbo slapped some sort of silver paint, well, grey really, on it and I went down in the basement and twirled. Later on, Momma hit the daily double on horses named Spin Dry and Silver Revolver and she said that was a sign so she gave me lessons at the Dainty Deb Dance Studio" (*Talking* 37).

The intensity and, ultimately, humor of reviewers' speculation about the identity of the playwright has escalated with the appearance of every one of her works, which include *Coup/Clucks* (1982), *Cementville* (1989), *Vital Signs* (1990), and *Criminal Hearts* (1992), among others, and particularly Martin's Pulitzer Prize–nominated drama *Keely and Du* (1993). Since 1982, headlines like "Jane Martin's Mystery Theater" (Hulbert 10), and "Who Is Jane Martin? None of Your Business" (Dodds 19) have run in newspapers across the country, chronicling the frustration of writers with the impenetrable wall the Actors Theatre has constructed around her identity. After examining many years' worth of such pieces, one realizes that the story of Martin's pseudonymous identity has evolved to the point where it is as important as the work itself—in fact, they are inseparable.

Not surprisingly, the media quickly began to speculate about likely suspects for the pseudonym. The most frequent guess was Jory himself, either alone, or in collaboration with other writers. Jory long retained a jovial outlook on these hypotheses, which often simultaneously refer to Jory's own work as a playwright as part of the evidence. Other journalists, having realized the futility of pressing Jory for specific details, have queried him simply about the sex of the playwright, which he also refuses to discuss. Told that he was "very good at keeping secrets," Jory explained to one writer, "I've had 10 years of practice. In the early days there was a lot of curiosity in these parts about Jane Martin's identity. But 10 years down the road, Louisville accepts that this is a Kentucky writer whose identity will not be revealed" (Evans 12). Jory's emphasis on Martin's geographical base may signal his desire to have her work considered within traditions of Southern writing, but it seems more likely to reflect his interest in reinforcing her regional ties to him and his theater.

My own attempts to get access to information about Martin's career may indicate a broader tension around her work in Louisville, however. When I sent a letter of inquiry to the theater, asking simply for a copy of Martin's standard program biography and some press clippings for my research, I was shocked to receive an early-morning telephone call from Mr. Jory himself, who cordially, but firmly, informed me that Jane Martin actively discourages scholarly explorations of her work.[3] Upon reflection, what really surprised me about this response was the level of anxiety it represented. Even though I had made it clear that I had no interest in trying to uncover Martin's identity, obviously my work represented some real threat. What might scholarly investigation of Martin's dramaturgy reveal that required as much deterring as the attempts to unmask the author? Jory's continued refusal to provide any information about the dramatist forces one to place the analysis of Martin's work in another arena, for which the trope of pseudonymy emerges, almost by default, as the central feature. And Martin's status as a pseudonymous writer is salient at this moment precisely because of the dominance of positional criticism within literary studies, as I will discuss shortly. By extension, then, the issue of pseudonymy itself may have something to do with Jory's anxiety, and it is to this subject that I now turn.

II

While both pseudonymy and anonymy date back to the beginnings of Western civilization, one might, for purposes of useful comparison, more profitably look to a moment when pseudonymy was a frequent literary practice —and a phenomenon inextricably related to questions surrounding gender identity. The history of the Victorian novel presents such an example; in her groundbreaking study *A Literature of Their Own,* Elaine Showalter links the rise of women's use of male pseudonyms to the professionalization of the "job of novelist" during the 1840s. Showalter sees this "role-playing" as "required by women's effort to participate in the mainstream of literary culture" (19). By analyzing reviewers' responses to texts according to the sex of their authors, Showalter demonstrates the assumptions and categorizations made by the critics. This applied particularly to novels known to be pseudonymous or anonymous; according to Showalter, "reviewers would break [them] down into [their] elements, label these masculine or feminine, and add up the total" in order to reveal the "true" authorship by sex (91). However, as Nicola Thompson shows in her study of gender and the critical reception of novels in the period, when the actual sexual identity of a pseudonymous author was revealed, as, for example, in the case of Emily Brontë's *Wuthering Heights,* the entire response to the work changes.[4] These historical reactions to unknown authorship highlight both the assumptions reviewers make about sex and writing and the commercial context in which one must pose questions about the practice of pseudonymy.

Quite conveniently, current criticism of Martin has stayed true to this historical form, generating journalistic commentary that obligingly foregrounds the masquerade along with a discussion of the work, and which echoes assumptions about authorial identity based on gendered conventions of writing well established in the Victorian era. A critic for the *Financial Times,* for example, after detailing the outlines of *Talking With . . .* comments, "Jane Martin seems to know about such things from the inside" (Young 17). And Glenne Currie of UPI maintains that Martin's "astonishing insight would almost assuredly mean she is a woman."

In her discussion of Victorian authorship, Showalter cites an even more personal reason for women to choose male pseudonyms: to protect themselves "from the righteous indignation of their own relatives" (58), whose assumptions about Victorian womanhood may not have included either a woman's professional activity or her potential to imagine the kinds of characters or situations present in the fiction she created. Showalter offers the example of one author whose reasons for writing pseudonymously "show both fear of discrimination and anxiety about causing pain, offending friends, or betraying affection" (59).

What interests me about this facet of the exploration of the use of pseudonymy by Jane Martin is the striking parallel between the critical construction of her situation and that of authors in the Victorian era. If one thinks of Jon Jory in his role of publicist, or spokesperson, for Martin, he becomes the prime conduit for our "knowledge" of her. In this way, regardless of the true identity of the playwright, Jory "becomes" Martin in terms of public representation. And, as with all other areas of Martin inquiry, Jory has constructed a narrative on the rationale for Martin's choice of pseudonymy—a narrative sounding very much like ones invoked by Showalter. When asked to explain Martin's reclusiveness, Jory routinely offers a sound bite like one of the following: "She honestly feels, for whatever reason, that she couldn't write plays if her people knew who she was and what she was" (Rizzo 4). "She doesn't want to talk about plays. . . . She doesn't want to deal emotionally with being a public figure. She thinks it would be bad for her" (Stayton 1). His constructions of Martin, relying on her close relationship to family and friends and the impact of that relation on her writing, as well as on images of sensitivity and emotionality, all serve calculatedly to invoke classic gender stereotypes of femininity and to cement the notion of an integral relationship between Martin's "real" sex and her dramaturgy. Jory's presentation of Martin, which so closely parallels Victorian ideas of femininity and female authorship, establishes a provocative tension with the thematic and narratological thrust of the works themselves, however; her scripts may appear modern, but as I will describe shortly, they betray notably regressive elements.

Yet the practice of pseudonymy in the Victorian period was even more complicated than Showalter describes. In their study of Victorian novelists and publishers, *Edging Women Out*, Gaye Tuchman and Nina Fortin studied the relationship between readership, market forces, and pseudonymy throughout the nineteenth century. Tuchman and Fortin's research reveals that, based on the targeted readership for novels, authors—or authors under the guidance of their publishers—would select either a male or a female pseudonym in order to appear to speak to their readership as one of them (53). Thus they show that "cultural expectations" may have been as significant a factor in the practice of pseudonymy as the more personally derived rationales proposed by Showalter (54).

Tuchman and Fortin's theories have certainly been borne out by the phenomenon of romance authorship in the late twentieth century—a more recent corollary for an analysis of pseudonymy. Perhaps the most forthright discussion of the issues and assumptions about gender surrounding romance authorship by men comes from Valerie Parv in her exploration of *The Art of Romance Writing*—a book targeted at aspiring authors: "Men can and do write romances successfully, although usually under a female pseudonym so their work isn't prejudiced on the basis of their gender" (4). Parv's synthesis of the editorial views on gender and writing, as well as her sense of the position of male authors within this market segment, strongly echo the findings of the more recent Victorian scholarship, showing that the historical assumptions are still very much with us.

While I have no evidence with which to dismiss the personal motives for Martin's pseudonymy, as suggested by Jory, I believe one might also speculate about such issues as market forces in the contemporary American theater, as well as the connection between dramaturgy and audience in the current moment, to determine the potential rationalization for the choice of pseudonym. Expressed more blatantly, might there be a demonstrable and growing market for "relevant" drama by "women" that could motivate artistry with an eye to financial gain or other marks of success? Similarly, one could explore the complex relationship among traditions of Southern female identity—coded similarly to ideas of Victorian womanhood, the construction of Martin, and the deeper, problematic structures in her dramaturgy, all of which may be interrelated.

In her well-known historical study *The Southern Lady*, Anne Firor Scott draws a direct parallel between men's images of Southern female identity and those of women from Victorian England (14), codes which emphasized "softness, purity, and spirituality," among other qualities (15). And as Peggy Prenshaw notes, these ideals continue to "maintain a spirited vitality" in the South today (74). Jory's invocation of tropes of Southern femininity for Martin thus shapes our sense of her, reinforcing the notion that "Southern women seem especially susceptible to mythmaking" (Wolfe 7). Even more importantly, however, these constructs may have much to do with Jory's endorsement of her writing, which, on its deepest levels, reveals a hostility to genuine feminist sensibilities or action—an attitude itself in keeping with a predilection for the tradition of Southern womanhood.

III

The *Oxford English Dictionary* defines a pseudonym quite straightforwardly as "a false or fictitious name, especially one assumed by an author." Extrapolating from this, one could argue that there is an inherent, irresolvable disjunction between "true" and pseudonymous authorial identity, a fissure marked by the nominative signifier. In other words, a pseudonym is designed to convey clear, but deflectionary, information about authorship, drawing attention from a form of stable authenticity to an alternative construct of identity that is clearly and calculatedly selected to convey and control the perception—and perhaps reception—of the writer. As the examples from the Victorian era and more recent romance writing show, this perception is perhaps most often linked to gender and sexual identity, but this is by no means the only option.

If one thinks about how pseudonyms work on the semiotic level, one may sometimes find that they are really quite pernicious, potentially dependent on the grossest forms of stereotype and convention to function. But a great deal more information can be conveyed pseudonymously. If an author wishes to be perceived as having a certain racial, ethnic, or geographical connection, then a name can be chosen accordingly. As Michel Foucault explains in "What Is an Author," that designation "is, to a certain extent, the equivalent of a description" (121). Such choices rely on shared social conventions and assumptions; they do not "prove" identity, despite the fact that they attempt to control it. Foucault reminds us that the name's "status and . . . manner of reception are regulated by the culture in which it circulates" (123). Taking Jane Martin as the example, one sees that the first name is the generic female signifier within American culture. And by using the last name "Martin" the author has opted *not* to be contained within an environment marked within our culture as "marginal" on the basis of the patronymic. Martin's name is thus "all-American," perhaps chosen calculatedly to appeal to the widest audience possible. One might even go so far as to suggest that through this pseudonym, the construction of Martin as a "Southern" woman can be extrapolated such that she becomes the "American" woman—a move in line with other recent trends in U.S. politics.

The structure of pseudonymy may further compel us to consider its relationship with a critical climate that often privileges reception over creation. On a fundamental level, we might say that pseudonymous texts, like anonymous ones, offer ideal examples of "authorless" works that would lend themselves neatly to a poststructuralist analysis that still considers constructs like "intentionality" problematic at best. The absence of a stable, verifiable authorial identity would seem to liberate the critic from the need to consider biographical criteria, yet this very freedom highlights, in its binary conceptualization of authored vs. authorless texts, the dynamic interplay between authorship and the very foundation of poststructuralist discourse. Indeed, as in the case of Martin, when pseudonymous authorship is so inextricably linked to the popular critical reception of a series of works, one might wonder about the prospects for a postmodern theoretical analysis of writing so closely tied to a constructed, essentialized biography.

I invoke the specter of essentialism here *intentionally* for two reasons. First, it is significant to note the relationship between pseudonymy and essentialism that the analysis of the former's structure reveals. The invocation of nomenclature with strong iconic, semiotic resonance points to the essentialized nature of that kind of pseudonymous identity. Exactly in the fashion most strongly critiqued in postmodern discourse, the pseudonym universalizes and reduces the constructed identity to conventionalized categories such as sex and ethnicity. At the same time, the author, through the selection of the pseudonym, attempts to control with these essentialized categories the reception and understanding of his or her work. Thus, on a basic level, Jane Martin *wants* her work to be read/seen as that of a (genericized) American woman dramatist. Interestingly, however, our national culture in the United States has no means of signifying regional identity through names, a convenience that furthers the extension of Martin as Southern writer to Martin as American writer. Martin's dramaturgy itself reflects this breadth. While about half her plays have Southern settings and feature clearly identifiable Southern characters and action, such as the "Tara Parade" in *Coup/Clucks,* the other half are set elsewhere or are not identifiable as regional pieces.

Theater critics have obligingly accepted and promulgated Martin's biographical image as a Kentucky woman writer through their journalistic commentary on her plays, although they ignore the potential connection between her Southern location and tropes within her dramaturgy. The provocative questions that remain, then, are why critics and scholars have eschewed the analysis of Martin's writing itself, and what, if anything, this might have to do with the tension between the structure and theoretical significance of pseudonymy and contemporary critical discourse. Issues surrounding essentialism may be integral to these queries.

In recent critical theory, the idea of the subject has crystallized into the examination of subject positions, a form of study associated with identity politics and the emergence of inquiry embracing race, gender, sexuality, ethnicity, and a host of other considerations. An interesting disjunction now exists between the very thoroughness of the exploration of the subject, and an under-theorization of the author with regard to the concerns of positionality when one is engaged in textual analysis. On the most basic level, the contemporary critical limitation on study of the author has led to a situation of scholarly assumptions or silence when it comes to invoking these same various critical discourses in analysis. It seems to be a given to apply the tools of positional literary criticism to texts by authors known or assumed to fit within a set of rubrics, for all intents and purposes skipping over the interrogation of that initial scholarly choice to move directly into textual exegesis. Swirling around this conundrum, of course, is the specter of essentialism, another term with connotations as negative, for many scholars, as intentionality. And although this practice is not universal, the dominant trend in such positional criticism is, fundamentally, essentialist in its linkage of discourse to authorial identity.

Thus a pseudonymous author would present an ideal opportunity for investigation under classic poststructuralist discourse, were it not for the connection of identity politics to poststructuralism in the contemporary critical climate. Ironically, the pseudonymous author instead highlights the very conflicts between these two discursive strategies, revealing the triangulated difficulties posed by indeterminate authorial identity, textual politics, and critical practice. How do we talk about avowedly pseudonymous texts without acknowledging their pseudonymy? And once we acknowledge that pseudonymy, we are forced to grapple with the essentialism potentially inherent to the calculation underlying the author's constructed identity and the intentionality linked thereby to the frame of reception for the text.

It might be useful here to recall by comparison the controversy arising in feminist critical circles from the analysis of the infamous *Portuguese Letters,* the series of missives "apparently written by a woman in a Portuguese convent to an unnamed French officer" (Kamuf 297). These writings were first published in 1669, and have subsequently been the topic of ongoing critical speculation, much of it revolving around the author's "real" sexual identity and the connections between that identity and the stylistics and content of the text. Scholars such as Peggy Kamuf and Nancy Miller have used this anonymous text to argue opposing feminist critical positions on authorship. Kamuf, in her well-known essay, "Writing Like a Woman," questions "how can one read a work in the absence of the concept of an author and hence authorial intention?" (297). She concludes that one must read "the author's 'intention' (and indeed the 'author') as itself already marked within the chain of differences which it can neither originate nor control" (297–98).

Miller, however, in response to Kamuf, maintains that one should not "foreclose as untimely discussions of the author as sexually gendered subject in a socially gendered exchange." She believes critics cannot "be too confident that non-discursive practices will respond correctly to the correct theory of discursive practice" (50), or ignore the social construction of gender and its impact on writing.

The more recent work of Diana Fuss, particularly her book *Essentially Speaking,* stands out for its cogent synthesis of these theoretical conflicts. Fuss perceptively reveals that the phenomenon of the subject position is the essentialist component of a social constructionist methodology (29). For Fuss, this has direct connections with the issue of authorship dismissed by poststructuralism: "The notion of subject-position reintroduces the author into literary criticism without reactivating the intentional fallacy; the author's interpretations of his or her own text is recognized as a legitimate position among a set of possible positions a subject might occupy in relation to the text produced" (35). Fuss explodes the bad critical karma around concepts like "intentionality" and "essentialism" by showing that the notion of "politics" is really *the* "essential component" of feminist discourses—not biology, gender, or other facets of identity—and that grounding analysis in feminist politics allows for the productive interplay of poststructuralism and feminism (36). Thus we might extend Kamuf's conclusion through Fuss to suggest that exploring the (political) context for both the creation and reception of texts, whether the author's "true" identity is known or not, may be the appropriate course for feminist criticism of Martin.

It may be that, more in the tradition of Miller, feminist theater scholars have not actively pursued explorations of her work because of exactly these theoretical complications involving essentialism and writing. The prevailing scholarly climate, which might assume a "natural" pairing between an author identified as female, and/or literary works closely concerned with female characters and/or "women's" issues, and feminist theory, would suggest the "appropriateness" of using feminist theater criticism in this instance. Almost all of Martin's plays have women as central figures, and their plots often revolve around conflicts in women's lives, such as inequities in divorce settlements, women's access to equal treatment in professional arenas, and the controversy over abortion rights.

The interplay of journalistic speculations on Martin's sexual identity and the critical pressure to engage with positional discourse may indeed have relegated Martin to a liminal status. This tension may be freezing Martin between the prevailing assumption that she is a man and the sense that identity renders moot the potential for any revelatory or meaningful feminist criticism of her work. Such conflict becomes more compelling when one considers the ongoing—and important—concern of establishing the significant contribution of women playwrights to the canon of American drama as well as the need to have this work produced regularly in the American theater.

However, another issue further complicates the discussion of Martin: the pressure linked to positional criticism that not only is concerned with sex and gender, but also with the politics of the dramaturgy itself—in other words, matters of plot, characterization, theme, etc., and their relation to assumptions about feminist authorship. One need only remember the controversy surrounding the endings of Norman's *'night, Mother,* with the suicide of the daughter Jessie, and Wendy Wasserstein's *Heidi Chronicles,* with the titular character's adopting a baby, to understand this critical dynamic. Thus one might hypothesize that the comparative feminist-critical silence on Martin stems from the double-whammy of her questionable sexual identity, coupled with the determination that her writing betrays questionable politics at best. Nevertheless, it is just as, if not more, important to apply feminist criticism to works purportedly by a female writer, especially if those works are mass-marketed or assumed to represent a feminist perspective, than it is to champion the creativity of perennially marginalized women writers, precisely because of the former's potentially wider cultural impact.

This mandate becomes more compelling when one looks carefully at the journalistic construction of Martin. It perfectly reflects a rudimentary, positional categorization of "her" work, first along sexual, then along the most elemental of interpretive lines, demonstrating the ongoing popular media's confusion between sexual and gender identity and politics. In a 1983 feature article in the *New York Times* magazine, for example, Mel Gussow profiles Martin's work along with that of numerous other new women playwrights in the theater, the sexual identity of these authors being the sole criterion used for his selection (Gussow, "Women Playwrights" 22). In another piece, Richard Dodds, writing for the New Orleans *Times-Picayune,* explains that "there is a provocative passion and a decidedly *feminine,* if off-center, point of view that unites the eclectic body of [Martin's] work," and that "despite [their] obvious *feminist* overtones," we should "reject a narrow label for the playwright's philosophies" (Dodds, "Who Is" 19; my emphases).

Dodds's analysis reveals another interesting aspect of the journalistic construction and interpretation of Martin: the questioning of exactly what kind of feminism her works demonstrate. In an article written in 1994, the critic for the *Columbus Dispatch* alludes to the feminist backlash, suggesting that "audiences will relate" to Martin's "sly sendup of feminism" (Grossberg 11). And in another piece of Dodds's, he claims "there is something phony about the feminism" in Martin's play *Criminal Hearts*, although "this actually winds up serving the cause of comedy. . . . If feminism isn't the right 'F' word, fresh, fun and flip will do" ("'Hearts'" 19).

This journalistic discussion actually underscores precisely both the issue central to the broader theoretical exploration of positional criticism posited by Fuss, namely politics, and the more narrow matter of how to talk about the increasing presence of Martin's work in the American theater. If one applies feminist reading strategies to the basic principles of theater semiotics, interesting but disturbing trends emerge from Martin's drama, as the following two brief examples may illustrate. A number of plays first produced in Louisville, including Martin's, which have subsequently received considerable critical attention and nationwide theatrical production, feature a central female character or characters who, while seemingly initially strong, are ultimately victimized, demonized, or objectified by the action of the play. A journalist writing in 1996 finally observed this technique in Martin's work. Hedy Weiss, of the Chicago *Sun-Times,* noted that Martin "has a grating tendency to put women characters in the driver's seat only to subversively undermine them. The tendency is evident in *Jack and Jill,*" the Martin piece that had recently premiered at the Humana Festival (Weiss 4).

Martin's *Keely and Du,* for example, portrays three antagonists in the right-to-life wars. Keely, a young woman who has decided to have an abortion, is kidnapped by anti-abortion crusaders, with the plan of confining her until her pregnancy is too far advanced for her to terminate. Her guard is Du, an older woman devoted to the right-to-life movement. Walter, the patriarch of the ideological family calling itself "Operation Retrieval," serves as the mouthpiece for the anti-abortion activists. The overcharged political atmosphere surrounding the drama's theme lends itself to the easy manipulation of the female characters by Martin, such that they inevitably oscillate between the demon and victim positions. Keely, initially confined to her bed, ultimately breaks free and secures Du's incarceration. With its overdetermined political charge, the ambiguity of the conclusion of *Keely and Du,* with each woman posing unanswered questions as to the other's motives and actions, should not be surprising, as it may have been one of the only ways to avoid agit-prop dramaturgy.[5]

Martin's comedy *Cementville* (1991) more graphically exemplifies the semiotic tensions within her theatrical texts for its clear disjunction between stage action and dialogue. The play chronicles the lives of a group of female wrestlers and is set in the locker room of a run-down arena where they are performing. While the audience hears the women detail their experiences, theoretically coming to self-empowerment through bonding and reveling in their physical strength, it simultaneously hears the grunts and moans of the offstage wrestlers—sound effects which are calculated to sound orgasmic—and sees the women parade through the locker room in various states of undress. Thus the action devolves to what can only be called a "tits and ass" show, while the dialogue blithely seems to champion these women's lives. Martin objectifies these characters, and the actors who portray them, in the guise of a humorous send-up of popular culture and women's potential to achieve success therein.

Obviously, a longer study could explore in detail the nuances of all of Martin's work and the relationship of her dramaturgy to that of the many other emerging playwrights launched by the Actors Theatre over the years. Such an exploration would not only have to look at Martin and her female colleagues, but also, even more significantly, at the strong thematic and semiotic connections between the work of Martin and that of male playwrights such as John Pielmeier (for example, his *Agnes of God*) and William Mastrosimone (for example, his *Extremities*) also produced in Louisville. Perhaps it is no wonder that Jory may want to discourage scholarly exploration of Martin, especially since there has already been considerable, negative criticism of some of the other female playwrights he has promoted, including Norman and Beth Henley. A detailed study of Martin, and her connections with Louisville and its associates, inevitably means an examination of Jory and his artistic choices. The scholarly revelation of Jory's taste in contemporary American drama, with its superficial championing of women masking a troubling backlash and decidedly anti-feminist sensibilities, could indeed be a liability. It may well be in Jory's best interests to perpetuate the game of masquerade, perhaps even by assuming the guise of irritation with it to continue to pique journalistic interest. For as long as critics and reviewers are preoccupied with unmasking Martin and linking her sexual identity to her texts, they may ignore larger questions about the cultural climate at the Actors Theatre of Louisville.

Notes

1. Since the completion of this essay, Jon Jory has resigned from this position. He now serves on the faculty of the University of Washington. It remains to be seen how his departure will affect the Actors Theatre or the playwriting career of Jane Martin.

2. Throughout the remainder of this essay the use of pronouns such as "she" or "her," or terms such as female or "woman," with regard to Martin should always be read

with the understanding that "her" sexual identity is indeterminate—despite the absence of quotation marks to call attention to this fact—and that feminine terms refer to the female pseudonym rather than indicate a verifiable authorial identity.

3. Telephone conversation, May 19, 1994.

4. See Thompson, chapter three.

5. One of the more fascinating aspects of *Keely and Du* is the fact that Martin never provides Keely with any argument other than her personal volition to counterbalance the diatribe of Walter. It is as if Martin is so sure that Keely's position would be clear to the audience that the need to express an argument for abortion rights appears superfluous.

Works Cited

Currie, Glenne. "Theater World: 'Cats' Composer Has Six Shows on Broadway and West End." UPI 13 Oct. 1982 n.p.

Dodds, Richard. "'Hearts' Alive with Sharp Comic Turns." *Times-Picayune* 14 Jan. 1994: L19.

———. "Who is 'Jane Martin'? None of Your Business." *Times-Picayune* 7 Jan. 1994: L19.

Evans, Everett. "Jane Martin: Theater's Best-Known Unknown." *Houston Chronicle* 23 Jan. 1994: 12

Foucault, Michel. "What Is an Author?" *Language, Counter-Memory, Practice: Selected Essays and Interviews.* Trans. Donald F. Bouchard. Ithaca, NY: Cornell UP, 1977. 113–38.

Fuss, Diana. *Essentially Speaking: Feminism, Nature & Difference.* New York: Routledge, 1989.

Grossberg, Michael. "'Hearts' Cavorts Through Laughs." *Columbus Dispatch* 27 May 1994: 11D.

Gussow, Mel. "Critic's Notebook: The Haphazard in Occupational Dramas." *New York Times* 19 Nov. 1981, sec. C: 24.

———. "Mystery Deepens at Louisville New Plays Festival." *New York Times* 4 Apr. 1982, sec. 1, pt. 2: 58.

———. "Women Playwrights: New Voices in the Theater." *New York Times* 1 May 1983, sec. 6: 22.

Hulbert, Dan. "Jane Martin's Mystery Theater." *Atlanta Journal and Constitution* 3 Apr. 1994, sec. N: 10.

Kamuf, Peggy. "Writing Like a Woman." *Women and Language in Literature and Society.* Eds. Sally McConnell-Ginet, Ruth Barker, and Nelly Furman. New York: Praeger, 1980. 284–99.

Martin, Jane. *Cementville.* New York: Samuel French, 1991.

———. *Coup/Clucks.* New York: Dramatists Play Service, 1984.

———. *Keely and Du.* New York: Samuel French, 1993.

——. *Talking With . . .* New York: Samuel French, Inc., 1982.

Miller, Nancy K. "The Text's Heroine: A Feminist Critic and Her Fictions." *Diacritics* 12 (1982): 48–53.

Mootz, William. "Playwright's Development Distinguishes ATL Festival." *Courier-Journal* 28 Mar. 1993: I1.

Parv, Valerie. *The Art of Romance Writing.* St. Leonards, Australia: Allen & Unwin, 1993.

Prenshaw, Peggy Whitman. "Southern Ladies and the Southern Literary Renaissance." *The Female Tradition in Southern Literature.* Ed. Carol S. Manning. Urbana: U of Illinois P, 1993. 73–88.

Rizzo, Frank. "Behind the Play, A Mystery Writer." *Hartford Courant* 14 Nov. 1993: G4.

Scott, Anne Firor. *The Southern Lady: From Pedestal to Politics 1830–1930.* 1970. Charlottesville: UP of Virginia, 1995.

Showalter, Elaine. *A Literature of Their Own: British Women Novelists from Brontë to Lessing.* Princeton, NJ: Princeton UP, 1977.

Stayton, Richard. "Theater's Old Kentucky Home." *Los Angeles Times* 25 Mar. 1993, home ed.: F1.

Thompson, Nicola Diane. *Reviewing Sex: Gender and the Reception of Victorian Novels.* New York: New York UP, 1996.

Tuchman, Gaye, and Nina E. Fortin. *Edging Women Out: Victorian Novelists, Publishers, and Social Change.* New Haven: Yale UP, 1989.

Weiss, Hedy. "Narrow Visions: Humana Festival of New Plays Contemplates Identity Crisis." *Chicago Sun Times* 7 Apr. 1996, fin. ed.: 4.

Wolfe, Margaret Ripley. *Daughters of Canaan: A Saga of Southern Women.* Lexington: UP of Kentucky, 1995.

Young, B. A. "From Minor to Major." *Financial Times* 15 Apr. 1982, sec. I: 17.

11

Dialectic and the Drama of Naomi Wallace

Claudia Barnett

"I love coming back here. It's where I get all my stories," Naomi Wallace said recently at her father's farm outside Louisville, Kentucky (qtd. in Egerton 14). With her Southern roots firmly established by birth and upbringing, Wallace is known, nonetheless, not as a Southern playwright, but as a London playwright. Four of her plays were successfully staged in England before she finally attracted attention in the United States, winning the 1996 Susan Smith Blackburn Prize, the 1996 Kesserling Prize, and the 1997 Obie Award for Best Play for *One Flea Spare*—which had moved from London to Louisville to New York. In 1998, *The Trestle at Pope Lick Creek* was her first play to premiere at home, at the Actors Theatre of Louisville's Humana Festival of New American Plays. Vivian Gornick, who featured the playwright in a cover story for the *New York Times Magazine,* has labeled her "an American exile in America" (27)—the perfect epithet because of its inherent contradiction, so characteristic of the playwright. Wallace's success in London is attributed to her political style—ironically the product of the rural South where her plays are rarely produced. Her dialectical consciousness developed in her youth; the family differed from their neighbors in terms of politics, education, and, as Wallace puts it, "Class. . . . It's all a matter of class. . . . We live in a culture where social forces are so present. They make us what we are" (qtd. in Gornick 28, 31). The product of liberal parents in a conservative society, of a comfortable upbringing among the poor, Wallace embodies contradiction in her life and her work.

Wallace may get her ideas from Kentucky, but she never sets her plays there. One drama takes place in London, another in Saudi Arabia and Iraq, another at "a place that could be the Mexico/Texas border."[1] "Slaughter City, U.S.A." and "somewhere in the United States" are the oblique settings for the two plays that grew directly out of Louisville. Slaughter City is modeled after the local Fischer Meat Packing Company. And a childhood friend, Mark Landrum, who as a teenager would "walk onto the narrow trestle east of Jeffersontown and race the train as it crossed," was the inspiration for *The Trestle at Pope Lick Creek* (Egerton 14). But Wallace shies away from representing her hometown, even her home region. "Accents of the characters should be as 'neutral' as possible," she notes the front matter for *Trestle* (309), echoing Marsha Norman's author's note for *'night, Mother:* "Under no circumstances should the set and its dressing make a judgment about the intelligence or taste of Jessie and Mama. . . . Heavy accents, which would further distance the audience from Jessie and Mama, are also wrong" (3). Perhaps both Kentucky playwrights anticipate audience prejudice against Southern characters. Paradoxically, Wallace may invite generic identification with her characters by cloaking their regionalism, but at the same time she creates very specific, even somewhat grotesque, characters, achieving distance and alienation.

Wallace's audience may never feel at home in terms of time and place. Not only are her settings foreign or vague, but several of her plays are set in the distant past. *One Flea Spare,* for instance, takes place in seventeenth-century London during the plague, a setting with which no one in the audience is directly familiar, so we may all feel alienated. "Wallace creates a degree of cultural and historical foreignness that allows for more disinterested reflection," writes William Over (254). On the other hand, while she creates distance between time periods, she also creates connections between the present and the past, suggesting that there are no distinctions. As Julia Kristeva suggests, "we confront two temporal dimensions: the time of linear history, or *cursive time . . .* and the time of another history, thus another time, *monumental time . . .* which englobes these supra-national, socio-cultural ensembles within even larger entities" (189). Wallace's plays may be alienating with regard to cursive time, but according to Kristeva's interpretation, they are all-encompassing in terms of monumental time—women's time. The forces that exist in Wallace's somewhat fictionalized 1665 world are very much alive in our contemporary society—including divisiveness among class, gender wars, and the plague. Wallace was reading Daniel Defoe's *A Journal of the Plague Year* when the Los Angeles riots broke out. As a result, she wrote *One Flea Spare,* in which she draws parallels between the events, including the fact that in spite of death and panic, the wealthy insist "on the prerogatives of [their] class" and that "in Los Angeles as well as London, calamity proved a great leveler" (Foley). Wallace amplifies Kristeva's theory of time as a continuum in which the same situations and similar people persist.

Wallace quotes Bertolt Brecht in an epigraph for *One Flea Spare:* "Corruption is our only hope"—an appropriate invocation not only because of the playwrights' common interest in Marxist politics, but also because the brief sentence sums up both their dramas. Succinct yet replete with contradiction, this line characterizes Brecht's theater, in which ideas are presented only to be inspected and overturned, in which optimism and pessimism symbiotically exist. Wallace employs Brechtian themes and techniques throughout her plays to become the consummate Brechtian feminist.

In *Unmaking Mimesis,* Elin Diamond theorizes the connection between feminism and Brechtian theory—a point of intersection which characterizes Wallace's plays. Noting the numerous standpoints reflected by the term *feminism,* Diamond suggests that "perhaps all theories that call themselves 'feminist' share a goal: an engaged analysis of sex and gender in material social relations and in discursive and representational structure . . . which involve scopic pleasure and the body" (43). She condenses the concerns of Brecht's theater, which focus foremost on "attention to the dialectical and contradictory forces within social relationships, principally the agon of class conflict in its changing historical forms" (44). While Brecht was perhaps not a feminist, his techniques facilitate feminist theater—a point proven in theory by Diamond and in practice by Wallace.

Wallace is a feminist playwright even though she tends to focus on male characters. Two of her plays have all-male casts, and, of a third, one critic has complained, "Ms. Wallace is better at male characters than female" (Rutherford).[2] Dominick Dromgoole, artistic director of the Bush Theatre, reads this as a strength: "She presents male violence and aggression without proselytizing about it, but baldly, as it is. She depicts what is despicable with enthusiasm. She understands it better than a lot of men do" (qtd. in Bassett). Wallace herself points out: "Men have created great female characters: Anna Karenina, Emma Bovary. Though women writers have been allocated a domestic dream, several have broken out" (qtd. in Bassett). Wallace has broken out, and in doing so, has drawn attention—in Brechtian fashion—to herself as a woman writer. Her "engaged analysis of sex and gender" tends to focus on the male, on what she cannot know firsthand but seems, nonetheless, to know so well—what she calls "writing from a different place" ("Poetry" 256). Her choices surprise, alienate, and, as a result, draw attention to her own gender. And her plays most certainly "involve scopic pleasure and the body." She is herself a contradiction in terms, the Brechtian dialectic incarnate.

Elin Diamond has developed "gestic feminist criticism" based largely on Brecht's theories regarding the *gestus,* a term which she defines as "the moment in performance when a play's implied social attitudes become visible to the spectator" (xiv). Brecht's most comprehensive definition of the *gestus* (or, in John Willett's translation, *gest*) appears in his "Short Organum for the Theatre":

> The realm of attitudes adopted by characters towards one another is what we call the realm of gest. Physical attitude, tone of voice and facial expression are all determined by social gest: the characters are cursing, flattering, instructing one another, and so on. The attitudes which people adopt towards one another include even those attitudes which would appear to be quite private. . . . These expressions of a gest are usually highly complicated and contradictory, so that they cannot be rendered by any single word and the actor must take care that in giving his image the necessary emphasis he does not lose anything, but emphasizes the entire complex. (Brecht 198)

The *gestus* is an action (typically a minor action) which exposes society's attitudes, including its sense of morality and class structure. Diamond adapts it to apply equally to gender: "When gender is 'alienated' or foregrounded, the spectator is able to see what s/he can't: a sign system *as* a sign system" (47). In order to achieve this effect, the actor must demonstrate how the character behaves as well as how the character does not behave. According to Brecht, "When he appears on the stage, besides what he is actually doing he will at all essential points discover, specify, imply what is he not doing; that is to say he will act in such a way that the alternative emerges as clearly as possible, that his acting allows the other possibilities to be inferred and only represents one out of the possible variants" (137). Diamond calls this Brechtian theory the "not . . . but," as it includes not only what the character is doing, but that which he or she is not doing (48). This "not . . . but" is the basis of Brechtian dialectic. Naomi Wallace embraces the "not . . . but" and its visual representation, the *gestus,* throughout her writing. While *gestus* may seem, according to its definition, less dependent on text than on performance, Wallace clearly writes many such moments into her dialogue and stage directions. *One Flea Spare* provides an excellent example, a series of scenes in which visual images underscore the language and create Brechtian alienation.

One Flea Spare begins with a report of the plague: "Sparrows fell dead from the sky into the hands of beggars," says the child, Morse. "Dogs walked in the robes of dying men, slipped into the beds of their dead Masters' wives. Children were born with the beards of old men" (2). Antonin Artaud, in his essay "The Theater and the Plague," likewise sees the plague as an agent of reversal:

"The obedient and virtuous son kills his father; the chaste man performs sod-
omy on his neighbors. The lecher becomes pure. The miser throws his gold out
the window" (24). Artaud likens the plague to his ideal theater, capable of
transforming the audience into their "doubles" by revealing to them their own
true natures. His plague affects individuals and transforms them from within.
But while Artaud's subjects (son, lecher, miser) are singular, Wallace's (sparrows,
dogs, children) are plural. She uses the metaphor not only to show the potential
change within each person, but also the essential changes among groups. Her
plague affects the whole society. In *One Flea Spare,* the world is thrust into
dialectic, and each *gestus* reveals the conflicted power structures upon which
this world rests.

Another theory of the plague also permeates *One Flea Spare*—a theory
which seems to conflict with Artaud's, thus enhancing the nature of contradiction within the play. "A whole literary fiction of the festival grew around the
plague," writes Michel Foucault. "But," he adds, "there was also a political
dream of the plague, which was exactly its reverse: not the collective festival,
but strict divisions; not laws transgressed, but the penetration of regulation into
even the smallest details of everyday life. . . . The plague as a form, at once
real and imaginary, of disorder had as its medical and political correlative discipline" (198–99). In *Discipline and Punish,* Foucault demonstrates how the
plague-stricken city resembles Bentham's Panopticon as a model of a perfectly
ordered society: "Each street is placed under the authority of a syndic, who
keeps it under surveillance; if he leaves the street, he will be condemned to
death. . . . Each individual is fixed in his place. And, if he moves, he does so at
the risk of his life, contagion or punishment" (195). The plague-stricken city is
the ultimate site of surveillance: "The gaze is alert everywhere" (105). The citizens are considered criminals not due to action, but to circumstance; the government punishes people because it cannot punish the plague. This dialectic
between carnival and control, between chaos and order, between Artaud and
Foucault's theories of the plague, is the basis of *One Flea Spare.*

Mr. William Snelgrave and his wife, Darcy, have been quarantined in their
home for four weeks to ensure that they have not caught the plague, but just
as they have nearly completed their time served, Bunce and Morse sneak into
the fortress one night—thereby extending the sentence by another four weeks,
for all of them. The Snelgraves do not observe the interlopers so they cannot
stop them; Kabe, the Panopticonic warden who walks the streets reading lists
of the dead, has seen them enter, but his job is to watch, not to act: "We're just
guards. We make sure no one gets out. If they get in, well, that's just luck" (6).

Bunce, a sailor, is easily conscripted into the Snelgraves' service, but Morse, a twelve-year-old girl who claims to be the daughter of the late Sir Braithwaite, enjoys acting as the Snelgraves' surrogate daughter. The four prisoners inhabit a microcosmic world in which societal rules are overturned. As Laurie Stone observes, "Wallace, by setting her play in plague-ridden London, 1665, has conceived a brilliant situation to level the classes, so that a pound of rich flesh is in just as much peril as a pound of poor flesh" (34). She summarizes the action: "The contest winds up four against one: a rich old white guy whose privilege can't protect him, besieged by females and underclass men" (34). For each battle of the class and gender war that ensues, Wallace creates a revelatory *gestus.*

In one gestic moment of *One Flea Spare,* Snelgrave teaches "history" to Bunce, his makeshift servant, by allowing him to try on his shoes and then informing him that he will never own such shoes because then people would not be able "to tell [their] feet apart. They'll look the same" (22). This *gestus* reveals class structures at an obvious level, but it also reveals the "not . . . but"; as Bunce observes, "I see the Master is without his shoes. And his new servant. He is wearing very fine shoes" (21). While we are told that Bunce will never have such shoes, we see him wearing the shoes. Snelgrave insists that this action is a game ("What we see here is not real" [21]), but Bunce asks, "What if I kept the shoes?" (21). Snelgrave seems nonplused, and in fact Bunce does return the shoes—but by the end of the play the shoes belong to Bunce. Snelgrave's ancient logic no longer applies to this world, at least not completely. While Snelgrave is mistaken about the class structure, he still understands gender codes: a woman could never wear his shoes, so he does not play this game with Darcy or Morse. Women are excluded from the charade; their class depends on their husbands' or fathers' shoes rather than their own.

On a theatrical level, the physicality of the *gestus* causes a shudder throughout the audience: when Bunce hesitates to try on Snelgrave's shoes and blames his dirty feet, Snelgrave insists, "Then have my socks on first" (21), and we see one character—and one actor—don the sweaty socks of another. A similar shudder is provoked toward the end of the play when Snelgrave has been tied to his chair by his wife, a girl, and a servant, three people whose lives he could easily have controlled—before the plague. Darcy, Morse, and Bunce delight in their newfound powers, having slowly realized that the master is no longer in charge. Snelgrave attempts to antagonize Bunce by insulting his own wife (with whom Bunce has been intimate), who was severely burned two years after their marriage at the age of seventeen: "Tell me, Bunce, what's her cunny like? . . . Bread that's been in the oven too long?" (57). In answer, Bunce stands silent for several moments, then shrugs and drinks some water. "He leans over Snelgrave as though to kiss him, and almost kisses him but instead lets the water trickle slowly out of his mouth across Snelgrave's mouth and face. Snelgrave is so shocked by the audacity and sensuality of this act that by the time he resists, Bunce is through" (57). Once again a physical action disrupts the line between reality and theater. Diamond examines a similar example in Caryl Churchill's *Traps,* in which a series of naked actors bathe in a stagnant tub of water. "At this point," she writes, "the spectator might also insist that the illusionistic surface has cracked; the orificial time-bound body of the actor, not merely the character, has become accessible" (87). The audience is forced into a horrible identification based on the physical action: we are arrested, like Snelgrave, by the audacity and sensuality of the act, which is not merely an act. And we are simultaneously repulsed by the character who would do this to another character, to an actor, to us. We are misaligned in our loyalties and hatreds, finding ourselves momentarily on the side of Snelgrave, whom we pity because the man playing Bunce has spit on him.

The class struggle in *One Flea Spare* is explicit not only because the servant is in charge, but because he is dressed in his master's clothes. Snelgrave tries to reclaim control by offering to pay Bunce to release him, but Bunce replies, "The child has already given me half your gold, sir" (56)—the polite "sir" serving to mock the man who is master in nothing but name. Money is meaningless in their isolated two-room world. This moment is shocking, too, within the realm of the play because of its elements of homoeroticism and voyeurism. Bunce lets the water trickle out of his mouth and onto Snelgrave's face while Darcy and Morse stand and watch. But they don't merely watch: they join in on Bunce's side, antagonizing Snelgrave and enjoying their new powers. In addition to class roles, gender roles also have shifted, and Darcy Snelgrave delights in freedom for the first time in her life; she is no longer somebody's wife or daughter. When Snelgrave informs her, "You do realize we can't go on after this as man and wife," she finally talks back (56). After years of neglect and abuse from her husband, who abhors the sight of her burned body, she not only helps tie him to a chair, but she initiates a sexual relationship with Bunce. By the end of the scene, Morse is orchestrating their foreplay and blindfolding Snelgrave. The child is in charge, the gentlewoman is unfaithful, and the gentleman is impotent; the world is topsy-turvy. Darcy's final line of the scene, "I don't want my husband to hear us," is punctuated by the stage direction, "Wanting Snelgrave to hear them" (60). What these characters say has little to do with what they mean; we hear Darcy say "not," while we see that she means "but."

Darcy's relationship with Bunce reveals Wallace's "engaged analysis of sex and gender in material social relations and in discursive and representational structure . . . which involve scopic pleasure and the body" (Diamond's definition of feminism) at the same time that it provides the most Brechtian moments of the play. The physical contact between these two characters is at once sensual and repulsive. Darcy's body is burned and numb, while Bunce wears a bandage around a wound on his stomach which he says is "years old" and "still bleeds" (4). They meet alone late at night; the first time, Darcy brings Bunce a shirt and fresh bandages, using the excuse, "I don't want blood on my floors" (24). Clearly, however, there is more going on, as Darcy refuses to leave. When she insists upon helping him with his new bandage, he holds his old bandage in place and says "No" (24). The servant-master dialectic is undone by sex and gender: Darcy cannot command Bunce because she is a woman. Furthermore, she is here as a woman, not as a master; she is here because she is attracted to Bunce. She asks him questions about his former lovers and he finally asks what she wants. When she says, "For you to answer me," he asks, "And if I don't?"—in the same tone as asks Snelgrave what if he were to keep the shoes (26). But the situation with Darcy is different: Bunce concedes, but not because she is in charge. Very clearly, he is in charge, and Darcy is asking for his help. Finally he tells her more than she wants to hear, and she threatens, "I could have you hanged for speaking of such matters to a married woman of my position" (28). Given the situation, whether she could or could not is quite questionable; what is clear is that she would not—and Bunce simply sings in response.

In Brechtian fashion, the nighttime encounter is replayed in broad daylight when Morse tells Snelgrave that she observed it. Morse begins to enact the scene, making slurping noises to show how Bunce lapped up Snelgrave's gin, then offering to show how Darcy checked his bandage. We see the meeting between Bunce and Darcy twice, once as a private moment and once as a public humiliation. The first time we are engaged in the seduction; the second time we observe from a distance, having the event replayed without romance. Brecht models his theater on the "street scene": a "demonstrator" observes a traffic accident and then "acts the behavior of driver or victim or both in such a way that the bystanders are able to form an opinion about the accident" (121). Brecht's ideal actor "forced the spectator to look at the play's situations from such an angle that they necessarily became subject to his criticism" (121), which is the same effect that Morse achieves by becoming an actor within the play: the audience is forced to relive and reassess the events. Morse is, in a sense, the Brechtian demonstrator who perpetually relates what she has seen with utter objectivity—although her motive is not to enlighten others but, always, to help herself; in this instance, she has been tied up and she wants to be untied. Snelgrave, rather than trusting her, attempts to disgrace the offenders. He directs Bunce to stand still and Darcy to demonstrate how she checked his bandage. Then, certain of victory, he commands Darcy to remove her glove, to reveal to Bunce "what's touched him in the dark" (31). Bunce, however, "does not react" when he sees the burned hand, and as a result, Snelgrave "deflates" (31). Moments later, when Snelgrave pathetically recalls the story of the long-ago fire, feeling sorrier for himself than for the victim, "Darcy puts her gloved hand on his head, she comforts him almost automatically" (32). Intrinsically playing the wife, she consoles him as he tortures her. In this gesture, we see the "not . . . but" marriage, what could have been but never was and never will be.

Darcy and Bunce's relationship reaches dialectical extremes when she later puts her charred hand beneath his shirt to feel his wound and states, "I've put my finger. Inside. It's warm. . . . It feels like I'm inside you" (50). When she removes her hand, blood is on her fingers. "The act is at once sexually charged and intimate, as though she were feeling his lifelong pain and remorse. It also suggests gender role reversal, since it is she who penetrates his softness and vulnerability," observes William Over (256). This *gestus* provides the most intimate and most alienating moment of the play—not only for the cringing audience but for the characters. In spite of their physical connection, Darcy forbids Bunce to address her by her first name (49), and Bunce tells her, "You people always want to fuck your servants" (50). Sex draws them together, but class divides them. Darcy maintains the nominal distinction of superiority, and Bunce condemns her as representative of her class. Later, when Morse suggests it might be safe for them to remain at the Snelgraves' home even after the plague, he seems incredulous: "Her word? Can't trust that the right story would stick in her mouth. Who's to say she wouldn't be front row just to see me rise up in me britches after I drop down and into hell" (64). In spite of moments of passion and warmth, trust between the classes is impossible.

The visual *gestus* and the aural narrative combine in *One Flea Spare* to challenge prescribed gender codes. Morse recalls the death of Sir Braithwaite's daughter: "I sat beside her, holding the bird. . . . It sang for hours and hours until its heart stopped in my hands. . . . It was Lissa's bird. . . . Even dead it was Lissa's bird. Not mine. . . . I opened her mouth and put the bird inside" (61). Morse's recollection is oddly tender, especially considering her lack of respect for the dead. She is never femininely squeamish; instead, she is always alert to opportunity, ready to make a deal to survive—ordering Lissa to give her her dress and shoes, asking Kabe to get her new linen from "the pits" (47). She has no sense of propriety about property, but the bird she sees as Lissa's, and she unites them physically by placing the bird in Lissa's mouth. The speech and the act are grotesquely sensual—which is true of many events in the play. For instance, Kabe sucks on Morse's toe and promises fruit in return for the favor: "Hey. I know an old woman who's got tangerines, still good, that she wears under her skirts. She says they stay fresh down there because she's hot as the tropics" (18–19). The sexuality permeating the language of the characters seems inappropriate and yet inevitable given their proximity to death. It draws attention to these de-gendered characters with their genderless names whose positions in society once would have been clearly defined by gender— gentlewoman, virgin child—but are now subverted, and sexualized, by circumstance.

Wallace employs Brechtian-feminist techniques again in *The Trestle at Pope Lick Creek,* which, like *One Flea Spare,* is set in the past (though not in a foreign land) in a time of desperation: 1936, in a town where most of the adults are unemployed and most of the children have no hope. The two plays are structurally similar, both framed by jail cell scenes in which the protagonists (Morse, Dalton) are encouraged to confess, while the main action flashes back to the events that have led them here. Both plays deal with issues of gender and class, and their messages in these regards are the same. Shoes are a prominent symbol in both plays, as when, in *Trestle,* Pace offers Dalton a semiotic prediction: "You're not going to college. . . . Look at your shoes. . . . If your Mom's putting you in shoes like that then you aren't going to college" (316). Both plays, too, revolve around questionable acts of murder: Darcy Snelgrave, having contracted the plague, pleads for death, and Morse, acting as the "angel of mercy" (Lahr 87), stabs her in the chest; Pace Creagan plunges to her doom from a trestle, and Dalton Chance, feeling responsible, claims to have killed her. But in *One Flea Spare,* the characters learn to change their identities: Morse becomes a Braithwaite, Bunce becomes Mr. Snelgrave, and Darcy becomes a woman. In *Trestle,* characters are fixed in their identities and don't want to change them; they want, instead, reinforcement. Dalton and Chance want witnesses, whereas Bunce and Morse delight in anonymity. Essentially, however, all four characters—like all Wallace characters—want the same thing: to survive. Circumstance dictates the superficial distinction, the teenaged need to be noticed.

Wallace's feminist concerns permeate *Trestle* as the two main characters struggle with sexuality and gender roles. Pace, a girl of seventeen, challenges Dalton, a boy of fifteen, to race the train across the trestle along with her. In many ways, as Dalton repeatedly points out, Pace acts like a boy: she pulls a knife on him, tells him what to do, wears her brother's clothes, and talks about train engines. She has raced the train before, with Brett, a boy who died, and she seems to be trying to compensate for his loss by reliving it—casting herself as Brett and Dalton as herself. When she and Brett raced the train, Brett looked back to make sure she was all right and he tripped to his death. Now she wants Dalton to run with her. The action of the play revolves completely around her trying to convince him to join her. Finally, he dares her to run it alone, and she does—as long as he watches. But then he turns his back, and when she yells at him to look, he covers his ears. He recalls: "But I wouldn't turn around. Pace must've slowed down. And lost her speed, when she was calling to me. . . . And then she did something funny. Pace couldn't even swim and there was no water in the creek, but she was going to dive" (352). She yells, "Watch me. Dalton" (352). And he does, as she dives one hundred feet to a dry creek bed. She has told him, "We can't watch ourselves. We can't remember ourselves" (352). But he rebels: "No! No way! I won't be your fucking witness!" (352).

The cause of Dalton's anger is sexual frustration—symptomatic of the sense of futility which permeates his life. Pace has refused to kiss him on the mouth because "that's common," so she kisses him on the back of his knee (for a full ten seconds, as Dalton counts). She refuses to have sex with him and instead, in the play's most provocative *gestus*, she stands still and instructs him to close his eyes and to touch himself as if he were touching her: "Yes. There. You won't hurt me. . . . Go on. Open your legs. . . . Do it. . . . Now touch me. There. Just touch me. . . . Can you feel me? I'm hard. . . . I want to be inside you" (355). She tells Dalton to close his eyes to facilitate imagination. This is the only instance when she does not require a witness, when seeing would be meaningless, as the act occurs only in their minds. After the back-of-the-knee kiss, Dalton, mortified and wounded, "starts to push [Pace]. He's pushing her hard backward but she keeps her footing. The potential for violence to escalate is evident" (334). Pace tells him, "You're mad at me 'cause you liked it" (335). After the imitation of intercourse, he feels the same but more extremely; he could kill Pace Creagan—and he effectively does so when he refuses to validate her by witnessing her run. But then, she has refused to validate him too. And in their world without hope, they need validation more than anything.

Laura Mulvey writes about the pleasures and powers of the cinematic gaze; her observations can extend beyond the realm of film and into Wallace's drama: "In a world ordered by sexual imbalance, pleasure in looking has been split between active/male and passive/female. The determining male gaze projects its fantasy onto the female figure, which is styled accordingly. In their traditional exhibitionist role women are simultaneously looked at and displayed, with their appearance coded for strong visual and erotic impact so that they can be said to connote *to-be-looked-at-ness*" (203). Mulvey's female is objectified by the male gaze, thus becoming the "unknowing and unwilling victim" (201). Pace Creagan, embodying the "not . . . but" with regard to Mulvey's male/female dialectic, attempts to subvert these roles to her own advantage—to be both active and the subject of the gaze, both male and female. She projects her fantasy onto the male figure, forcing Dalton to undress and to submit. She also longs to be looked at, but not fetishized. In fact, one of the first tricks she uses to get Dalton's attention is to objectify another girl in her stead: She suggests that if Dalton were to cross the trestle with her, then Mary Ellen Berry would like him. She has seen Mary Ellen naked ("I once told her to take off her clothes and she did" [315]), and she answers Dalton's queries in stereotypical schoolboy fashion: "I'd say she's on the menu. Front, back, and in reverse. You'd like her" (315). Pace, who unself-consciously changes clothes in front of Dalton, knows she is not on the menu. "You're not good-looking," Dalton tells her. She seems not to mind: "Yeah. But that's got nothing to do with trains" (315). Dalton will not look at her the way he (or she) would look at Mary Ellen, but he will look at her; her race with the train is her plea for attention. She tries to be two things at once, but then she finds the combination impossible: she dies trying to conflate the male and female roles, trying to force Dalton to make her the object of his gaze.

Wallace takes up this theme explicitly in *Slaughter City* with a female character who pretends to be a man, exciting the attention of a female co-worker and, more importantly, earning a higher wage because of her supposed sex. "Working like a man," she says in true Brechtian fashion, "I feel more of a gal" (81). But her masquerade does not bring victory or freedom; no matter how hard she tries to escape her identity (in terms of gender and also history), she is destined to repeat—or remain in—the past. *Slaughter City* is set "now and then" (xiii) at a meat-packing plant, where (at least in its first production) "the heads of carcasses circle the stage on meat hooks" (Butler 15); and yet, Wallace says, this play too is about love, sex, the body. "I'm interested in challenging notions of what is erotic and what is sexy, and how you portray it on stage. . . . If you work in a place that doesn't protect you and your body is destroyed, that affects how you love, how you make love and who you may choose to love" (qtd. in Hemming 13).

In *Slaughter City,* gender is equated with class—and so is race. In one comical *gestus,* a black woman named Roach orders a white man named Brandon to put on a dress. He plays the *femme* to her *butch.* "Please, sir. Avert your eyes. . . . No peeking!" he flirts (67). "Roach rips the dress open so that Brandon's chest is exposed. This should be done how we've seen it in countless melodramatic films" (68). Countless layers of the "not . . . but" are at work here regarding issues of class, age, and gender. Brandon has little work experience compared to Roach, but he is promoted because he is white, privileged (college-educated, in spite of the fact he can't read), and loud. She takes this opportunity, only partly in jest, to reverse their roles, to play the master. In an earlier *gestus,* Roach is forced to "play" the slave when the company manager, calls her, her friend Maggot, and their supervisor to his office. The manager complains that the women's uniforms are not clean and he commands them to take them off, but then he signals Maggot, who like him is white (as her name implies), not to undress. Roach is left standing alone in her slip. He asks repeatedly if Roach is clean. "It's hard to tell," he explains, so he has her stand on a chair to inspect her (39). When he spots dirt, he has the supervisor, who is black, scrub her. The black woman and man are forced into intimate physicality, while the white woman "looks away" (39). The white man subjugates the others to his whims, shaming them all, so that images of the slave plantation reverberate in the *gestus.*

Throughout her dialectical drama, Naomi Wallace distances her audience while drawing them into the action. Time and place are both distant and present. The repetition of horrors does not imply inevitability, however. Unlike Kristeva's monumental time, which is "without cleavage or escape" (191), the Brechtian continuum of history is malleable. With her conflation of past and present, Wallace suggests that the world has not advanced with time; she also, however, offers change as an ever-present possibility. "The best work does make us yearn toward that, toward change—not only political change, but changing ourselves," she says ("Poetry" 258). Her best work makes us yearn toward change by revealing our world with distance and hindsight, by providing views of far-off reality and then exposing them as our own. Her South is disguised, not so she can hide it, but so she can ultimately expose it. The purpose of her theater is to incite evolution.

Notes

1. *One Flea Spare, In the Heart of America,* and *The War Boys,* respectively.
2. *The War Boys* and *Birdy* have all-male casts. *In the Heart of America* is the third play.

Works Cited

Artaud, Antonin. *The Theater and Its Double.* Trans. Mary Caroline Richards. New York: Grove, 1958.

Bassett, Kate. "A Woman Behind the Lines." *Times* [London], 2 Apr. 1994. Lexis/Nexis. 21 Aug. 1998.

Brecht, Bertolt. *Brecht on Theatre: The Development of an Aesthetic.* Ed. and trans. John Willett. New York: Hill and Wang, 1964.

Butler, Robert. "Danger: Poetry at Work." Review of *Slaughter City,* The Pit, London. *The Independent* [London], 28 Jan. 1996: 15. Lexis-Nexis. 21 Aug. 1998.

Diamond, Elin. *Unmaking Mimesis: Essays on Feminism and Theater.* New York: Routledge, 1997.

Egerton, Judith. "Writer Naomi Wallace Draws on Her Kentucky Home." Louisville *Courier-Journal* 8 Mar. 1998: I1, I4.

Foley, Kathleen. "*Flea* with a Bite." Rev. of *One Flea Spare,* Studio Theatre of the Shannon Center, Los Angeles. *Los Angeles Times* 18 June 1998. Lexis-Nexis. 21 Aug. 1998.

Foucault, Michel. *Discipline and Punish: The Birth of the Prison.* Trans. Alan Sheridan. New York: Vintage, 1979.

Gornick, Vivian. "An American Exile in America." *New York Times Magazine* 2 Mar. 1997: 27–31.

Hemming, Sarah. "Drama at the Cutting Edge: Sarah Hemming Talks to Controversial American Playwright Naomi Wallace." *Financial Times* (London), 19 Jan. 1996: 13. Lexis/Nexis. 21 Aug. 1998.

Kristeva, Julia. "Women's Time." *The Kristeva Reader.* Ed. Toril Moi. New York: Columbia UP, 1986. 188–213.

Lahr, John. "Death-defying Acts." Rev. of *One Flea Spare,* Joseph Papp Public Theatre, New York. *New Yorker* 24 Mar. 1997: 87.

Mulvey, Laura. "Visual Pleasure and Narrative Cinema." *Narrative, Apparatus, Ideology: A Film Theory Reader.* Ed. Philip Rosen. New York: Columbia UP, 1986. 198–209.

Norman, Marsha. *'night, Mother.* New York: Hill and Wang, 1983.

Over, William. Rev. of *One Flea Spare,* Joseph Papp Public Theatre, New York. *Theatre Journal* 50 (1998): 254–57.

Rutherford, Malcolm. "Lost in the Heart of America." Rev. of *In The Heart of America,* Bush Theatre, London. *Financial Times* (London), 8 Aug. 1994. Lexis/Nexis. 21 Aug. 1998.

Stone, Laurie. Rev. of *One Flea Spare*. *The Nation* 19 May 1997: 34–35.

Wallace, Naomi. *One Flea Spare*. New York: Broadway Play Publishing, 1997.

———. "Poetry, Plays, Politics, and Shifting Geographies." *Tony Kushner in Conversation*. Ed. Robert Vorlicky. Ann Arbor: U of Michigan P, 1998. 255–65.

———. *Slaughter City*. London: Faber and Faber, 1996.

———. *The Trestle at Pope Lick Creek*. *Humana Festival '98: The Complete Plays*. Eds. Michael Bigelow Dixon and Amy Wegener. Lyme, NH: Smith and Kraus, 1998. 307–55.

12

Amparo Garcia and the Eyes of Tejas: Texas Community through Mexicana Eyes

Carolyn Roark

Amparo Garcia is a native Texan whose work often deals with both the daily lives of Mexicanos in the South and Southwest United States and with her personal experience of growing up in Texas. In her plays, both as text and as performance, Garcia seeks to recreate and to give representation to her community and herself in a forum that often excludes her or minimizes her significance. Her plays merit critical analysis (and popular attention) because she successfully combines contemporary characters and plots with lyrical dialogue, skillfully blends spiritual quest and revelation with life's innate sensuality and vulgarity, and finds humor in tragic social situations without dismissing their importance. Her work can enhance discussions of Southern drama because it reveals the inner workings of communities that limited notions of Southern identity and writing have often rendered invisible.

Scholars examining the region must acknowledge that, historically, the creators and critics of Southern art and literature have not been broadly inclusive in determining who represents the experience of Southern life and identity. According to Mary Ellis Gibson in her introduction to the anthology *New Stories by Southern Women,* "Southern literature was originally defined in terms that were white and largely male and has taken the notion of southernness at its center; from this center it has accommodated work by white women, black men, and less often black women" (6). Richard Owen Geer, a theater practitioner who works with community performance in the South, notes a similar homogeneity in the traditional theater-at-large, which includes Southern drama: "American Theater carried no local information. Instead it broadcast a 'one size fits all' brand of entertainment created by a cultural elite. This professionalized performance-genre used play to cloak its culture-shaping work. Theaters were factories for the production of mass culture" (29). While Southern theater *does* carry a notion of local or regional information, the concept of a "cultural elite" imposing a single standard for subject matter and socioeconomic viewpoint still applies to the Anglocentric focus that Gibson pinpoints and that scholars and practitioners must attempt to overcome.

Greater inclusiveness comes with time and the active efforts of writers, performers, and scholars to broaden categories. Gibson affirms Southern women's literature as "tak[ing] gender as the defining center . . . not depend[ing] on exclusion by race" (4). Even such movements for inclusion, however, continue to see the world quite literally in terms of black and white, as Gibson's quote intimates; many people of color still are excluded from a wide range of discussions involving Southern writing and performance. Ramón Saldívar, in his book *Chicano Narrative: The Dialectics of Difference,* holds that "[d]espite its long-standing cultural presence, Mexican American heritage has either been excluded from or relegated to the margins of American political, social, and literary history" (23). Though Mexican Americans, among other groups, have a strong presence in parts of the South, such as Texas and Louisiana, the tendency among scholars and writers alike is to place their work automatically in specific "minority" genres. *I do not suggest that Chicano Studies lacks strength or importance as a genre within literary and artistic circles;* however, persons attempting to study the region must overcome this fallacious and limiting tendency to consider the work of Latinas and others as applicable only to discussion of "ethnic art." Scholars and writers alike might begin to examine the work of Latinos and other people of color whose work deals with life in the southern United States, including such authors as Elena Carrillo (Latina), Paul Bonin-Rodriguez (Latino), Judy Lee Oliva (Native American), Carolyn Cole Montgomery (African American), Regina Taylor (African American), and Sterling Houston (African American).[1]

I have chosen to focus my own work on Amparo Garcia, an emerging Chicana playwright whose work centers on Texas, my home state. Her plays have won several awards, been produced off-Broadway, and one has been included in an anthology of Latina play writing. In addition, she has been very open to discussing her work. The critical attention she is beginning to receive and her accessibility make her an excellent candidate for the kind of inquiry I propose.[2] She has lived all of her life in Texas and is both subject to and engaged in the same social and political situation as other Texas citizens. She interacts on a daily basis with other Texans of many ethnicities: European American, African American, Latino, Asian American, and others. Yet she and many other Texas citizens emerging from a bilingual, bicultural background remain absent in discussions of Texas art and performance as Southern cultural artifacts. This discussion attempts to integrate "Tejas" with Texas, to examine the vision of this very familiar locale through eyes too long disregarded.

Garcia became motivated to write for the theater during her young adulthood, in the midst of difficulties in finding acting work. She recalls being told by directors and agents that "White is in" and learning of the tenuous position of minorities in the arts from a Screen Actor's Guild study that explored percentages of race and gender as represented on television shows. She describes its intense impact on her theatrical development: "The big results came out in the *L.A. Times* and now, finally, on paper, Latino characters show up on television, as of '92, one percent of the time, and they're equal to extraterrestrials. That was the statistic, so every time you see someone from Mars, you might possibly see a Latin person. I mean, I was shocked." The lack of representation and opportunity she felt personally led Garcia, as a minority, to begin writing plays. "I started writing so that I would have something to do where I could play Chicano characters," she has said (Personal Interview).

These desires to make visible and viable a culture often ignored and to give herself more opportunities as a theater professional and as a person combine in Garcia's plays with a desire to explore mythical, transcendent themes and ideas that cross cultural boundaries. She ascribes this desire to her experience growing up: "I'm a very intense dreamer. . . . I've had extraordinary precognitive information. I mean, just this incredible, personal, universal world of archetypes and dreams that I had never consciously studied, so I'm more interested in the universal, in mythic proportions. They happen to be Chicanos wrestling with mythic proportions" (2). Her unpublished play "Under a Western Sky" (1997) reflects these experiences and Garcia's understanding of the Texas town she calls home.

Particular issues, themes, and characteristics significant in the geographic area of the southern United States frequently surface in Southern drama. Important aspects of the genre include political and social concerns of local communities, the centrality of family and heritage, the landscape and natural conditions of Southern locations, and culture. In his *History of Southern Drama,* theater historian Charles Watson borrows from T. S. Eliot for a definition of culture. This definition includes "all the characteristic activities and interests of a people" (qtd. in Watson 1). Building on this definition, Watson establishes a set of characteristics specific to Southern plays: they are created by Southern writers with Southern audiences in mind; make use of distinctive social types, violence, heritage and legend, religion, recognizable forms of speech stressing rhythm, pronunciation, and idiom; and evoke a sense of local color (2–3).

Like Watson, Gibson indicates that the perception of Southern identity in literature may be perceived through "generalizations about themes and form, about stylistic affinities, and about literary history" (6). In her introduction to *New Stories,* Gibson identifies as characteristic of Southern (women's) writing "an emphasis on dailiness, on the nature of living within a social fabric, a fabric that may seem hopelessly torn but which it is always somebody's duty to repair" (6). Quoting Ellen Glasgow's "prescription of Southern fiction"—"blood and irony"—Gibson explains that Southern women's writing often addresses "Blood families and other families; their food and communal occasions; their disintegration and reconstitution in a changing culture; relationships between mothers and their children, between women, between classes; the illusory nature of maturity" (6). These themes all point to the centrality of community in Southern writing; all of the aforementioned activities and behaviors arise during group interaction. Geer defines community by three factors, which may work separately or together: location, spirit, and tradition: "Communities of location are neighborhoods or towns. Communities of spirit convene around beliefs or values. . . . Communities of tradition are groups constituted around shared activities and maintained over time through these activities" (29). In "Under a Western Sky," the inhabitants of the town occupy and form a community in all three senses.

These characteristics articulated by Watson, Gibson, and Geer situate Garcia's dramatic world within the realm of Southern drama. The action occurs in the South, in Texas. Shared culture, beliefs, and activities determine the characters' dramatic reality. Thematically, the action addresses family and group dynamics, social disruption experienced by the town, and relationships between mother and child, between townspeople, and between classes. The community's defining characteristics include its focus on collective unity and consciousness, Mexicano cultural influence on language and values, and relegation of Anglos to the margins of the society. Garcia bases the action of the play on real incidents in Texas; through her fictionalized account of true events, she explores the inner workings of a small, primarily Mexicano town. Taking the hardships of the small community where she was raised and the painful events that are a part of its (and her) history, Garcia creates a fictional picture of Texas as she has known it.

The play focuses on an event of far-reaching, community-wide consequences: the gang rape of a local woman in Garcia's hometown of San Diego, Texas. Garcia says that the play is, in part, about "coming to grips with the intense violence there. It doesn't happen every day, but when it does, it's extreme" (Percal 3). Bringing to mind Glasgow's evocation of "blood and irony," Garcia affirms the influence of her own background in her work, and the importance of dark humor in retelling the events: "I don't come from migrant farmers, but I come from very poor people—I nearly starved to death—where it's a lot of violence. You know, my father was murdered, just extraordinary catastrophic situations, so perhaps my interest in the lyrical was a kind of transcendence at that point" (2).

Recently produced at the off-Broadway venue INTAR (International Arts Relations, Inc.) Theatre, "Western Sky" reflects the Southern genre's focus on violence and on the community. The character Yolanda Vasquez has been attacked at an illegal cockfight and raped by a number of the men in attendance. During the play, the town learns of the attack and attempts to deal with it collectively through the eyes and ears of its citizens. According to Garcia, the play "is not about the rape. It's about people reacting to the rape" (20). The actual event, therefore, is far less important to the play than Garcia's exploration of the community that experiences it and how it responds. She focuses on the relation of the individual to the group and the behavior of the group, rather than the behavior of the individual and the group's relation to the one. The technique creates a heightened sense of collectivity and community as part of Garcia's world, and of the picture created of her "corner" of the South. In a sense, her community *is* Garcia's landscape. The people of this small town and their interactions create a strong group dynamic which does far more to determine the world of the play than the *physical* locale in which it occurs. The town collective thus becomes Gibson's "social fabric in constant need of repair" (6).

Garcia highlights the focus on the community and guides the audience's perception of her locale primarily through the use of narrative asides, which are given by characters during the course of each scene. As the action progresses, each speaker announces (in third person) the character that he or she portrays, how this person fits into the scenario, and what that character thinks and feels at that dramatic moment. For example, in the first scene, the actors portraying Yolanda and Javier address the audience:

Actress One announces simply:
Somewhere in this space a young Mexican-American woman, Yolanda Vasquez, 18, sleeps and dreams, alone. . . .
Actress One continues:
Her slip is torn and filthy. There are scrapes and scratches on her elbows and knees. Her body is caked with dirt and other debris.

Actor One announces simply:
Elsewhere, Javier Zuniga appears. He is a lanky thirteen year old boy with
tattoos all over his fingers. His face broken out and a straggly mustache
is starting to darken over his full lips. He chews gum and is very nervous
to tell his story to the authorities. (2)

In the play's introduction, Garcia indicates that the major part of this description, the torn slip and bruises, and the tattoos and mustache, need not be physically present on the actors; as with the setting, they exist primarily in description. The third-person, descriptive nature of these asides serves to familiarize
the audience with the character and the action as seen through the eyes of the
community. Through these lines, actor/characters describe themselves as others
perceive them, as well as the emotions they personally feel in the scenes. That
Garcia, in her introduction, stresses that the asides should not be "declamatory"
but "natural" and in character, suggests that she wishes the asides to remain
within the world of the play. The technique is not a Brechtian alienation device
intended to separate the audience from the story, but rather a means of deliv-
ering information within the story, reminding the audience that the community is intimately close to, and aware of, its members. Four actors, all Chicanos,
portray all characters, supporting the notion that the characters deeply connect
with one another as a community, as parts of the same whole.

This emphasis on community also results in shifting the focus away from
the rape victim as a human individual, locating it instead on the victim's place
in her society. The shock wave that the attack sends across her town takes prece-
dence over the rape's effect on Yolanda's person. The audience learns far less
about Yolanda's reaction than about the responses of the town toward the attack
and toward her, both before and after the incident. In fact, most of what we
learn about Yolanda emanates from narrative asides and from other characters.
In dialogue with other characters, she never speaks about herself or how she
feels. Only one time does she show any powerful feeling at all, during the opening scene in which a teenage boy reports the rape to the town sheriff (2–4). As
Javier describes the event on one side of the stage, Yolanda simultaneously pan-
tomimes it on the other, showing fear and anger as she attempts to ward off
invisible attackers with screams and physical resistance (3–4). This is Yolanda's
only extended outburst. Even during her report of the incident to the sheriff,
she refrains from describing either the event or its effect on her. She simply,
though tearfully, announces the names of her attackers.

The names that she tells the sheriff signify more than just the individuals who carry them; they reveal that several segments of the community have participated in the act. As Yolanda, her husband, Frankie, and the sheriff discuss the men, the audience learns the position each attacker holds in the community. Among the assailants are Roel Paiz, the mechanic; Armando Rodriguez, Dairy Queen employee and son of local restaurateur Sammy Rodriguez; and Sergio Villanueva, whose father is the town judge and whose uncle is a prominent lawyer. So Yolanda has not simply been raped by Armando, Sergio, Roel, and other men, but by the town's mechanic, food service personnel, influential families, and so forth. The connections between the rapists and the roles they perform for their community bring the town itself closer to the rape than would be the case if both victim and attackers were perceived as simply individuals and not as part of the collective body.

Because the play considers them more than private individuals, the role of society in the young men's corruption cannot be ignored. Elisa, a ninety-year-old wise woman with a talent for speaking uncomfortable truths, reveals that the crime of the rape belongs to the whole group as well as to the individual perpetrators. While her granddaughter, Veronica, argues for individual culpability, Elisa points out that such crimes can begin with the influence of a flawed society on its members:[3]

> ELISA: The day they started to put women to sleep, mijita. When they bring their babies into this world, that's when the bad was done.
> VERONICA: They're saying they raped her three times, ama. Three different places. After the cock fight.
> ELISA: If the mother does not feel the pain, the child comes in feeling nothing too.
> VERONICA: Ama, I'm talking about those boys. They beat up the ones that WOULDN'T touch her. What kind of devil is that, ama.
> ELISA: Pos, that's what I'm saying.
> VERONICA: This has nothing to do with their mothers.
> ELISA: If they cannot feel their mother's pain, they will never feel anybody's pain. That's why they can cause it. (10)

Elisa ends the conversation with a summation of the social problem as she (i.e., the author) sees it:

> ELISA: For all of the bad to stop, mothers are going to have to remember their jobs in this world.

VERONICA: Not everybody is here to take care of babies.

ELISA: Pos no, but my babies never slept alone, mijita. They stayed in the bed with me. Where they were born. Till they were not afraid. Those boys died, alone. The moment they were born. That's why motherless animals have ears but no souls to feel. That is what the end of the world is about. I never thought I would live to see it. (11)

Veronica, and the rest of the community, miss the significance of Elisa's words. When the collective fails its members on some level, individuals will fail in their responsibility to the community. Both Yolanda and these young men have been failed by the community. Ironically, the same townspeople that convict Yolanda's attackers also force her family into exile through persistent gossip about her morality.

Forced to move to Corpus Christi, Yolanda and Frankie try to escape the public scorn and derision they encounter in their hometown. The collective cannot deal with the ugliness of the event or the involvement of so many townspeople and reacts by seeking to place the blame on Yolanda. In a sequence of performed conversations, various townspeople debate Yolanda's potential involvement in her own violation, speculate about her sexual habits and fidelity to her husband, and question her past relationships to her attackers. The importance of their community, in spite of its cruelty to them, becomes apparent as Yolanda and Frankie discuss, in an interview, their discomfort at separation from their collective:

YOLANDA: But the people here. They're nice. The counselor. I like her a lot, but . . . I don't know, it's . . . different I guess.

FRANKIE: Down there [in his hometown] I fit in. Here in Corpus I'm just another Mexican. I mean it's a dumb town, there's nothing to do down there, but I've been there all my life. The people here are nice, I guess, but they act like they're our good friends or something. We don't even know them. (51–52)

Another important aspect of "Western Sky" concerns the interaction of community members with outsiders. Saldívar suggests that, as the result of "bicultural experience" and of being forced into the status of "other" by majority influences, there exists an inherent set of differences between Chicanos (and other minorities) and Anglos. He asserts that in Chicano/Mexicana literature, both writers and written material announce themselves as "other" by acknowledging the differences ascribed to them by majority elements. They then subvert the ideas by placing these same elements in the position of "other" and thus oppose the culture/literature/ideas of the majority, i.e., Anglo-dominated, culture in which the authors exist.

Garcia also sets up a relationship of contrast between Anglo and Mexicano characters; in her world, the Anglos are the outsiders, the exotic others. Her writing does not stage an overt protest such as those Saldívar describes, but Garcia emphasizes the notion that the two groups are opposite and unable to connect. Anglos exist only at the edges of Garcia's landscape, and within the play, only in their relation to the Mexicana characters. In fact, only one Anglo character, reporter Mandy Feinstein, actually appears bodily in the play; others, like politician George Parr, exist only in the words of Garcia's characters. That Garcia intends Mandy to be portrayed by a Chicana actress reinforces the notion that Anglos function only in relation to Mexicanos in this story, as her character exists as an Anglo as interpreted by a Chicana.

A meeting between Mandy, a reporter for *Texas Monthly,* and town lawyer Beto Aleman immediately establishes the polarity between Mexicano and Anglo. The narration sets the characters up as opposites from the beginning by physical description—she is Anglo and female; he is Mexicano and male. Beto confirms her position as an outsider by announcing, in a narrative aside, "Everybody knows everybody in this town, so when Beto spots Mandy, he assumes without question that she is the one he has been waiting for" (21).

The interaction between Mandy and Beto exemplifies the distance between Anglos and Mexicanos. From the beginning of the scene, Beto establishes control and turns the ethnic tables on Mandy by pretending to be unable to pronounce her Anglo surname. Neither truly answers the other's questions, nor can they agree on what has happened in the town. The stage directions indicate that the one possible connection between them, sexual attraction, becomes a further barrier: "Beto stands up to greet her. Oddly, they find each other, unexpectedly, attractive. That doesn't make either of them feel excited. In fact, it makes them feel mean" (21). That meanness results from transgressive feelings on the parts of both characters; each perceives the inappropriateness of an attraction between one person within the collective and another from outside the margins.

Mandy's position as an Anglo outsider does not, however, make her an antagonist. She sympathizes with Yolanda's experience and feels compelled to defend her against Beto's (the town's) accusations. However, that sympathy and sustained focus on the individual woman's experience do not accord with the town's impulse to protect its collective existence. The debate that ensues between Beto and Mandy reflects the irreconcilable differences between the inside/community and the outside/society.

> BETO: That's a tabloid mentality and you know it, Ms. Feinstein. I don't want to try the case in the newspapers but that young woman had been keeping company with one of the accused on the QQT. That's the story you got to get right.
> MANDY: And that gives TWENTY men permission to violate her?
> BETO: The press, my dear, is making the young woman appear innocent, a young, virginal mother. That's a contradiction in terms unless you're the Holy Mother of God herself. (He laughs.)
> MANDY: One of the accused is related to you?
> BETO: He's the best example for what I'm saying, yes. His uncle is on the school board, his whole family is devoted to the good of this community. (24)

Mandy's conversation with Beto reveals another aspect of the Anglo/Mexicano dichotomy, the legacy of politician George Parr, a real and controversial historical figure from Garcia's part of Texas:

> MANDY: I don't believe any story can be told about this town or the rape without talking about the last of the white, benevolent Patrones.
> BETO: I'm sorry but I fail to see the connection.
> MANDY: What the Parrs did to this town, politically. It's not that different than what those boys did to Yolanda, emotionally. (Beto laughs uproariously.)
> BETO: Call it whatever you like but I can tell you this rape business would have never happened if George Parr was still alive.
> MANDY: Because nobody would have been able to talk about it without his permission, you mean? (23–24)

Mandy's defense of the ostracized Yolanda and her condemnation of the deceased Parr, a powerful influence on the town, do nothing to remedy her own status within the community. If anything, they separate her further from those whom she seeks to interview. Beto, acting as a member of the collective, defends the town's values, or "spirit," and its leaders, living or otherwise.

The conversation reminds the audience of an all-too-real part of the playwright's growing-up experience, the existence of "white Patrones" such as Parr, a Big Daddy–like figure reminiscent of the creations of Tennessee Williams or Harper Lee. The dialogue concerning him reflects a Southern thematic concern with political power and corruption, as racial majority status and wealth allowed such men powerful influence in towns like San Diego, Texas. Beto defends Parr to Mandy because his power benefited some segments of the town (like Beto) and gave him access to the collective, including marriage to a local Mexicana woman and the Spanish nickname "Cho-che" (27). However, Garcia makes it clear that Parr's Anglo status separated him from the community in many ways. In narrative asides, she contrasts the description of his home:

> Actress Two announces simply:
> An hour later, Mandy drives up to the biggest house in the town. It is a two-story white-washed Spanish colonial just a short distance from where the town gives over to the brush country to the southwest. Bald palm trees lean in toward the house; a brick fence encloses a swimming pool. Clearly at one time, it was grand. It was the home of George Parr, and it is for sale. (24)

with a later description of a neighborhood in town:

> Actor Two announces simply:
> The Sheriff approaches the house of Estella Gomez and her son Jesus. They live in a neighborhood known to the locals as "Naked City" because so many children run dirty and wild with only a shirt or shoes on. A mangy pit bull guards the porch. (53)

The description of Parr's wife also signals his removal from the people he has governed:

> Actress One announces simply:
> Parr's widow, Evelina, gives Ms. Feinstein a tour of the mansion. She is a bit over-dressed for the occasion. Tall heels, expensive gold jewelry, looking like she might go out on the town instead. She wears a little too much make-up for her age and dyes her hair blonde to make herself appear whiter. (27)

Parr's wealth amidst the poverty of the town and his wife's effort to associate herself with Anglo rather than Mexicano identity reinforce the true separation between him and the community he controlled. These factors suggest the notion of Anglo-dominance and oppression that Saldívar notes in his discussion of Chicano literature. Beto might defend the dead man to Mandy, who is not a local. However, Parr participated in the community only by exercising political power, not through any shared culture and values nor by intermingling with the collective. Ultimately, he maintained a separation based on race and class. After his death, the community's hostility to this invader begins to reveal itself, especially to Evelina. She tells Mandy that many locals no longer speak kindly of Parr, and some imply that he has gone to hell for his misdeeds (28).

Another example of the Anglo as the "exotic other" occurs as the sheriff's daughter, Carmen, describes her new Anglo boyfriend during a phone call to a friend. In a previous "telephone" scene (15–18), Carmen espouses the community's contempt for Yolanda and echoes the general sentiments of fear and discomfort about the episode. Her next conversation reveals that she has begun dating a member of an Anglo news team covering the trial of the rapists (59–60). She now condemns the act and the perpetrators, even as she discusses her budding romantic fascination for this young man who has a degree and "uses words I have to look up in the dictionary." She begins to refer to the local people as "low class" and holds up her new friend as superior to the local boys, citing as an example his willingness to use condoms. Further, she announces her desire to be "like Murphy Brown" (60). The new association with this exotic Anglo man has precipitated a 180-degree shift in Carmen's thinking, including a new cynicism and disdain for her collective and the replacement of local icons with Anglo role models.

Garcia's vision of her community necessitates positioning the Anglo as the outsider, the "exotic other" that intrudes into this Southern town. The Anglo, though not inherently an antagonist, always stands apart from the collective. Her vision displays the Anglo through Mexicana eyes, and Anglos exist only in the locals' verbal description and through interpretation by a Chicano actor.

The relationship between Anglo and Mexicano, between outsider and local, are part of the South depicted by this Mexicana playwright. Garcia has chosen to explore the world of the Mexicano community, where the violence and events that occur are not the central focus of the play, but rather a litmus test of community dynamics. Through it she reveals their values and their customs and examines the group's ability to handle disruption and social change. Garcia's hometown collective and the relationships among people within it compose "the South" as Garcia knows it. In "Under a Western Sky," the sky itself and the land bring the audience into the Texas that she evokes, but the citizenry existing within its suggested borders embody the place. They comprise the world as Garcia understands it. The "blood and irony" of the piece—the themes of violence, community interaction, and local flavor—place the play within the traditional realm of Southern writing. That Garcia is Mexicana should not exclude her work from discussions of Southern drama; rather it should displace the traditional Anglo lens that usually provides the focus and replace it with a vision of the South through Chicana eyes. Discussions of performance and writing in the South can only benefit from analyzing "non-traditional" Southern authors such as Garcia, those playwrights whose ethnicity scholarship has not defined as Southern, even though they inhabit and explore the region in their work. This does not mean that their ethnic identity should be subsumed in an overarching Southern identity or that work in various Ethnic Studies areas should be abandoned. However, it does suggest that the boundaries of Southern Studies should be broken down to allow material to move in and out of the genre with greater flexibility. By broadening our base of interpretation and by uncovering different viewpoints, artists and scholars will further cultural and social understanding between the different peoples who share this rich region.

Notes

1. I received many suggestions for minority playwrights to suggest as subjects for further study. Most of those I have named live in or near Texas, as that is my primary region of interest. There are, however, many others. I also received suggestions that discussions of Southern theater might benefit from examining South*western* playwrights, especially those now working in New Mexico and Arizona, like Leanne Howe, Roxy Gordon, Terry Gomez, and Elvira and Hortensia Colorado.

2. Prior to the 1997 off-Broadway premiere of "Under a Western Sky," Garcia won the Larry L. King Play Writing Award for her play "Cocks Have Claws and Wings to Fly," a work that later premiered at Latino Chicago. She has also written for the Mark Taper Forum and won a NEA/TCG Directors' Fellowship in 1991.

3. The dialogue uses both English and Spanish phrasing, as is common in the speech of many Latinos in Texas and elsewhere. "Pos" is slang for "pues," which means "well" (as in "Well, if you insist"). "Ama" is a term of affection for a mother or grandmother. "Mijita" is a diminutive for "Mi hijita," which means "My little daughter." I quote all dialogue as written in the unpublished script of "Under a Western Sky," given me by Garcia.

Works Cited

Garcia, Amparo. Personal Interview. 4 Mar. 1997.

———. "Under a Western Sky." Unpublished script, 1997.

Geer, Richard Owen. "Of the People, By the People and For the People: The Field of Community Performance." *High Performance* 16.2 (1993): 28–30.

Gibson, Mary Ellis. *New Stories by Southern Women.* Columbia: U of South Carolina P, 1989.

Percal, Balka. "In Dialogue with Amparo Garcia." *Women's Project and Production Newsletter* Spring 1997: 4.

Saldívar, Ramón. *Chicano Narrative: The Dialectics of Difference.* Austin: U of Texas P, 1990.

Watson, Charles S. *The History of Southern Drama.* Lexington: UP of Kentucky, 1997.

13

Reconfiguring History: Migration, Memory, and (Re)Membering in Suzan-Lori Parks's Plays

Elizabeth Brown-Guillory

Since the mid-1980s, the two-time Obie Award–winning Suzan-Lori Parks has revolutionized Black women's theater tradition with her plays. In some ways, Parks's plays resemble the mutative and vertiginous stage poetry of Adrienne Kennedy's *Funnyhouse of a Negro* (1962) and of Sonja Sanchez's *Sister Son/ji* (1969), both of which experiment with language and theatrical space and, in effect, reconfigure the boundaries of the American stage. Parks extends Sanchez and Kennedy's experiments with language and form in an attempt to challenge a very conventional, conservative, and impenetrable American stage. Her plays call for a theater that will embrace theoretical artists, namely playwrights like herself who wish to offer audiences the possibility of multiple meanings in nonlinear, multidirectional works.

Parks's plays have been produced at such places as Yale Repertory Theater, Actors Theatre of Louisville, BACA Downtown in Brooklyn, New York, and the New York Shakespeare Festival. Her plays have also received the imprimatur of a number of institutions, including the National Endowment for the Arts, the Rockefeller and Ford Foundations, and the New York State Council on the Arts and the New York Foundation for the Arts. Having received an Obie in 1990 for *Imperceptible Mutabilities of the Third Kingdom* (1986–1989) and one in 1993 for *The America Play* (1992–1994), Parks is recognized as one of America's most dynamic, experimental, and passionate playwrights. Two other plays by Parks deserving of serious critical attention are *The Death of the Last Black Man in the Whole Entire World* (1989–1992) and *Venus* (1996).

Though viewed by many as representative of a new and challenging strand in American theater, Parks's detractors claim that "her work is extremely difficult and esoteric" (Gin 39). While Mel Gussow named Suzan-Lori Parks the "year's most promising playwright" in 1989 in the *New York Times* (qtd. in Jacobus 1351), Tony Kushner, in his "The Art of the Difficult," noted that Parks "is the only American playwright I know who makes use of footnotes, which . . . present a conundrum for the production team . . . [and her plays] are full of these sorts of provocations" (qtd. in Gin 39). Alisa Solomon notes that Parks's plays resemble "long, dialogic poems" with movement "contained in the speech itself" (76). Solomon also notes that Parks is "fond of leaving out punctuation," letting "words run together to find their own rhythms" and manipulating spelling to "imply stage action" (76). Solomon best sums up what audiences think of Suzan-Lori Parks's work: "Though it is so abstract in form and language as to make any attempts at interpretation provisional at best, it is, at the same time, clearly and firmly rooted in a forthright political sensibility, one absolutely concerned with African-American experience under the weight of a hostile world" (73). This maverick's political sensibility links her to such theorists as Frantz Fanon, Homi Bhabha, W. E. B. Du Bois, and Gayatri Spivak.

A postcolonial critique of Parks's plays reveals that she primarily concerns herself with the African American experience of migration, racial memory, and remembering. The form in her plays inextricably links to the content. The nightmarish, detritus objects that comprise the props of her plays represent the fragmentation of Blacks induced by forced racial migrancy. Parks rejects, confuses, distorts, and complicates language in an attempt to subvert the discourse of dominance and to mirror the stresses and strains of Black life in a hostile world. Parks represents, reenacts, or replicates racial migrancy in poignant Middle Passage scenarios in much of what she writes to suggest the destabilizing effect of the African holocaust. She seems intensely interested in exploring the synergies between racial memory and healing or remembering of Blacks.

Crucial to understanding Parks's plays is the recognition that she concerns herself with reconfiguring American history to include the lives and accomplishments of Black people. Parks's plays suggest that as long as Blacks are relegated to the "hole" (read "absence") of history, the possibility of wholeness becomes limited. While her characters, generally speaking, do not achieve wholeness, the playwright attempts to dramatize the struggle, the resistance to nullification. She does this with nonlinear representations that challenge audiences to decipher experiences and identities of Blacks working toward agency in a world in which their subjectivity is subordinated by hegemonic discourse. By foregrounding Black migration, which is a cultural continuity of the African American experience, Parks is able to demonstrate that the rupture created as a result of slavocracy continues to be manifested in the lives of present-day Blacks at both the subconscious and conscious levels. This collective racial memory, Parks posits, provides the impetus for the continued sense of disconnection and displacement that Blacks experience. Her plays repeat hegemonic historical representations of Blacks while simultaneously revising and reconfiguring those representations to include the souls of Black folk. In much of her work, Parks manages to stage double consciousness, "two warring souls, two thoughts, two unreconciled strivings; two warring ideals in one dark body . . . " (Du Bois 45). The ambivalence that Parks stages is articulated by Homi Bhabha, who notes that "the colonial presence is always ambivalent, split between its appearance as original and authoritative and its articulation as repetition and difference" (32). The ambivalence, the double vision, directly relates to dislocation.

Parks's own migrancy may well be thematized in her plays. Though Southern-born in Fort Knox, Kentucky, in 1963, the playwright lived during her formative years in Texas, California, North Carolina, Maryland, Vermont, and other places in the United States, as well as in Germany. After completing a double major in English and German at Mount Holyoke College, she moved to England to study acting in 1985. Parks is fond of referring to herself as an alien because of the frequent moves her family made during the years her father served in the military (Jiggetts 310). Sometimes her family stayed behind; perhaps her military father's periodic leaving and returning might account for Parks's preoccupation with migration/movement as well as her interest in "absence and nurturing, mourning, and renewal" (Rayner and Elam 458).

Parks's keen interest in reconfiguring history matches her equally strong commitment to reshaping the stage, making it more malleable and open to avant-garde presentations. In a sense, her plays serve to stage reform while simultaneously reforming the stage. In an interview with Drukman, Parks speaks of her impatience with the American theater. She feels that the theater lags behind other arts in its reluctance to embrace change (61). She, however, will not allow the American stage to bar her from representing African Americans in history in what Michele Wallace calls "extraterrestrial blackness" (31).

Though earlier shorter pieces, including *Betting on the Dust Commander, Fishes,* and *The Sinner's Place,* all produced in 1987, drew modest recognition, *Imperceptible Mutabilities of the Third Kingdom,* Parks's first full-length play, brought her to the attention of the American stage. Jacobus notes that Parks has a "special interest in language of speech and gesture—in almost equal measure" (1352). Alisa Solomon posits, "There's little that could be called plot here. Indeed, the idea of sequence is subverted again and again. Time is subverted, past and future conflated into the simultaneity of the theatrical present" (qtd. in Jacobus 1357). Solomon argues that "nothing is spelled out in Parks's liquid writing" (76). Elam and Alexander contend that Parks is "abstract both in form and language" and uses "symbolism, metaphor, humor, and irony to probe the relationships between African-American history and the construction of contemporary African-American identity" (14). A close study of Parks's plays reveals that her work is shaped by a migratory aesthetic. Elam and Alexander's assessment of the influence of the Middle Passage on Parks's work substantiates the migration theory:

> According to Parks in *Imperceptible Mutabilities,* when the white slave traders, the "Bleached Bone Man," brought blacks to the New World, they created a "third kingdom," a liminal space between the world of Africa and America. Parks observes this "third kingdom" through history and suggests that the changes, the evolutions, or the mutabilities in African-American identity and self-knowledge are virtually imperceptible. African-Americans still suffer from the feelings of isolation, dislocation, and alienation experienced on being brought from Africa and jettisoned into the "third kingdom." (14)

The form of Parks's play appears, in fact, constructed to illustrate the angst experienced by Blacks as a result of this historical rupture, this forced migration.

Imperceptible Mutabilities divides into four sections, all of which Solomon suggests are linked by "slavery, genocide, and gentrification" (74). The first section, "Snail," examines the lives of three contemporary Black women who are scrutinized and manipulated by a white naturalist and pseudo-exterminator who spies on them from a cardboard box modeled after a giant cockroach. Here, Parks's work substantiates Frantz Fanon's critique in *Black Skin, White Masks* of the destructiveness of the (white) gaze on Blacks. Fanon comments that such a gaze can seal the Other in "crushing objecthood" (109). Liz Diamond, who has directed several of Parks's plays, describes the women in "Snails" as trying "to define themselves beyond the gaze of the white world" (87). The women's self-esteem disintegrates after being bombarded repeatedly with verbal attacks, past and present, from the naturalist, who represents hegemony. One of the effects of the gaze is that the women become mutative, donning new but slippery identities to win the approval of the colonizer. To illustrate double consciousness and the destabilized identities of her characters, Parks relies upon the musical motif of "repetition and revision" (rep & rev) or refrain (Gates 105; Solomon 78; Diamond 86; Frieze 524; Bernard 693). She admits that rep & rev allows her "to create space for metaphor. . . . Characters refigure their words and through a refiguring of language show that they are experiencing their situation anew" (qtd. in Bernard 693). For example, Parks relies on rep & rev to reconfigure Molly, who says, "Once there was uh me named Mona who wondered what she'd be like if no one was watchin" (597). Later Molly adds, "Once there was uh me named Mona who wanted tuh jump ship didn't" (597). Molly's *parole* conjures up images of Black men and women who flung themselves overboard from slave ships rather than live in subjugation. The playwright's characteristic use of rep & rev on this theme presents the Black woman who considers suicide but chooses survival. The encoded utterances made by the three women, such as the repetition of words such as "splat," articulate insurgency in the way that Spivak speaks of it: "When we come to the concomitant question of the consciousness of the subaltern, the notion of what the work cannot say becomes important. . . . Elaborations of insurgency stand in the place of utterance" ("Can the Subaltern Speak?" 28). With her creation of the women in "Snails," Parks achieves what Margaret Homans articulates about women writers in "Her Very Own Howl": "Simultaneously appropriating and rejecting the dominant discourse, they formally duplicate the female experience that they thematize, the experience of both participating in and standing outside of the dominant culture" (205).

The second section, "The Third Kingdom," which Elam and Alexander argue represents a "threnody of the Middle Passage" (14), reenacts the rupture caused by the separation of Africans from their homeland. Kin-Seer says, "I was standin with my toes stuckted in thuh dirt. Nothin in front of me but water. And I was wavin. Wavin. Wavin at my uther me who I could barely see. Over thuh water on thuh uther cliff I could see me but my uther me could not see me" (608). Shark-Seer describes the humiliation and feelings of powerlessness that the slaves felt when he utters, "Black folks with no clothes. Then all thuh black folks clothed in smilin. In between thuh folks is uh distance thats uh wet space. 2 worlds: Third Kingdom" (610). Parks's topographical narrative of this liminal space explains the confusion that the Seers experience: they are displaced in both the historical past and the present. Both Kin-Seer and Shark-Seer's feelings of separation from their country, their culture, their family, and themselves are juxtaposed with the constant motion of the boat, which is couched in performative language. This disintegration that Parks speaks of is articulated by Homi Bhabha, who comments, "The contour of difference is agonistic, shifting, splitting" (32). Soul-Seer moans, "Rock. Thuh boat. Rock. Thuh boat. Rock. Thuh boat. Rock. Thuh boat" (611). Clearly, the space that the Seers inhabit is a signifier on diasporic living. James Frieze argues that

Parks's Seers "are themselves icons out of focus, mangled archetypes, ellipti-
cal points of reference . . . [which] embody the confusion of living in limbo"
(527–28). It is, however, in this liminal space that new identities are constructed. Shark-Seer chants, "My new Self was a Self made by thuh space between" (610). Parks's characters take on multiple identities, which mirror fragmentation.

The next section, "Open House," focuses on the nightmare of a dying former slave whose memories of the stench and overcrowded conditions aboard
the slave ships become interspersed with her recollections of a white Mrs. Faith,
who symbolically snatches her memories, her history, from her via a series of
brutal tooth extractions. Blanca, the dying former slave, says of the slave ship,
"They're sitting in their own filth because they haven't been changed they
haven't been fed they haven't been aired they've gone without sunshine" (612).
The forced migration from Africa clearly links to the pain associated with the
extraction of teeth. The conflation of the present and past suggests the imperceptible changes in the relationships between the colonizer and the colonized.
This scene parallels Fanon's critique of the colonizer in *The Wretched of the
Earth* in which he references the Middle Passage and slavery, commenting that
"the settler never ceases to be the enemy, the opponent, the foe that must be
overthrown" (51). Parks's representations then may be seen as performances of
resistance. Her graphic portrayal of the migration/dislocation, devastation, and
fragmentation of Blacks gets repeated in the second part of "Open House,"
titled "Third Kingdom (Reprise)."

The final section, "Greeks" (or 'The Slugs')," continues the images of dislocation, the sense of Blacks living piecemeal in a world somewhere between
Africa and the New World. In this section, a Black marine sergeant who strives
for distinction overseas finally returns home without legs to find a wife who
has gone blind and children who have multiplied in his absence. This section,
like the others, reinforces Parks's view that Blacks are splintered. No tidy ending here or in any play by Parks! The characters in *Imperceptible Mutabilities*
struggle toward agency but seem mired in a miasmic, liminal space punctuated
by the chaos, pain, and disruptiveness of living between worlds, in the third
world, where Blacks are, in the words of Mr. Sergeant Smith, "Slugs. Slugs.
Slugs. Slugs" (643).

If *Imperceptible Mutabilities* serves as an exploration of the harrowing effects
of transplanting Africans in America and the double-voiced discourse that accompanies such a rupture, *The Death of the Last Black Man in the Whole Entire
World* extends the dialogue. Parks's preoccupation in this play is that Blacks

have been written out of history. She suggests that historical records inscribe lack of value upon the Black psyche: "Once upon a time you weren't here. You weren't here and you didn't do shit" (qtd. in Drukman 67). Outraged at subaltern positionality, Parks reconfigures what postcolonial feminist critic Gayatri Spivak refers to as "the fabrication of representations of so-called historical reality" (245).

Parks signifies on the stereotypes created within hegemonic discourse by naming two central characters Black Man With Watermelon and Black Woman With Fried Drumstick; they interact with such characters as Before Columbus, Queen-Then-Pharaoh Hatshepsut, Lots of Grease and Lots of Pork, and Yes And Greens Black Eyed Peas Cornbread. Louise Bernard posits that Parks's Black Man With Watermelon is "at once written out of history, yet placed at the center of his own (postmodern slave) narrative" (688). In this play filled with hallucinogenic imagery, Black Man With Watermelon repeatedly is almost killed. In prismatic representations, he experiences being plucked away from Africa, falling off of a ship, becoming an object of an auction block, bursting into flames, carrying a tree attached to a noose around his neck, recalling an electrocution, and speaking of falling twenty-three stories to his death. Black Man With Watermelon, however, is not allowed to die because he has to undertake a journey during which he must be told of his history before he can arrive at his final resting place.

The various tortures that Black Man With Watermelon experiences are, in the main, reenactments of the atrocities that happened to Blacks during the Middle Passage and afterward on American soil during slavery, Reconstruction, and beyond. While Parks's text, on one level, speaks of the absences or holes in history, it simultaneously fills those holes with icons of Blacks throughout history who have subverted racist imagery. Her characters speak into and through the hole of history, and as Fanon states, "to speak is to exist" (17) and "to speak a language is to take on a world, a culture" (*Black Skin, White Masks* 38). More importantly, Parks's characters reconstruct or remember themselves with stories of their past. This racial memory that Parks interweaves in the play serves as the impetus for the healing of the once fragmented, dislocated bodies.

While Parks may be compared to Beckett, Brecht, Adrienne Kennedy, Faulkner, James Baldwin, James Joyce and others, she is perhaps more closely linked to Flannery O'Connor because of her deep interest in the grotesque, namely physical and emotional disfigurement predicated upon dislocation and disconnectedness. Parks seems to borrow from O'Connor's short story "A Good Man Is Hard to Find," in which the Misfit bemoans the fact that he cannot match his crime with all that he has been punished for and blames the abuse on the fact that he did not record his personal history. Parks's characters in *Death of the Last Black Man in the Whole Entire World,* like the Misfit, cannot fathom what they have done to warrant devaluation in America. But, like the Misfit, they view the narration of their lives as crucial to making sense of the chaos. Yes And Greens Black-Eyed Peas Cornbread says: "Mmmmm. Yes. You should write that down. You should write that down and you should hide it under uh rock" (263). Later, the cautionary tale of writing things down appears again but with a twist of certainty. Yes And Greens Black-Eyed Peas Cornbread says, "And you will write them down" (277). Finally, he says, "You will write it down because if you don't write it down then we will come along and tell the future that we did not exist. You will write it down and you will carve it out of a rock. You will write down thuh past and you will write down thuh present and in what in thuh future. You will write it down" (278). The shift in tenses serves to collapse the borders of time and space and, as Bernard argues, "reconfigures the metaphysical landscape of racial memory" (688). Characters in *Death* find themselves in the hole of history where the present, past, and future are indistinguishable, which suggests that for Blacks the (w)hole of history has been exclusionary. Rayner and Elam note that the writing down of Black history allows Black Man With Watermelon and Black Woman With Fried Drumstick to move on, to escape liminality, to gravitate toward subjectivity (456).

The play successfully executes its missive at the end when Black Man With Watermelon tells Black Woman With Fried Drumstick: "Re-member me" (279). She, in turn, responds to and echoes his call, "Re-member me. Call on me sometime" (279). The very last line of the play points to Parks's commentary on Blacks' search for wholeness in a postmodern world. All of the characters in unison chant, "Hold it. Hold it. Hold it. Hold it. Hold it. Hold it. Hold it" (279). The morphophonemically designated chant signifies on wholeness. The characters insist upon accurate, whole representations of themselves in the hole of history. Bernard correctly sums up Parks's intent when theorizing that the playwright "revises the historical trope of 'fabricated absence' and so synthesizes the personal and the political into a prophetic journey that acts as libation to the ancestors and a call to present/future generations to carve out their histories, restore knowledge, and take their rightful place in the eternal struggle for representation" (696).

Parks's third full-length play, *The America Play,* won for her a second Obie. While characters in *The Death of the Last Black Man in the Whole Entire World* repeatedly refer to the hole in history, characters in *The America Play* are physically situated in a hole in the stage from which they dig up detritus objects while searching for themselves. In Parks's phantasmagoric play, a Black man named The Foundling Father who looks like Abraham Lincoln digs a gaping hole, "the Great Hole of History," and in it he earns a living by allowing himself to be shot repeatedly with blanks as a reenactment of Lincoln's assassination. Marc Robinson points out that "Every time the Foundling Father sits in 'Lincoln's Chair' at 'Ford's Theater' and 'dies,' he is doing more than merely returning to a legendary moment. He is forcing the past back into the present, and thus enabling himself to revise history" (39).

Parks's reflections on *The America Play* elucidate what has throughout her oeuvre become a growing concern: the construction—or misconstruction—of history: "Since history is a recorded or remembered event . . . theater, for me, is the perfect place to 'make' history—that is, because so much of African-American history has been unrecorded, dismembered, washed out, one of my tasks as playwright is to—through literature and the special strange relationship between theater and real-life—locate the ancestral burial ground, dig for bones, find bones, hear the bones sing, write it down" (qtd. in Gin 41).

The Foundling Father, also known as The Lesser Man, sits in for The Great Man, Abraham Lincoln, as people parade through the giant hole paying a penny each to take a shot at him. The Foundling Father, alias fore/foe/faux–father, who symbolizes omissions in history, slumps dramatically and enthusiastically in his chair each time he is shot. Satisfied customers shout epitaphs which are repeated and revised, a device Parks uses to produce a gradual progression in the text. A Man shoots The Foundling Father and shouts, "Thus to the tyrants," and B Woman shoots him and shouts, "LIES!" (29). One might argue that the shooting of The Foundling Father is O'Connoresque, particularly if the shooting is viewed as a riff on the cleansing/purging of The Foundling Father's sins of omissions in history. By way of a brief summary, the grandmother in "A Good Man is Hard to Find" is a consummate liar until, faced with death, she embraces Jesus and reaches out to the Misfit. At the precise moment of her reaching out, he shoots her. Like the grandmother in O'Connor's story, The Foundling Father is forced to atone for his sins of omission with each shot to his head. Riffing on O'Connor, Parks implies that The Foundling Father "would of been a good [man]"—i.e., included Blacks in history as subjects—"if it had been somebody there to shoot [him] every minute of [his] life." The irony is that The Foundling Father gets shot repeatedly but neither dies nor learns from the symbolic gaping hole in his head. If anything, he shows signs of amnesia, which is precisely Parks's commentary on America's faux/foe–fathers. John DeRose speaks for other critics when he questions the "cathartic function" of The Foundling Father for the many shooters/Misfits whose history has been dismembered, washed out, written over in order to make place for the lies (410).

While the first act focuses on the sins of the faux-father, the second act dramatizes the life of the son of The Foundling Father, Brazil, who eventually climbs out of the pit, the great hole. Having spent his whole life digging for evidence that his father existed, he realizes that he has found only fragmented pieces of a life. Parks here suggests, as she does in *Death*, that history as recorded in America is and has been exclusionary. Todd London argues that "by replaying the death of Lincoln, Parks brings American history into collision with the absence of African-American history" (44). Brazil in the second act emerges from the hole/whole "after trying to excavate a history for himself where there is none" (London 44). He comments on the continuum that one inherits: "In thuh beginning there was one of those voids here and then 'bang' and then voila and here we is. . . . But where did those voids that was here before we was here go off to? Hmmm. In thuh beginning there were some of them voids here and then: KERBANG-KERBLAMMO! And now it all belongs to us" (34).

The entire process of recognition forces Brazil to turn his efforts to creating his own representations of self, to write his own history, to avoid following in his father's footsteps, which submerged The Foundling Father into the "Great Hole of History," where he play-acts someone else's history and is ritualistically shot.

Parks's *Venus* offers in some ways a slight departure from her earlier plays in that its central character is a female. The play is based upon the true story of a South African woman, Saartjie Baartman, whose unusually large buttocks stigmatized her. Brought to England and displayed in a circus as The Venus Hottentot, she later was taken to France and further exhibited until she fell ill and died of smallpox or tuberculosis. In 1817, a French doctor, Georges Cuvier, dissected The Venus Hottentot to study her buttocks and genitals.

Parks's Venus finds herself under the control of the vindictive, materialist Mother Showman who cages and displays the oddity in a sideshow of "Nine Human Wonders." Mother Showman's cruelty goes unabated until Venus escapes to Paris, where she is seized by Baron Docteur as an object of study. Here Parks revisits her concern about the gaze, which she explored earlier in the "Snails" section of *Imperceptible Mutabilities*. Though the Baron Docteur assures his colleagues that he plans to make Venus the subject—actually object—of his research, he falls in love with her. When Venus dies, his fellow doctors urge the Baron Docteur to help advance the knowledge of the scientific community. The Baron Docteur succumbs to the pressure, dissects Venus, and grows in stature as he reports his findings about this commodified Black female.

Park's fictionalized version of the story, namely the love scenario, has shocked and angered some critics who feel that Parks romanticized the utterly reprehensible Baartman story by constructing Venus as a subject of complicity in her own destruction. Jean Young has been most critical of the playwright's portrayal of Saartjie Baartman: "Baartman was a victim, not an accomplice, not a mutual participant in this demeaning objectification, and Parks's stage representation of her complicity diminishes the tragedy of her life as a nineteenth-century Black woman stripped of her humanity at the hands of a hostile, racist society that held her and those like her in contempt. In other words, Parks's Venus reifies the perverse imperialist mind set, and her mythic historical reconstruction subverts the voice of Saartjie Baartman" (700).

However, Parks's own explanation for her representation of Saartjie Baartman seems equally powerful: "I could have written a two-hour saga with Venus being the victim. But she's multi-faceted. She's vain, beautiful, intelligent, and yes, complicit. I write about the world of my experience, and it's more complicated than 'that white man down the street is giving me a hard time.' That's just one aspect of our reality. As Black people, we're encouraged to be narrow and simply address the race issue. We deserve so much more" (qtd. in Young 700).

While the issue of representation of Saartjie Baartman appears, indeed, controversial, Parks succeeds—as she does in her other plays—in staging migration, dislocation, and dismemberment. Michele Wallace's reading of Park's *Venus* accurately notes that the author "draws upon a wide range of divergent, comparatively new and unexplored discourses: stereotypes of race and gender in Western culture, the plight of the black female body in representation, and the ethnographic subject of the social sciences as a by-product of colonial power, wherever there were inconveniently located indigenous populations who couldn't or wouldn't get with the program" (31).

The cartographizing of Venus's body, using her buttocks and genitals as sites of exploitation, renders Parks's play a brilliant riff on Victorian puritanism and allows Venus agency. Parks researched Saartjie Baartman's life and represented her as if she had a choice in determining the course of her life. At one point, while being propositioned by exhibitors, Baartman/Venus (The Girl) asks, "Do

I have a choice? I'd like to think on it" (17). This one sentence speaks volumes in identifying a woman, as figured in Parks's imagination, who conceivably could have chosen between subjugation by the Dutch colonizers in her native South Africa and exploitation with the possibility of some monetary reward in England and France. One way to read Venus—alias Saartjie—is as an insurgent female character who understands that though she remains an object of patronymic exchange, she also remains capable of resistance. Interestingly, borrowing from the Black vernacular, Venus chooses to "show her ass" as a strategy of resistance. Parks's perception of female resistance is articulated by Brown and Anderson, who note that "the black woman's reaction to despiteous social conditions and the tactics she uses to acquire seemingly unattainable goals were examples of active resistance" (247).

Young cites Brustein's comment that Venus portrays "the humiliation of Blacks in white society without complaint or indictment" (706). While Parks may not be articulating the rhetoric of complaint, one can hardly read this play and see it as anything but an indictment of those who colonize and those whose complicity, regardless of the consequences, might be perceived to some people as victim positionality.

In looking back over this study, one might argue that Parks's four plays constitute a tetralogue, a rep & rev dialogue that begins in *Imperceptible Mutabilities* and is finely tuned in the three succeeding plays. While her four plays are narratively distinct, they are thematically and theoretically linked. *Imperceptible Mutabilities,* with its four segments, "Snails," "The Third Kingdom," "Open House," "Greeks" (or "The Slugs"), is replicated and enlarged in each of Parks's succeeding plays. "Snails," which portrays three women under the gaze of the white, colonizing naturalist who poisons them with his disinfectant and essentially diseases/dis-eases them, gets reenacted in *The Death of the Last Black Man in the Whole Entire World* when Black Man With Watermelon is besieged by a plethora of violent acts, including being kidnaped from his homeland, colonized, and lynched. "The Third Kingdom," which represents a threnody of the Middle Passage, is reenacted in both *Death* and *The America Play.* In the latter, the entire "Great Hole of History" symbolizes the rupture created by the Middle Passage. When Africans were forcibly removed from their homeland, many of them literally dropped off the face of the earth into the "black hole" of the Atlantic Ocean. Those who survived helped build America under the gaze and whip of the colonizer, but, says Parks, their histories get erased: "You weren't here and you didn't do shit" (qtd. in Drukman 67).

The third section of *Imperceptible Mutabilities,* "Open House," wherein a former slave has nightmares during which her teeth are extracted, parallels the grotesqueness of *The America Play*, whose The Foundling Father is shot repeatedly. In both instances, digging serves as a powerful metaphor for absence or silences in history. Finally, the fourth section, "The Greeks" (or "The Slugs"), becomes revisioned in *Venus*. In "The Slugs," Sergeant Smith comes home from war without legs, having fought a battle to unearth his history. *Venus* is dissected, having her buttocks and genitals removed and pickled as an illustration of Black female sexual deviancy. The missing parts, in both instances, speak to the fragmentation that characterizes Black life.

One senses in the language of Parks's four major plays the utter devastation of Black people. Parks's characters are dismembered, dislocated subalterns who cannot speak, to borrow from Spivak, who argues in *A Critique of Postcolonial Reason* that "simply by being postcolonial or the member of an ethnic minority, we are not 'subaltern.' That word is reserved for the sheer heterogeneity of decolonized space" (310). Parks's characters inhabit a liminal space and are unable to articulate within the dominant discourse. A classic example of what some see as esoteric language can be realized in the much-quoted Queen-Then-Pharaoh Hatshepsut in *The Death of the Last Black Man in the Whole Entire World*: "Before Columbus thuh worl usta be roun. They put uh/d/on thuh end of roun makin round. Thusly they set in motion thuh enduh. Without that /d/ we could uh gone on spinnin forever. Thuh /d/ thing endiduh things endiduh" (263). This example demonstrates Parks's refusal to "spell out" the experience of rupture in the discourse of dominance. She rejects any attempt at representing the unrepresentable in European-based discourse. While much of what her characters speak supplies a performative rendition of their splintered selves occupying a liminal space, she makes use of stage instructions, such as "pause," "rest," and silences indicated by listing characters without utterances next to their names. For example, note the instance of silence in *The America Play*:

Brazil:
Lucy:
Brazil:
Lucy:
Brazil:
Lucy: (34)

When Brazil regains his voice, he enumerates the items he has found in the "Great Hole of History," including Mr. Washington's bones, his wooden teeth, and a bust of Mr. Lincoln, none of which proves useful in helping him unearth his past. Lucy, Brazil's cohort, speaks even less. Her utterances seem frequently punctuated with pauses. The silences, then, serve as Parks's riff on an American history that is exclusionary. Parks's "silences" substantiate Spivak's assertion that "if, in the context of the colonial production, the subaltern has no history and cannot speak, the subaltern as female is even more deeply in shadow" ("Can the Subaltern Speak?" 28).

One sees Fanon's ideologies reverberating in Parks's characters, particularly when circling back to Fanon's comment that "to speak a language is to take on a world, a culture" (*Black Skin, Black Masks* 38). Parks's characters refuse to participate in the discourse of dominance—to take on the culture in totality— for that would reinforce dominance. They speak the language of the liminal. Suzan-Lori Parks has chosen to create her own howl, one which allows her to reinscribe value upon the Black psyche.

Works Cited

Bernard, Louise. "The Musicality of Language: Redefining History in Suzan-Lori Parks's *The Death of the Last Black Man in the Whole Entire World*." *African American Review* 31 (1997): 687–98.

Bhabha, Homi. "Dissemination: Time, Narrative, and the Margins of the Modern Nation." *The Post-Colonial Studies Reader*. Eds. Bill Ashcroft, Gareth Griffiths, and Helen Tiffin. New York: Routledge, 1995. 29–35.

Brown, Delindus R., and Wanda F. Anderson. "A Survey of the Black Woman and the Persuasion Process: The Study of Strategies of Identification and Resistance." *Journal of Black Studies* 9 (1978): 233–48.

DeRose, David J. "The America Play." *Theatre Journal* 46 (1994): 409–12.

Diamond, Liz. "Perceptible Mutability in the Word Kingdom." *Theater* 24.3 (1993): 86–7.

Drukman, Steven. "Suzan-Lori Parks and Liz Diamond." *Drama Review* 39 (1995): 56–75.

Du Bois, W. E. B. *Souls of Black Folks*. New York: Signet, 1969.

Elam, Harry, Jr. and Robert Alexander, eds. *Colored Contradictions: An Anthology of Contemporary African-American Plays*. New York: Plume, 1996.

Fanon, Frantz. *Black Skin: White Masks*. New York: Grove Weidenfeld, 1967.

———. *The Wretched of the Earth*. New York: Grove Press, 1961.

Frieze, James. "Imperceptible Mutabilities in the Third Kingdom: Suzan-Lori Parks and the Shared Struggle to Perceive." *Modern Drama* 41 (1998): 523–32.

Gates, Henry Louis. *The Signifying Monkey: A Theory of African-American Literary Criticism*. New York: Oxford UP, 1988.

Gin, Willie. "Suzan-Lori Parks." *Current Biography.* 1999 ed.

Homans, Margaret. "'Her Very Own Howl': The Ambiguities of Representation in Recent Women's Fiction." *Signs: Journal of Women in Culture and Society* 9 (1983): 186–205.

Jacobus, Lee A., ed. *The Bedford Introduction to Drama.* 2nd ed. Boston: Bedford, 1993.

Jiggetts, Shelby. "Interview with Suzan-Lori Parks." *Callaloo* 19 (1996): 309–17.

London, Todd. "Epic-cure: History That Heals." *American Theatre* July 1994: 43–45.

O'Connor, Flannery. "A Good Man Is Hard to Find." *Flannery O'Connor: Collected Works.* New York: Library of America, 1988. 137–53.

Parks, Suzan-Lori. "The America Play." *American Theatre* Mar. 1994: 27–39.

———. *The Death of the Last Black Man in the Whole Entire World. Moon Marked and Touched by Sun: Plays by African-American Women.* Ed. Sydne Mahone. New York: Theatre Communications Group, 1994: 249–79.

———. *Imperceptible Mutabilities in the Third Kingdom. Colored Contradictions: An Anthology of Contemporary African-American Plays.* Ed. Harry Elam, Jr., and Robert Alexander. New York: Plume, 1996: 593–643.

———. "Parks: On the Dangers of Schmaltz." *American Theatre* 12.6 (1995): 86.

———. *Venus.* Theatre Communications Group: New York, 1997.

Rayner, Alice, and Harry J. Elam, Jr. "Unfinished Business: Reconfiguring History in Suzan-Lori Parks's *The Death of the Last Black Man in the Whole Entire World.*" *Theatre Journal* 46 (1994): 447–61.

Robinson, Marc. "Four Writers." *Theater* 24.1 (1993): 31–42.

Solomon, Alisa. "'Signifying on the Signifyin': The Plays of Suzan-Lori Parks." *Theater* 21.3 (1990): 73–79.

Spivak, Gayatri Chakravorty. *A Critique of Postcolonial Reason: Toward a History of the Vanishing Present.* Cambridge: Harvard UP, 1999.

———. "Can the Subaltern Speak?" *The Post-Colonial Studies Reader.* Eds. Bill Ashcroft, Gareth Griffiths, and Helen Tiffin. New York: Routledge, 1995. 24–28.

Wallace, Michele. "The Hottentot Venus." *The Village Voice* May 1996: 31.

Young, Jean. "The Re-objectification and Re-commodification of Saartjie Baartman in Suzan-Lori Parks's *Venus.*" *African American Review* 31 (1997): 699–708.

14

The Memory Palace in Paula Vogel's Plays

Alan Shepard and Mary Lamb

Gore Vidal quipped in 1971 that "Americans hate history" (qtd. in Brownrigg 26). It is often observed that that caricature took root in Puritan society. Four centuries ago, those who landed in what would become New England were eschewing the past, or at least parts of it. Two centuries later, Tocqueville would praise the American habit of looking forward: "Democracy shuts the past to poetry but opens the future" (485). Notwithstanding his affection for America, however, Tocqueville also saw how democracy makes "men forget their ancestors" (508) because it privileges pragmatic self-interest, which often requires that the messy complexities of the past be cast off so as not to fetter an aggressive pursuit of the future. What Tocqueville marked as a tension between blinkered optimism and willful forgetting in nineteenth-century America has often been made painfully explicit in the subsequent two centuries. The Civil War, emancipation, suffrage, the depression, the modern Civil Rights movement, feminism, gay and lesbian liberation, Vietnam—these cataclysms have forced Americans to grapple with the nation's collective past.

Paula Vogel collects shards of these events from America's past to make historical landscapes for her plays. America's uninterest in history is sometimes even an opportunity for whimsy. Take, for example, an exchange between Anna and a lover du jour in an imaginary Amsterdam in *The Baltimore Waltz*. Anna, dying of Acquired Toilet Disease, a comic analog of AIDS, is encouraged to visit the city's Van Gogh gallery and the Rijksmuseum. Replying to his advice, Anna sighs, "What's the use? I won't remember them, I'll have no memory." Her beau, The Little Dutch Boy at Age 50, extrapolates cynically: "So you are an American?" (33). It's not simply that Anna is being pegged as a philistine who spurns Art. The Dutch Boy blunders across one of the principal topoi in Vogel's plays—the lack of interest in memory in contemporary American culture. Ironically, Anna is obsessed with memory. Only two scenes earlier she had wondered whether, after death, one's memory is able to resist what Jonathan Boyarin calls "the disintegration of consciousness" (27), much as a computer battery keeps time even when the machine is unplugged. She had asked her brother Carl a Faustian question then: "I wonder if there's any memory in the grave?" (28). When The Dutch Boy associates a lack of memory with American identity, he unwittingly takes Anna to be an example of Americans' infamous indifference (if not open hostility) to memory, history, and art.

Yet Vogel appears to be less invested in pronouncing openly on the role of art as a vehicle of memory and history than are many American playwrights, such as Tony Kushner, Lorraine Hansberry, Lanford Wilson, or Chay Yew. Kushner, like Vogel also a Pulitzer winner, has been most insistent in *Angels in America,* having Ethel Rosenberg warn, ominously, that "History is about to crack wide open. Millennium approaches" (112). Vogel reaches ground akin to that cultivated by these "playwrighting" contemporaries by assembling montages of historical events, pop culture, and family tales. But her metatheatrical claims about history and memory are interstitial, linked to her experiments with form: borrowing bits of film and canonical lit to broach transgressive subjects such as pedophilia, porn, AIDS, and sexual orientation; staging complexly achronous vignettes whose structures are every bit as complex as their thematic material. As Vogel has told Stephanie Coen, "theatre is about structure and sequence, and not about words" (26). We propose that Paula Vogel's formal experiments, together with her studies of transgressive subjects, create an atmosphere that opens spectators to the possibility of reimagining and sometimes rescripting a number of America's myths and historical "truths."

By way of staging these bits and pieces from the past, Vogel puts pressure on the future of America's self-narrative. As part of the project of reimagining and rescripting, Vogel makes her characters preoccupied with the topos of memory itself as well as with a wealth of memories they recollect on stage: Anna's imaginary grand tour in *Baltimore Waltz;* the sex workers' good times in New Orleans' red light district, Storeyville, in *The Oldest Profession;* Myrna's flight as a sixties radical in *The Mineola Twins;* and Li'l Bit's tableaux of Uncle Peck's advances in a car in South Carolina and a motel in Maryland, in *How I Learned to Drive.* Such characters walk us through their memory palaces. As they open up symbolic spaces that house some piece of their history, they vicariously engage us in their efforts to tell the memories anew in light of the personal and national changes that form the backdrop of the action. Hearing and seeing their memories come to life against those changes, we are invited to imagine how America's future could be scripted differently:

"*American Graffiti:* There's never been a movie made that's even close to how I'm gonna live. I'm making it up from scratch."

(Myra, *The Mineola Twins* 122)

Myra's indie-film attitude is ironically, even quintessentially, American. An adolescent bad girl as the play begins, she spurns the possibility that her rebellious ways might not be original. She is indebted to the sui generis fantasy that is, these days, most often planted in the American imagination by the Hollywood entertainment industry. Movies figure prominently in Vogel's work. Sometimes they function as a kind of graffiti, marking boundaries, signifying zeitgeist, as one of Vogel's Germany-obsessed characters might say. More often than not, they shape the action—her characters and their plots are fashioned by the movies they know, and that we may know.

But Vogel's use of film is also tinged with ambivalence. Her representations of cinema and photography implicitly warn that they can distort or sanitize the recorded moment or otherwise rob reality of its complexity by making a two-dimensional object. A powerful example of that critique is lodged in the photo shoot in Peck's basement in *How I Learned to Drive.* When Peck lets slip his plan to sell the photos to *Playboy* when Li'l Bit turns eighteen, she is enraged: "Any *boy* around here could just pick up, just go into The Stop & Go and *buy*—" . . . "If I look at you—if I look at the camera: You're gonna know what I'm thinking. You'll see right through me—" (65). Fearing that the camera, in Peck's hands, will steal her privacy and perhaps her identity, Li'l Bit seizes this moment to mark the first overt rupture in their relationship. It's not clear, though, that Peck is motivated by commercial opportunity. He's a pedophile, not an entrepreneur. As such, he is interested in capturing on film images of Li'l Bit that defy the complexity of their relationship. He wants her image to gratify himself. He is engaged in making what, in another context, Frederic Jameson has dubbed "pastiche," "history subordinated to the signifiers of style" (Worthen 164). Jameson has described pastiche as the "transformation of reality into images, the fragmentation of time into a series of perpetual presents"; it is an act that signifies "the disappearance of a sense of history, the way in which our entire contemporary social system has little by little begun to lose its capacity to retain its own past, has begun to live in a perpetual present and in a perpetual change that obliterates traditions of the kind which all earlier social formations have had in one way or another to preserve" (125). In contemporary western culture, film has become so familiar a genre that most of us do not stop to think about its effects, as pastiche, on our sense of history, for instance. Even some commonplaces about the effects of film elide the dangers associated with flattening three dimensions into two. When movie critic Gene Siskel died in 1999, for example, he was eulogized on National Public Radio by his first producer, Maria Della Santos, who observed that images from films become inscribed on our hearts. But is that a good thing? Vogel is skeptical.

Vogel's Jamesonian respect for "a sense of history" and her suspicion of the consumerism of late modernity are at the heart of *The Oldest Profession*. The comedy presents vignettes of a collective of sex workers in New Orleans who have shared living space and clients since before the Second World War. The episodic plot incorporates many reminiscences as, one by one, the women exit, then die. These recollections reveal long-simmering differences in point of view toward life and The Life. At one pole is Ursula, of implied Germanic heritage, who favors trafficking in the nostalgic romanticism now embraced by their aging clients as a way to make a buck. "Advertising's the soul of the modern marketplace," she says cheerfully, en route to suggesting that as elderly prostitutes they should cater to a niche market; Ursula's referent film is *Harold and Maude* (142). At the other pole is Edna, who wants nothing to do with Ursula's promotion of such late-capitalist virtues as hyper-efficient worker productivity and profit maximization. Whereas for Ursula nostalgia is simply one more consumer good, and one that is much in demand, for Edna romantic idealism is genuinely an ideal. Edna's last movie? *The Sound of Music* (166). At first glance this blip may seem to be merely a sign of Edna's dated cultural literacy, akin to Vera's love for "Donny and Marie" (134). But the allusion to Robert Wise's 1965 musical obliquely raises the specter of the Third Reich, a subject that exerts a controlling minority interest in most of Vogel's other plays. *The Sound of Music,* like, say, TV's *Hogan's Heroes,* romanticizes the pleasure of foiling fascism, makes risk somewhat glamorous. In such venues, the threat of the Third Reich's expansion is appropriated to impel a plot and thereby subdued as pastiche, reducing the historical threat into a saleable American entertainment product.

However much the women profess wanting "to remember" (156), as Mae says, the art of taking each other and us on tours of their rich lives in Storeyville during the Great Depression and the Second World War necessarily demands narrative selection and suppression. As in *Sound of Music,* in *The Oldest Profession* war is transformed into a mere trope by such remembering, as we can see when Ursula and Lillian quarrel in the first scene. Ursula, whose pursuit of the future has no respect for the past, baits her: "You were just a scrawny virgin with big eyes in Storeyville while I was satisfying the troops——." Lillian, whose clients include a Mr. (Willy?) Loman, who still pays in chocolate and silk stockings as if he's stuck in 1945 (145), is unimpressed by Ursula's longer tenure as a prostitute: "Seniority be damned . . . who cares if you were fucking at Gettysburg!" Ursula snorts in reply: "Gettysburg!" (152). That Civil War battle had proved to be a decisive moment in American history, as much so as the Great Depression and victories over the Japanese in the Pacific theater, other events that form the casual historical backdrops for *The Oldest Profession*. Against that history Vogel has offered some new scripts that challenge a few commonplaces. She revises the literary representation of the whore, for example. Mae, Edna, Vera, and the rest are neither early modern vixens enslaved by unholy passions nor impoverished Dickensian creatures down on their luck. They are instead philosophically engaged workers with vanilla interests in the personal, physical effects of large, impersonal events on the world stage.

The filmic graffiti in *And Baby Makes Seven* is much bolder, more complex. *Baby* aims at nothing less than thinking through an alternative to the nuclear family in the late twentieth century. Not only does *Baby* presuppose the dysfunction of the Ozzie and Harriet model that is also a target in other Vogel plays ("obscenity begins at home," quips the epigraph to *Hot 'n' Throbbing* [228]), but *Baby* also confronts some of the potentially serious snags created by more fluid models of familial and parental organization. In *Baby*, the new community is constituted by a pair of lesbian lovers and their gay friend (and sperm donor). "They" are pregnant, yet we discover that Ruth, who is not pregnant, feels threatened by the biological bond between Anna and Peter. The plot, which veers toward the representation of psychosis in a number of places, takes us through the tumultuous feelings (rather than through historical events per se) that erupt during the pregnancy. The tumult is intensified by Vogel's experiments with form, for the lesbians move rapidly in and out of the characters of small imaginary boys (Cecil and Henri), and Ruth adopts a second "character," the inarticulate Orphan.

By playing off its intertextual referents, *Baby* ponders the question of whether a story, script, or cultural narrative can be fundamentally changed in mid-course. Can an adult who suffered a miserable childhood, such as Peter, for example, plot a different course as an adult? Can adults steeped in traditional notions of family dynamics and parental roles invent new ones? And what is the role of memory in such a process of inventing a new script for oneself and one's children?

In the midst of killing off their imaginary children to make way for the "real" baby that arrives in the final scene, Ruth and Anna dispute a narrator's agency: "I don't see why we can't change the . . . the narrative at this point,"

Ruth muses. To which Anna replies, "We can't stop now. Not in the middle of the story" (105). Later, Peter makes the request of Cecil: "Look—do you think maybe we could . . . change the ending?" (113). Ironically, Ruth and Anna can stop the story of Henri and Cecil's deaths. For them, creation of a script is not an "originary" act; however, they import bits and pieces of *The Exorcist, Lassie,* and *Macbeth,* for example, to compose a script that explores the anxiety and even grief that grips them as they prepare for their baby's imminent arrival. Scene 6 in particular fuses these various sources; what these have in common is that all are didactic narratives of human responses to acute experiences of loss. They differ markedly in the responses they propose. Scene 6 closes by taking spectators across that spectrum. Anna and Ruth (playing Orphan) are self-consciously theatrical, as Orphan's "grand mal" seizure stops when Ruth takes off her gag and rope to announce, "(Cheerfully): The End!!" (89). The grand mal itself is likewise self-referentially hammed up. The "strange buzzing noises" in Orphan's throat, à la *The Exorcist,* give way to echoes of Ibsen's *Ghosts* ("Mother, g-give me th-the-sahh-sun"), another play about sexual and familial transgression that provoked a stormy response in its day; and *Macbeth* ("Out, d—damned Spot!!"). Then Orphan hums the theme song from *Lassie* and beckons, "L-l-lassie c-come..hh-omme. . . . " (88). Orphan's paroxysm conveys Ruth's anxieties that are brought about by Anna's pregnancy and her new biological bond with Peter. But as this scene comically suggests, Ruth's stress is not abated by the sentimentality of children's stories, the purgative effect of Renaissance tragedy, or the mock exorcism of modern horror films.

A more satisfying narrative model had been introduced much earlier in the play (68), and attempting now to mediate the stress, Ruth and Anna return to that story—*The Red Balloon.* Published in Paris in 1956 and filmed as a silent movie that year, Albert Lamorisse's tale presents Pascal, a lonely boy befriended by a magical balloon. It brings him quiet companionship and comfort. When a group of bullies destroy it, all the captive balloons in Paris come to Pascal's house; from there he rides the balloons around the world. In the tradition of magical realism, the story offers a fantasy of escape from an otherwise banal existence punctuated by genuine oppression. A recent volume on magical realism describes its effect: its "ontological disruption serves the purpose of political and cultural disruption: magic is often given as a cultural corrective, requiring readers to scrutinize accepted realistic conventions of causality, materiality, [and] motivation" (Zamora and Faris 3).

Henri's retreat into the story of *The Red Balloon* in *Baby* is integral to the way the play challenges the ideal of the nuclear family. As Henri experiences a vision of "My balloons!!" Anna speaks for those who prefer mundane realism. She judges that Henri is having "a relapse" worthy of another visit to "Dr. Weinstein" (107). Unlike the mock-tragic madness of scene 6, this retreat into fantasy is more disturbing for spectators to watch because the conventions of causality and materiality are so obscured; but Henri's retreat into magical fantasy is ultimately more palliative to him than any mock-tragic madness can be. While Anna calmly recites the plot of *The Red Balloon*, Henri insists, "It wasn't a movie!! It was my life" (108). Just when Henri's psychosis threatens to break the bounds of make-believe, however, Henri silently becomes Ruth again and, climbing in from the fire escape, "holds out a deflated red balloon" (109). As subsequent scenes demonstrate, however, Henri is not extinguished as a character when the (real) balloon deflates. Nor is Cecil. For in spite of Cecil's suicide in scene 12, performed to the script of "*Julius Caesar*, Act Five" (113), Cecil is also resurrected in another act of magical realism. The imaginary children survive as tokens of the escape that fantasy provides, but also as signs of the effects of children's memories, which can be fertile ground for imagining a different life as the millennium approaches.

When Peter confides that being abandoned as a boy by his own father has ill-prepared him to father Nathan, Cecil advises "just make it up on your own" (113). And they do. Anna, Ruth, and Peter constitute a version of the nuclear family that was almost unimaginable (outside the avant garde, perhaps) only a few years ago. Making it up, or changing the ending, as Peter proposes, demands the capacity to accept the presence of the magically real. The play ends on such a moment. While Anna and Ruth look on, Nathan giggles and squeals as Peter "makes gobbling noises" and says, "I'm eating you up, yummyyummyyummyyummy—yummmm—Nathan's all gone" (125). What is implied in the contrast between Peter's playing with Nathan and Peter's memories of his own father's cold indifference is that it is possible, as it were, to rescript the future. And that is a goal Vogel endorses, as she explained to Stephanie Coen: "This is a racist, misogynist, homophobic society, and after a while it becomes the air you inhale. . . . I believe we [playwrights] have to get out there and write flawed plays that disturb everybody, and change the atmosphere" (26).

The most dynamic weaving of classic films, metatheatrical pondering, and national narratives occurs in *The Baltimore Waltz* and *Hot 'n' Throbbing*, which make an unlikely pair. In the first, the Cold War thriller *The Third Man* (1949) supplies a background screen of bomb-riddled Vienna, where only the black market (13) and deep pessimism flourish. But the action takes place not in time past or time present, but time future, for as we learn in the final scene, most of the play is taking place in Anna's mind. This makes for thrilling theater, but it does not lead to utopian optimism. Quite the opposite. In the words of Harry Lime, a crossover character who is in the business of fencing scarce penicillin in Graham Greene's script, "In these days, old man, nobody thinks in terms of human beings. Governments don't, so why should we?" (112). Vogel borrows Lime for *The Baltimore Waltz,* where he is selling hope. As he tells Carl, "Listen, old man, if you want to be a millionaire, you go into real estate. If you want to be a billionaire, you sell hope" (50).

Nourished in part by *The Third Man*'s film noir ambiance, film noir being "a cinema of moral anxiety," *Baltimore Waltz* posits that, in half a century, little has changed in America's response to what it perceives to be its internal enemies (Cook 469). Paranoia and prejudice are still rampant. In the opening scene, for instance, Carl is fired from his job as a children's librarian at The San Francisco Public for coming out and acting up. Later, Anna frets about being marked as an untouchable with ATD, as Carl rehearses the line of argument used in the 1980s to defend PWAs' civil liberties: "[ATD]'s not a crime. It's an illness" (17). The U.S. government's lackadaisical response to the HIV epidemic during the Reagan administration, especially its Dick-and-Jane campaign of uncandid sex education, is also briefly mocked (18). The analogy between Cold War–era anxieties about subversive infiltration and Reagan-era anxieties about the risks posed by those infected with HIV, such as Vogel's brother, Carl, is funny, but sobering. America feeds on disenfranchisement.

The ironic tone of *Baltimore Waltz* circumscribes the emotional effects associated with thrillers. So the play is more black comedy than spy thriller. Because *Waltz* is also an elegy for Vogel's brother, the cultural work done by the play—making fun of the American fear of invisible evil agents, expressing some of the intense grief felt by people touched by the HIV epidemic—such aesthetic work nevertheless does not cross over into an exercise in style alone. To the last, the play retains its awareness of personal as well as public history. It never sacrifices Carl to the stylish creation of art for its own sake. However much Anna fears being unable to remember her French—"'I have no memory.' (*Reads from the Berlitz*) 'Il n'y a rien à faire'" (7)—the play remembers multiple languages and histories so very well. The Berlitz lesson suggests, in fact, that memory provokes action.

The second of the pair, *Hot 'n' Throbbing,* Vogel's grimmest play, is quite a different kind of story: a mock-up of a porn-slasher movie; a pastiche of sado-masochistic filmmaking; a very sober inquiry into the roles of horror films such as *Halloween* (1978) in the psychodynamics of domestic abuse; a play about snuff films; and a snuff play. *Hot 'n' Throbbing* presents the final hours in the life of a middle-aged woman signified only as Woman in the script apparatus but known to her teenage children and estranged husband (Clyde) as Charlene. She is juggling single motherhood with a career in B-movies, writing, acting in, and producing pornography, or what she insists is "*adult entertainment*" (238). While Charlene holds that there is "a mile of difference" between the two, the plot collapses the distinction. In doing so, the play suggests that contemporary feminists who dismiss the link between pornography and violence may be collaborating with apologists for mass media's implicit sanctioning of violence against women. Charlene's inability to come to terms with the memory of her own history with Clyde dooms her.

For even as Charlene pronounces that the film company she has created from scratch, Gyno Productions, aims "to create women as protagonists in their own dramas" (262), the metaplot of *Hot 'n' Throbbing* is unfolding as an all-too-familiar narrative of domestic violence, disguised as the spousal reconciliation that Clyde says he craves, and that ends in her murder. The plot recapitulates the history of their entanglement in domestic abuse. As the play opens, Charlene is observed under deadline, cranking out the first forty pages of a new s/m script. It features a dominatrix: "He needed to be restrained. Tied Down. . . . She was hot. She was throbbing. But she was in control. Control of her body. Control of her thoughts. Control . . . of him" (235). These last words also conclude the play. There, they are typed into the computer by daughter Leslie Ann, who seems unmoved by Woman's [aka her mother's] cooling body on stage as she enters and picks up where Charlene had stopped in the first scene. The parallel suggests that Leslie Ann's adolescent enthusiasm for contemporary horror movies such as *Halloween* and its spinoffs, including *Friday the 13th* (280), has normalized for her not only Charlene's career as a porn star but also the larger slasher-s/m American subculture, and has sped Leslie Ann toward a life in porn as well.

Yet both Vogel's *Hot 'n' Throbbing* and Charlene's play-of-the-same-name-within-the-play do not only repulse the slasher-s/m genre but also open up disturbing questions about the role of art in replicating romanticized violence against women. *Hot 'n' Throbbing* shows that it is a shorter distance than is usually acknowledged from *Ulysses, Plexus, Lolita,* or *Othello,* passages of which all make cameos, to its own final scene. There, an insanely jealous Clyde strangles Charlene on what had been their marital bed, reenacting Othello's murder of Desdemona, while the disembodied Voice Over recites the juicy bits from *Ulysses* where Molly Bloom experiences an orgasm (or surrenders to reconciliation with Leopold). The superimposition of Molly's pleasure on Charlene's death is disturbing. As the timing suggests, the intertextual borrowings in *Hot 'n' Throbbing* are coyly agonistic. One question raised by Molly's aria as Charlene dies: If Joyce's modernist implosion of received western culture is complacent in its treatment of the status of women, then what can be hoped for from art that is not experimental, such as *Othello*?

The "snuff" film acted in the final minutes of the play peels back the usually more romanticized western narrative of women as men's chattel so often reproduced by mainstream Hollywood entertainment. The denouement trashes Charlene's earlier confidence that Gyno Productions can shoot porn that liberates women. As the filming starts, Charlene protests that the pain is too real: "Wait a minute, guys—that really hurt. Larry—stop the camera" (288). As the play suggests, the medium of film especially accommodates male disembodiment from the violence of that narrative. Objecting to Charlene's acting in any Gyno film, Clyde explains his obsession with controlling Charlene as a "tape loop. It's torturing me. I'm standing outside my body, watching this actor doing that to you. A stunt man who's got my face" (264).

Unlike *Desdemona*, which goes to blackout before we can be sure that the modern version will end as the Jacobean one does, *Hot 'n' Throbbing* leaves no room for audiences to disconnect from what is happening. "Shut. Up. . . . Now—get on the bed like a good wife" (291) the Man lip-syncs to the Voice Over, as Charlene and Clyde roleplay his fantasy that she is a prostitute for hire. It is a fantasy she has agreed to act out because her cultural training to please her man overrides both her memories of their relationship and her instincts. By the time her instincts kick in and she is standing "stock-still, smelling the change in the atmosphere" (288), she has lost control of the screenplay. As Man and Woman lip-sync, The Voice asks for Man, "Do you remember the last time? I asked you a question. Do.you.remember.the last time." The Voice replies for Woman: "When . . . we . . . made love?" For Man: "No. When I beat you to within an inch of your life. You didn't learn did you. . . . I'm going to have to teach you all over again" (290–91). Man "savagely hits" Woman (290), verbally humiliates her, ropes her with his belt, then strangles her with his "bare hands" (294). The dialogue is heavily stylized, as in some episodes in *Baltimore Waltz*. But here the effect is raw and painful.

As the action rushes toward a grisly finale, the techniques create great stress and alienation. In lieu of direct speech, the characters lip-sync while their lines are artificially amplified by The Voice Over; the stage directions note that "*we watch their mouths move like puppets, mechanically and exaggerated"* (290). The Woman cries in pantomime. At one point all the voices together cry, "a strange keening" (292). The Voice on tape is slowed as it reads again from Joyce as Woman dies; then there is a flash of light, a blackout, and the return of Girl.

These techniques draw on Vogel's knowledge of the Russian formalist Viktor Shklovsky, from whom "Brecht purloined the Alienation Effect," as David Savran observed in introducing the first collection of Vogel's work, *The Baltimore Waltz and Other Plays* (xi). "The purpose of art, according to Shklovsky, is to restore visibility, to *defamiliarize* the commonplace so that we notice it again" (xi; italics original). What is startling in *Hot 'n' Throbbing* isn't the talk of pornography or the domestic violence—it's the stagecraft, which isn't easily digestible. The events are not today's installment of TV news' shrink-wrapped tale of the tragedy of a battered woman. When as a final action Girl plucks Woman's sunglasses from the corpse and takes up Charlene's work on the screenplay of *Hot 'n' Throbbing,* the hint that Woman may have died in vain is difficult to ignore. The ending may cause us to wonder whether a traditional tragedy such as *Othello* does more to replicate violence or purge our impulse to do it.

The Body as Memory Palace

"His heart beating Dixie— "
(Li'l Bit, *How I Learned to Drive* 83)

To the extent that Vogel's plays evince a "theory" of memory, it might be paraphrased thus: that memory is recorded and recalled through sensory experiences, that the human body is an archive of its past, that the past is sometimes known to the body generally but not to the mind itself. A corrupt version of the theory is voiced in *How I Learned to Drive* when Peck aims to coax Li'l Bit into yet one more hotel bed by reasoning that "sometimes the body knows things that the mind isn't listening to" (81). As it turns out, Peck is more right than he might wish. The mature Li'l Bit who narrates the play sums up the effect of the first instance of his molestation by reporting that "that day was the last day I lived in my body. I retreated above the neck . . . " (90). Li'l Bit's recovery from the abuse does not depend on her telling her story as a kind of therapy. The story is not blurted out. It emerges in a controlled, distanced way. As that form suggests, Li'l Bit's work on stage is not unmediated recollection, not the return of the repressed.

Rather it is a complex, retrospective reconstruction of a complicated family history of incest, in which she has been taught to play the role of the solicitous female who in effect invites Peck to abuse her. But she is only twelve when she offers to play his confidante and surrogate wife (71), having no notion that her offer highlights the age-inappropriateness of Peck's contact. The moment distills how insidious the script of female behavior can become.

In that environment, memory stores the unspeakable in the body's bank of sensory stimuli for later examination. In the opening scene of *How I Learned to Drive*, for example, Li'l Bit invites us to join her on a trip down memory lane, the landmarks for which are visual and other sensory memories. It's a warm summer night in Maryland, 1969. But as she sketches the scene, Li'l Bit contrasts contemporary images of the "revival churches, the porno drive-in, and boarded up motels" that she sees in her mind's eye with what someone a century earlier might have seen: "You can still imagine how Maryland used to be, before the malls took over. This countryside was once dotted with farmhouses—from their porches you could have witnessed the Civil War raging in the front fields" (7). The allusion to the Civil War hints at the internecine struggle yet to come in Li'l Bit's narrative.

For his part, Peck later tells his history to Li'l Bit by way of analogies to South-North relations that draw on olfactory memories. "I was stationed in D.C. after the war, and decided to stay. Go North, Young Man, someone might have said" (26). Echoing the expansionist cry "go west!" Peck initially glosses over why he has emigrated from his native South Carolina to Maryland. In a soliloquy he hints to us, however, that South Carolina is the scene of his first crime, the sexual abuse of his nephew, Bobby, while teaching him to fish. Peck remembers South Carolina as a physical place: "There's a smell in the Low Country—where the swamp and fresh inlet join the saltwater—a scent of sand and cypress, that I haven't found anywhere" (34). Picking up on the geographical designation of the Low Countries, also the early modern name for what is now principally Holland and Belgium, Peck marshals what he understands to be Amsterdam's reputation for sexual permissiveness to excuse his "present" ploy to get Li'l Bit drunk in a Maryland motel bar. "This establishment reminds me a lot of places back home," he muses, as she gulps her martini. For Peck, "South Carolina" signifies a libertine space that winks at incest and pedophilia: "In South Carolina, like here on the Eastern Shore, they're . . . *(Searches for the right euphemism)* . . . 'European.' Not so puritanical" (23). Peck's memory, like his judgment, is ever dubious. But his association of South Carolina with the scents of Low Country waters and the misguided notion of this sort of supposed European permissiveness illustrates what J. Gerald Kennedy and others have suggested, how we "reconstruct the past largely through the imagery of place," and also how "memory is less the retrieval of bygone time than a recovery of symbolic space" (500).

The sprezzatura of the South behind which Peck takes refuge is explicitly satirized much later in the play when the Male and Female Greek Choruses join Li'l Bit in a mock-blazon, "Recipe for a Southern Boy," whose rhythms echo the call-and-response of a Baptist revival. "Bedroom eyes—" says the Female Chorus. "A dash of Southern Baptist Fire and Brimstone—" declares the Male Chorus. "The slouch of the fishing skiff in his walk— . . . and under the wide leather of the belt—Sweat of cypress and sand—Neatly pressed khakis— His heart beating Dixie—The whisper of the zipper—" (82–83). With its chirpy tempo, its appeal to the scent of cypress, and its erotic attention to the Southern young man's body, the mock-blazon registers both what is appealing and disgusting about a formula for masculinity that is intertwined with nationalistic nostalgia for the South.

As in the adult Li'l Bit's return to a warm summer night in Maryland, however, memories of the body's sensory experiences are shown to have healing potential as well. Thus in *Baltimore Waltz* Anna comforts the Munich Virgin: "The human body is a wonderful thing. Like yours. Like mine. The beauty of the body heals all the sickness, all the bad things that happen to it. And I really want you to feel this. Because if you feel it, you'll remember it. And then maybe you'll remember me" (41).

Historical memory as recorded in the human body is likewise depicted as a strength in *The Oldest Profession,* where Mae, for example, defends her turf against an upstart by shouting, "We're built to last! We give service we're proud of!! Unlike you, your plastic twat is gonna fall out in the road five years from now" (137). The sex workers, like Vogel herself, reject the strictures of political correctness. Indeed, in the penultimate scene, Vera and Edna, the last survivors of Mae's coterie, think momentarily about the plight of laborers in other jobs. Gazing on a BLT sandwich, Edna is no longer able to see it as a simple sandwich. For her it's a sign of the exploitation of labor, of the "union struggles for lettuce workers in California" and in the slaughterhouse and the mill (171). These thoughts do not lead toward political action, however, but instead toward Vera's fond memories of her late mother's red beans and rice, cooked every Monday while the laundry was washed. The olfactory pleasures of the dish are lovingly described, crowding out the politics of exploited labor. In the final scene, Vera, now the lone survivor, simply "sits, plaintively quiet" (172).

The question when the curtain comes down seems not to be "will Vera join a union?" but, like Anna in *Baltimore Waltz,* "will she have any memory of her life from within the grave?"

In Mae's house there is none of the theatricalized sadomasochism said to be practiced in the brothel in *Desdemona* and parodied in *"the beating scene"* (211) in which Bianca *"lightly straps"* Desdemona while Emilia, horrified, prays the Hail Mary (212). This scene reaches for the comic potential of lesbian s/m; Vogel is no Pat Califia. If the scene mocks the putative pleasure of submitting to a dominatrix, it also comically inverts the ancient western antipathy for the human body, for its ability to function as a pleasurable subject. Physical stimuli, recollected on stage, trigger the characters to speak about, and sometimes act out that antipathy. In *How I Learned to Drive,* for example, the Catholic doctrine that the pain of childbirth is punishment for Eve's sin is evoked when Li'l Bit's mother, Lucy, disputes her own mother's fear that the frank discussion of sexuality will encourage Li'l Bit to sleep around. Speaking for the community, the Female Greek Chorus says, "I'm not scaring her with stories about Eve's sin and snakes crawling on their bellies for eternity and women bearing children in mortal pain—" (43).

Desdemona is rife with western culture's hostility toward women's pleasure. When Bianca is praised by Desdemona as a "free woman—a new woman—who can make her own living in the world, who scorns marriage for the lie that it is," Emilia responds with a tag that belies her negative Catholic fixation on the corporeal destiny of all women: "No matter how you dress up a cow, she's still got udders" (194). Thus Emilia advises her mistress to give up the pleasures of moonlighting at Bianca's brothel for the "peace and love Our Lady brings" (192). But praying to the BVM is no salve against domestic violence, as Emilia knows. She explains it away as an effect of men's "itchy heat rash in th' crotch"; "they get all snappish, but once they beat us, it's all kisses and presents the next morning" (189).

The learned behavior of pathological dissociation revealed by Iago's treatment of Emilia shows up in other Vogel plays, too. Typically some manifestation of dissociation surfaces when characters get too stressed by the tension between their present reality and their consciousness of memories past, when those two seemingly cannot be integrated. One example of the scrambled brain comes in *The Mineola Twins* when the "good" twin Myrna endures a momentary "comatose seizure" (132) during an argument with her son, Kenny (132). While she writes it off as a "residual effect" of electroshock therapy done to her years ago, its timing is suspicious. For it interrupts Kenny's harangue against militarized civic authority, which he sees all around him in contemporary American society (this is 1969). His metaphor for that is the Third Reich. With adolescent hyperbole Kenny complains that "I have to dress like a Hitler Youth all day in school because of our Nazi principal and his Nazi dress code" (131). And the Chicago police at the 1968 Democratic Convention were "Mayor Daley's stormtroopers" (132). Initially Myrna objects to his "countercultural nonsense" (131) by recalling the sacrifices of Kenny's "grandfather and other men like him who fought for your freedom." Otherwise, she says testily, "you'd be singing 'Deutschland Über Alles' every morning in home room. —Nazis! Hitler Youth!" (132).

In the midst of complaining to Kenny that teenagers exist in a dichotomous moral universe that allows "no gray. Nothing relative" (132), Myrna is incapacitated by a seizure. It's as if her brain cannot process Kenny's ahistorical misappropriation of the Nazi mentality and legacy. For her, the specter of Hitler is a repressed memory of evil incarnate, and not simply a linguistic sign for all that is authoritarian, as it is for her son. Myrna's nephew, young Ben, the neoconservative son of a sixties' radical, later reiterates Kenny's speech, but from precisely the opposite political pole. He whines that he is tired of being taught to be ashamed of being a white male—at school "we get hit on the head about the holocaust and date rape" (156). Like Kenny, Ben reduces the holocaust to a pastiche. Both speeches suggest just why history must be taught, to keep alive a historical memory, to prevent the hijacking of history for narrow political purposes, as when, for example, people deny that the Holocaust actually happened. As Jonathan Boyarin insists, "it would be perilous to ignore [Walter] Benjamin's lesson that one of the ways that life is maintained is through a constant effort to retain the image of the past—to rescue the dead and oppressed ancestors by giving their lives new meaning. Much as genetic information is a 'narrative,' memory resists the disintegration of consciousness" (27).

We get a more disturbing version of the sequence of memories of Nazis being juxtaposed with physical evidence of pathological dissociation in *Baltimore Waltz*. Chasing a cure for ATD, Anna submits herself to the ministrations of a deranged Viennese urologist, Todesrocheln ("death-rattle"). The etymology is one sign of the humor with which Vogel defangs the memory of the Nazis' notorious "medical" experiments on Jews and other condemned people. Even while Todesrocheln laments the loss of data "senselessly annihilated" at Ravensbruck (53), he struggles not to taste the urine provided by Anna. He is mad, an alchemist gone over to the dark side, outfitted in a toupee, wig, and big glasses, as if in a Marx Brothers' movie. Vogel's comic rendition of The

Physical Exam, the penultimate imaginary event before Carl's death is announced, alleviates plot stress that was induced early on, when Anna had asked Carl, "Just what was he doing from, say, 1938 to 1945?" (15). While the question does invite us to recall what the Nazi physicians did, it also discriminates between their war crimes and the legitimate experiments of research physicians who work on the HIV epidemic, whose treatments at times may only seem barbaric. One way to preserve an enduring international horror and outrage over Nazi atrocities is to protect the words used to describe it from being used casually.

Todesrocheln's struggle illustrates that perpetrators carry the psychological damage of war crimes in spite of themselves. Compulsively he drinks from Anna's urine sample, symbolically acting out a kind of cannibalism. If his history remains shadowy to us, nevertheless it clearly continues to warp his functioning in the present. His personality is so compartmentalized that he presents two personalities: during The Physical Exam his left hand repeatedly grabs for Anna's urine flask while his right hand tries to prevent it. When the left hand sneaks the flask below a table, "the right hand is puzzled" (55), and loses the very funny psychomachic "struggle" that Todesrocheln cannot suppress (53). The symbolic action of hand fighting hand invites spectators to witness the doctor's partial regression into a childlike state.

Baby provides earlier evidence that Vogel turns to the physical gesture of the psychomachic hands in order to dramatize the matrix of German nationalism, dissociated personality, and regression that fascinates and repulses her. In *Baby*, though, the matrix is comic rather than sinister. Ruth generally plays two boys at once, the French lad Henri and the younger, less articulate Orphan. Making lunch one day, Ruth/Henri/Orphan acts out the stresses of incipient and surrogate motherhood and the complexities of her liaisons with Anna and Peter by having Henri and Orphan fight over a peanut butter sandwich. The stage directions are revealing: "*Ruth's hand does a* Dr. Strangelovian *battle with her other hand, fighting for possession of the peanut butter and jelly. In the midst we hear her sing Wagner*" (81). What is Wagner doing in this scene with Dr Strangelove? It's not quite that an allusion to Wagner supplies an auditory trace of German nationalism, for the historical events that led to the development of the atomic bomb are remote from the issues being explored here. More likely, Ruth's impulse to sing Wagner hints at how a musical score—a script—can offer an aesthetically mediated response to stress. Rather than articulate her anxieties directly, Ruth sings opera.

Among children it is obviously a sign of health to be able to make believe. At its best, the game can be played only by the young, however, for the pretender must be largely unconscious of history and be lacking long-term memory. "The problem with being an adult," says Anna, waiting in Dr. Todesrocheln's exam room, "is that you never forget why you're waiting" (52). Indeed, Todesrocheln's comically sinister psychomachia is perhaps triggered by his watching Anna re-enact a childhood game she invented to entertain herself before she could read—before she became conscious of herself as a subject within the master narratives of history and her own memory. "I would make up stories about my hands—Mr. Left and Mr. Right." "Mr. Left would provoke Mr. Right. . . . The trouble would escalate, until my hands were battling each other to the death." Finally they would become "friends again, and they'd dance" (52). Hands dancing—a waltz?—would bring the child Anna from a condition of internal strife to order. As the self-conscious experiments with form and language suggest in *The Baltimore Waltz,* however, order itself is often precariously contingent upon an adult game of make-believe.

Exilic Memories of Childhood

> "It smelled of Crayola wax, crushed purple and green—"
> (The Third Man, *The Baltimore Waltz* 46)

This ekphrastic memory of the classroom where Anna teaches first grade is characteristic of the weight Vogel puts on the sensory dimension of characters' recollections of childhood, their own as well as other people's. More than any contemporary playwright, Vogel populates plays with virtual children: the doll Ruth and Peter practice bathing in *Baby;* the kids at the San Francisco Public Library in *Baltimore Waltz* whom Carl teaches to sing "here we go round the mulberry bush" as they cut out pink triangles to memorialize homosexuals killed by the Nazis; the allusive traces of biblical youth such as the Prodigal Son and Jacob and Esau in *Mineola Twins* (137, 145); *The Little Prince* in *Baltimore Waltz* (24); Pascal from *The Red Balloon* in *Baby* (68, 106); and Bobby and younger versions of Li'l Bit in *How I Learned to Drive.* Vogel's memory-obsessed adults are often refugees from ugly childhoods. They bring to the stage exilic memories of loss. Remembering how it felt to be abused or deprived, they frequently resurrect incarnations of their much younger selves.

If Vogel's adult characters travel childhood paths to heal old wounds, their memories of childhood also recuperate the significance for their adult selves of playing make-believe. In the theater, the firewall between fantasy and reality, between childhood and adulthood, instantiated in American culture is temporarily opened. Doing so allows the adult characters to experiment with rewriting some powerful childhood narratives, for themselves and for the culture at large.

The clearest examples of aesthetically mediated revisions are to be found in Ruth's plans for killing off the imaginary boys in *Baby*. When Peter insists halfway through the play that the imaginary children be performed no longer, Ruth proposes to script their deaths, so as to "get my last inch of fantasy out of them" (84). Yet the last half of *Baby* is focused on plots to kill off the boys as well as conversations about the value of allowing them to survive even after baby Nathan is delivered. Rather, as the boys' deaths are acted out, Anna and even Peter come to agree with Ruth's position that, through regressive fantasy, they can safely traverse very adult obligations and stresses.

For example—the physical changes and mental accommodations of pregnancy. Even before Anna erupts in anger at being "bloated and tethered like some goddamn Good Year blimp" (96–97), miserable in New York in August, Ruth acts out Anna's loss of control over her own body by making an ironic spectacle of it, much as Carl's HIV in *Baltimore Waltz* becomes Anna's ATD. Similarly, Ruth gives Orphan rabies, and stages a comic death scene that distracts Anna. Her mock sympathy is directed instead toward Ruth/Orphan, who convulses and cribs lines from *The Exorcist, Macbeth, Hamlet,* and *Lassie.* If being pregnant is a form of alien engorgement, as Peter later suggests after witnessing Nathan's birth ("Before tonight in that delivery room, I though[t] *Aliens* was science fiction" [115]), then Orphan's "death" by rabies allows Anna and Ruth to displace such alienation from the pregnant body onto the non-pregnant partner.

Moreover, Ruth's control of the narrative development of the fantasy gives her a gestational, creative role in the household alongside Peter and Anna's biological ones, thereby diminishing her twinges of being excluded from the pregnancy. Even as Ruth offers Anna comfort through fantasy, however, she also bids for control of how the imaginary boys are disposed of. Through such bids, which Peter and Anna also make, Vogel invites spectators to become more self-conscious of the ways that adults borrow canonical scripts about childhood for their own purposes. One fascinating instance: Ruth's resurrection of the ghost of Orphan as act 2 opens. The ghost awakens Cecil (Anna) in the deep of night to stutter a few lines from the first act of *Hamlet,* in which the ghost of Old Hamlet admonishes the Prince to "remember me." Sometimes in *Hamlet* criticism their exchange is read psychoanalytically as an Oedipal warning not to forget the Father. In *Baby,* where such anxieties mutate with a new idea of family, Orphan's quoting Old Hamlet sets up an ironic transgenerational parallel in which an inarticulate child speaks as a patriarch who demands that he not be removed from the narrative.

This stubborn impulse not to be removed is also on Henri's mind as he waits with Cecil to be killed off. Indeed Henri declares to Anna that *he* (not Peter) is "father to your child" (102). By having Henri attempt to horn in on the fact of paternity, Vogel suggests the ways in which even those not capable of "fathering" a child may work to create and claim some paternity through fantasy, whether that be by composing poetry or other posthumous markers of one's life, or by attempting as Henri does to gain other people's assent to wishful thinking.

As in *Hamlet,* then, in *Baby* the characters wrestle with the obligation to remember the past as they embrace the future. Thus in a funeral prayer for Orphan just before his ghost enters, Cecil (Anna) has affirmed "I'll never forget you. You'll always be with me" (91). This is said not from Christian fright, as in *Hamlet,* but from the "Laws of Physics," namely that "matter can't be destroyed, but only changed" (91). This turns out to be more true than Cecil/ Anna could have foreseen. For as the play ends, Peter himself regresses into the character of Orphan as a way of remembering the child within, who is buried under the adult burdens of his career as a marketing specialist. But Peter's breakthrough into fantasy comes as something of a surprise, for he and Anna have insisted all along that a story, once launched, needs to be completed along its prescribed trajectory. Now even Peter is playfully rewriting the trio's history.

For Vogel, finally, the stage, with its capacity for intertextual and historical echos and its live performance medium, is a vibrant site of the human act of remembering. The three-dimensionality of the actors' bodies resists the flattening out of complex realities that other media such as film and still photography effect. Vogel's plays draw spectators to see the necessity and sheer complexity of remembering. For the act of remembering is never a simple event, but a process of imposing narrative order, drawing boundaries in retrospect, tying together sequences of what were once to the mind's eye apparently unrelated moments, perhaps even inventing a more perfect history.

Works Cited

Boyarin, Jonathan. "Space, Time, and the Politics of Memory." *Remapping Memory: The Politics of TimeSpace.* Ed. Jonathan Boyarin. Minneapolis: U of Minnesota P, 1994. 1–37.

Brownrigg, Sylvia. Rev. of *The Essential Gore Vidal. Times Literary Supplement* 30 Apr. 1999: 26.

Coen, Stephanie. Interview with Paula Vogel. *American Theatre* 10:4 (1993): 26–27.

Cook, David A. *A History of Narrative Film.* 2nd ed. New York: Norton, 1990.

Della Santos, Maria. "Latino USA." National Public Radio, broadcast 28 Feb. 1999.

Greene, Graham. *The Third Man: A Film by Graham Greene and Carol Reed.* Intro. Andrew Sinclair. Modern Film Scripts. New York: Simon, 1968.

Jameson, Fredric. "Postmodernism and Consumer Society." *The Anti-Aesthetic: Essays on Postmodern Culture.* Ed. Hal Foster. Port Townsend, WA: Bay, 1983. 111–25.

Kennedy, J. Gerald. "Place, Self, and Writing." *The Southern Review* 26 (1990): 496–516.

Kushner, Tony. *Angels in America, Part One: Millennium Approaches.* New York: Theatre Communications Group, 1993.

Tocqueville, Alexis. *Democracy in America.* Trans. George Lawrence. Ed. J. P. Mayer. New York: Harper, 1988.

Vogel, Paula. The Baltimore Waltz *and Other Plays.* New York: Theatre Communications Group, 1996.

———. *The Mammary Plays:* How I Learned to Drive *and* The Mineola Twins. New York: Theatre Communications Group, 1998.

Worthen, W. B. *Modern Drama and the Rhetoric of Theater.* Berkeley: U of California P, 1992.

Zamora, Lois P., and Wendy B. Faris, eds. *Magical Realism: Theory, History, Community.* Durham, NC: Duke UP, 1995.

15

Postmodern Monologues in Regina Porter's *Tripping through the Car House*

Mary Resing

Regina Porter's 1997 play *Tripping through the Car House* is a hybrid formed of several theatrical categories. In the tradition of American realism, *Tripping* provides a compelling domestic drama, dealing with love, kinship, and betrayal. However, as a postmodern work, it mixes a linear plot with a variety of oblique and fanciful elements. With this play, Porter borrows from the traditions of Black and Southern women writers to compose a unique and non-holistic world and culture. Set in an environment half house/half car, the play combines moving narrative and strong characterization with a pastiche of images. Several monologic scenes which involve the characters Dee, Dale, and Nita Myers clearly reveal this world.

Tripping through the Car House progresses on two distinct but related levels. On the first level, it presents a coming-of-age story—the tale of twelve-year-old Nita, who struggles to come to maturity as the marriage of her restless parents, Dee and Dale, deteriorates. On the second level, the play embodies the internal conflicts of the three main characters. Memories, dreams and deeply imbedded bits of popular culture make up the identities of these characters; their divergent identities are embodied, given movement and voice, through conversations with "ghost" characters. The multiple identities of these characters betoken the fragmented world in which they live.

In *Performance: A Critical Introduction,* Marvin Carlson, citing an argument by Fredric Jameson, states that "in postmodern expression, the traditional unified work of art expressing a unified personality gives way to a 'schizophrenic' art, reflecting a shattered and fragmented culture" (135–36). *Tripping*'s playwright, Regina Porter, herself embodies a number of separate identities. Born and raised in Savannah but a resident of New York, an African American but also a woman, Porter represents no single category. She discloses her multiple identities in the disconnect between herself and her dramatic characters. Although Porter herself is highly educated, her characters speak in slang. As the following examples illustrate, the playwright herself often writes in standard English. Even her stage directions use a grammar that reflects her education:

> The hint of a smile creeps across Dee's face. She sways from side to side for A BEAT, catches herself and stops. (3)
> Dee crosses into the kitchen humming "Habanera" from Bizet's *Carmen.* CARMEN emerges ankle-deep in water in the kitchen sink. (22)

Contrarily, Porter's characters employ a nonstandard grammar native to parts of Georgia—which reflects not the playwright's education but her Southern background. The speech of the character Beryl exemplifies this grammar usage: "I'm fixing this customer's hair a certain way like she asked me to. And then she says she don't like her hair that way. And I say, honey, then why did you ask for that style in the first place? I told you it wasn't gonna work! You got one of those big pie faces. Don't necessarily do well with that style" (34).[1] Alone, neither the standard English of the stage directions nor the nonstandard grammar of Beryl encapsulates Porter's narrative voice. Her voice remains multi-vocal, a compound which reveals the playwright's own experience and imagination, but this revelation appears fragmented, broken up into distinct grammars.

Through her adherence to the dramaturgical traditions of both African American and Southern women, Porter's work reflects her multiple identities in another way. Obviously, the categories of African American women and Southern women overlap considerably. Historically, this overlap was reflected in their dramaturgical conventions. In their work, both sets of playwrights focus on the home and on the lives of strong women. Kathy Perkins, writing of early-twentieth-century African American playwrights Zora Neale Hurston, Georgia Douglas Johnson, and Eulalie Spence in her introduction to *Black Female Playwrights: An Anthology of Plays before 1950,* states that "The main characters in plays by black women were usually female. . . . The action for the most part occurred in a domestic setting—the kitchen, dining room, or living room, and the play usually opened with a woman sewing, cooking, cleaning, or praying—rarely outside or far from the home" (2). Milly S. Barranger in "Southern Playwrights: A Perspective on Women Writers" makes a similar claim for Southern playwrights Lillian Hellman, Carson McCullers, Alice Childress, and Marsha Norman: "The center of the universe for these playwrights is a woman (or women) and the family" (8).

Although both sets of playwrights find the home a provocative setting for the exploration of mother/daughter relationships, some African American writers, both playwrights and novelists, perceive these relationships as problematic in a very specific way: often the daughter serves as the vehicle for her mother's displaced dreams. Lucille Fultz, writing of the work of African American novelist Toni Morrison, observes, "The mother often sees herself as enabler and her daughter as the agent of promise and change" (228). The mother's displaced ambitions serve as a source of tension for both the mother and the daughter. Awareness of life's hardship tempers and confounds the mother's ambition for her daughter, arousing in the younger conflicting emotions. Longing for her daughter to escape the bonds of family and home, which have confined her, the mother also urges her daughter to find security through the love of a man and a comfortable home life. According to Patricia Hill Collins in *Black Feminist Thought: Knowledge, Consciousness and the Politics of Empowerment,* such mothers "encourage their daughters to be independent and admonish them to get married and raise children. This apparent cognitive dissonance emerges from these mothers' attempts to create buffers for their daughters against a hostile world and at the same time pass along a legacy of love and service" (126).

Porter explores this dilemma through the characters of Dee and her older daughter, Beryl. Passionately ambitious for her daughter, Dee's own past nonetheless tempers her hopes. Nineteen-year-old Beryl won't go to college and has trouble holding a job "fixing hair" (34) but has plans more ambitious than working for the "ranky-dank beauticians" of Savannah (73). Telling her mother that she wants her own business, Beryl cautions her: "I just don't know if Savannah's gonna necessarily be the place" (74). Although Dee admires her daughter's independence, it frightens her, for she wants Beryl to hold a steady job, get married, and settle down. Fixating on the handsome musician Frazier as a husband for Beryl, Dee advises, "A life in other people's hair is hard. A life in your own hair is hard. This boy is a good catch, Beryl. He could open up a whole new world for you" (40).

Dee alternately encourages and thwarts Beryl in her efforts to leave Savannah. Her own unhappiness complicates her mothering of Beryl. Although Dee feels that she has been "raised to go places" (4), she lives within the confines of the city of Savannah. Increasingly frustrated and bitter, Dee ultimately performs an act confusing in its mix of selfishness and motherly love: she seduces Beryl's beau, the womanizer Frazier. This act causes a rift in her relationship with Beryl and jeopardizes Dee's own marriage. Although destructive, Dee's seduction of Frazier has its beneficial side. The excitement of the moment assuages, at least temporarily, Dee's need to break out of her stifling domestic role and allows her to continue in her roles as wife and mother. Furthermore, Beryl's resulting disillusionment with Frazier prevents her from repeating Dee's own mistake—that of sacrificing her dreams for a man unworthy of her love.

Although both Southern and African American women often use the home as a setting for their plays, Southern women frequently expand the scope of their work to include a wider sense of place. Dialects, social customs, and references to specific locales reveal and celebrate Southern culture. According to Barranger, women playwrights "have transposed to the theatre such distinguishing marks of Southern life and cultures as the importance of family, a specificity of place . . . gothic humor [and] regional dialects" (7). *Tripping* clearly belongs to this tradition. Set in the Myerses' home in the city of Savannah, the narrative revels in its coastal Georgia location, and the characters' speech is redolent of Georgia. Even the obscure Gullah dialect of coastal Georgia becomes a source of humor—when Dale asks for help getting rid of his "ghost," his friend Grease replies, "Then you gonna have to do what the old folks did: buy yourself some sulfur—(with an intentional hint of Gullah) *Burn he out*" (87). Furthermore, the food the characters prepare and eat potently evokes Southern life: "Collard greens. Candied yams. Fried chicken . . . special recipe macaroni and cheese. Okra gumbo—and Mississippi mud pie" (18). For the Myerses, however, Savannah exists not as a closed-off and parochial world but as a place of some sophistication, a city of opera and jazz, of beauty parlors and stock car racing, of longshoremen and trips to France.

Contrasting elements make up the evocative and complex world of *Tripping*. The Savannah of the play is, within itself, disjointed. The visiting Frazier finds the city romantic and welcoming: "Every corner I turn, there's a square to sit in. Azaleas in bloom. Spanish moss dangling from weeping willow trees" (44). But for Dee, a native of Savannah, "the wrong turn on a downtown side street . . . can take you from cobblestone to dirt in the blink of an eye. From brownstones and renovated mansions . . . to shacks on stumps with barefoot children running everywhere, and women who still use brown paperbags as hair curlers" (45). The Myerses' house, the Car House of the title, is also fragmented—half race car, half house. Porter describes the house as "a world where nothing is ever as it seems. Central to this place is a Vintage Ford Race Car. In the real world, it would be nestled safely in a garage. In this one, it is an extension of the house, literally built into it, protruding out of it, distorting its interior and exterior" (1).

Representing dual worlds and multiple functions, the Car House signifies, simultaneously, the allure and danger of the national racing circuit and the comforting world of home and hearth. The house functions as a place to eat, to sleep, and to exchange confidences, a place of sudden flashes of violence and tenderness. The car serves as a hobby, a gathering place, and a vehicle for fantasy. When Dee comments to Dale, "Would be nice if we could ride in it—instead of you always working under it," she is greeted by an invitation to sit in the car: "Close your eyes," he says, in an invitation to dream (4). The car both brings the family together through imaginary journeys and ultimately breaks the house apart through real ones.

In addition to evoking place, many plays by Southern women share another element: they embrace the style of the well-made play. From Lillian Hellman to Marsha Norman, Southern women playwrights, similar to many of their male counterparts, have adopted the style's linear plotting and single climax. With the narrative of *Tripping*, Porter too adopts the well-made-play format. At the beginning of the *Tripping* narrative, stasis exists—the Myers family is intact and functional. With their jobs as longshoreman and seamstress, Dale and Dee provide a stable and comfortable home for their family, a stability that includes rewards: their daughters Beryl and Nita are well loved and self-confident. The action starts, classically, when a stranger, the jazz saxophonist Frazier, enters town: "Not from around these parts, are you Frazier?" Dale asks when they meet (16). "Just passing through?" he inquires (17). Frazier's arrival creates an immediate fissure in the Myerses' home life. Soon after he arrives, Dee turns to her daughter Nita, and "smacks her good and hard" (20). The fissure in the family widens as incident builds on incident to create the climactic scene in which Dale leaves Savannah to return to the professional car racing circuit and the Car House, literally and metaphorically, blows apart. In the play's final scene, with Dale dead and Frazier gone, a stasis returns. The house is now just a house, and a newly constituted family unit becomes haltingly functional: "It's too quiet here," Nita complains, "We gone and got ourselves a quiet house" (119).

In adopting the well-made-play format, Porter separates herself from many of her African American contemporaries. Although, traditionally, African American women playwrights too have borrowed from the well-made-play format so enmeshed in the modernist style of American realism, recent dramas by African American women have eschewed that format. Dramatic works by Kia Cothron, Robbie McCauley, and Anna Deveare Smith have rejected a single linear plot in favor of a multiplicity of narratives. A variety of individual voices intermingle to create a work unified by rhythms, themes, or tone, but not by plot. Instead of following a single narrative to its logical climax, these women present a variety of elements which may or may not lead to a single and holistic conclusion. Syndé Mahone in the introduction to *Moon Marked and Touched by the Sun* refers to each of these women as a "word weaver" and "wor(l)d weaver" who "has created a testament of Originality, defining theatre on her own terms. Borrowing from a wide range of styles and genres, they create a new matrix for the narrative of the ever-evolving human spirit" (xiv).

Although Porter avoids the nonlinear format of contemporary African American writers, neither does she limit herself strictly to the well-made-play form. A number of stylized elements coexist with her linear and realistic plot. These elements comment on and stand in contrast to the high emotion of the plot. The key stylized element in *Tripping*'s departure from modern realism lies in the series of scenes involving "ghost" characters, for these scenes depart from the realistic narrative to reveal the inner conflicts of the three main characters. Each scene with a ghost character takes place at a time when Dee, Victor, or Nita struggles with conflicting emotions. Their conversations with their ghost confidantes allow them to voice their concerns and justify their viewpoints.

The character of Dee holds these conversations with the "ghost" of Carmen, a character from Bizet's opera of the same name. Bold, brassy, sensual, and doomed, Carmen can express her sorrows and joys in emotive songs. Prior to her marriage, Dee sang too. In fact, she had hopes of becoming an opera singer. Dee's hopes for a professional singing career were intertwined with her difficult relationship with Victor, a successful and determined race car driver. When Victor changed from the man with whom she fell in love to a cruel womanizer, Dee became bitter and self-destructive: "No longer the sweet boy I knew in high school, he was screwing everything under the sun and a few things in the shade. First, I turned a blind eye to it. Told myself it was just a phase. But then he got to flaunting his woman in my face. Made it so, I wanted to hurt him same way he was hurting me—" (106). When Dee began an affair with Victor's brother, Dale, and Victor subsequently died in a race, she shut herself off to music and excitement. Turning her efforts toward establishing a home life and raising her daughters, she dedicated herself to keeping her home intact and to being a faithful wife to Dale.

After Victor's death, Dee becomes "a serious woman." In her public character, she shows herself as a loving but strict mother—inside her house, she "rule[s] the day" (9). She is an industrious seamstress and a demanding spouse. Carmen becomes Dee's private side, her sensual nature. Dee tells her daughter Nita: "Carmencita is a friend who sometimes keeps me company. She was with me before you or Beryl was born. From the minute they first lowered Victor into his grave. And my singer's voice just cracked—shriveled up. Giving me one more reason to boo hoo cry. And that's all I did was boo hoo cry. Then Carmen came to me . . . I'll sing for you, she said. I'll dance for you, she said" (88). Carmen provides Dee with an outlet for artistic expression, providing relief from the tedium of her everyday life. Carmen's presence, however, is not completely benign—she constantly taunts and tempts Dee, leaving her restless and uneasy. Dee sees Carmen as her freed spirit, yet Carmen holds Dee back and keeps her from living in the present. "How do you stand being cooped up?" she asks Dee, "Something's got to give" (22). Carmen constantly reminds Dee of her lost career and guilty sensual desires, calling her, "Sweet Dee. Guilty Dee" (49, 90). Dee initially resists, saying, "But I've changed, you know. Settled, Carmen. I'm not that kind of woman now" (23), but finally gives in to her suppressed desires.

Similar to Dee's conversations with Carmen, Dale's discussions with the "ghost" of Victor have to do with thwarted dreams. Victor, "the best looking boy at Beach High" (92), has haunted Dale since his death twenty years earlier. Partners in success, Dale and Victor were two young black men who achieved prominence in the white-dominated field of stock-car racing, "finishing in the top ten on the National Circuit two years in a row" (63). Dee found the very idea impressive, remarking, "Now, that was enough to make anyone laugh. Notion of two good-looking colored men thinking they could get away with driving fast" (92). Dale played the role of the little brother, the good boy, the one Victor sent "to cover for him" (106). In life, Victor was a con man, a daredevil, and a betrayer of trust, but through his death, he has gained mythological status and power.

Although Victor's ghost has become Dale's constant companion, the bond between the two brothers lacks the veneer of friendship which characterizes Dee's relationship with Carmen. Victor does not provide Dale with an escape from the drudgery of daily life. Rather, functioning as Dale's ever-present tormentor, Victor becomes inescapable. "How you figure you can just shut me out when and wherever you want. Like I can't come in when and wherever I want?" Victor says (30). He undercuts Dale's happiness by casting doubt on all that Dale values, including his love, both platonic and erotic, for Dee; his relationship with his daughters; and the worth of his friends. As a result of his conversations with Victor, Dale eventually begins to see himself as "a race car driver doing menial work" (52) and not as a satisfied family man.

Dale claims that Victor belongs to the past and not the present, and he tries to deny Victor's power over him, saying to Dee, "I ain't Victor. I ain't my brother" (50). Attempting to drive Victor away, he conducts an exorcism. But

Victor reappears, gaining even more power over Dale. Dale tells Victor, "Get out of my fucking head" (114), but Victor does not. When Dale says to his friend Grease, "I can put Vic in his grave," Grease replies, "He's already in his grave" (115). However, the Victor Dale sees will not rest until Dale joins him in death.

If the conversations between Dale and Victor clearly reveal antagonism, the conversations between twelve-year-old Nita and her "ghost" confidante, Clint Eastwood, reveal both more playfulness and more ambiguity. Clint Eastwood exists as a poster on her wall and a visitor in her bedroom. For Nita, Clint Eastwood represents adventure, excitement, and romance. He serves as both a model for her own behavior and an object of desire. If Clint Eastwood acts bravely, Nita can too. If Clint Eastwood is sexy, so is Nita. For Nita, Eastwood represents the androgyny of childhood and the lack of emotional boundaries. Nita can say in one breath that Clint Eastwood reminds her of her father: "Y'know what I like about Mr. Clint Eastwood? I like that sort of look he gets. Like right before he gets into trouble. Like right before he's gonna maybe die. All wise and faraway. Kind of reminds me of Daddy. You ever notice how Daddy gets that look? He does—all the time—most of the time, really. You wouldn't think their eyes would be so similar—especially since his are brown and Mr. Clint Eastwood's are blue. But they got that distance thing going. That faraway thing. Don't you think?" (12) and in the next say that she likes to imagine him as her boyfriend: "Why, sometimes at night, I sit up and lift my arm just like this. (She lifts her arms toward her.) And I kiss it just as long and hard as I can. I imagine it's Mr. Clint Eastwood done stepped out of his poster world right smack into mine" (36). Her admiration for him is both filial and sexual, romantic and autoerogenous.

His movie roles serve as a model for her behavior. The actions of Clint Eastwood in his "Harry-got-a-magnum-thing" movies lead Nita to face down the neighborhood boys who threaten her (2). And Eastwood as a "handsome Yankee soldier" in *The Beguiled* on whose account a little girl, "just swoons and swoons—like any sensible girl would" (57) leads her to speculate about her own sexuality, never considering her sister Beryl's caution that "little black girls don't fit squarely into the lives of the Mr. Clint Eastwoods of this world" (37). But the Clint Eastwood with whom Nita converses is neither the actor himself nor a character in any movie. As he says to her: "This isn't any former mayor of Carmel standing before you. I'm the bits and pieces lost along the way. The scenes that gave way to editing floors. The small exchanges in between shooting on studio lots. Before the director said cut. And after that still. I'm the stuff little boys and girls construct in their minds on idle days. Construct, and yes, outgrow. The way you're outgrowing me now" (76).

Clint Eastwood functions in three dimensions, but not as an autonomous being. Rather, he reflects Nita's needs. Like Victor and Carmen, he represents a composite of memories, dreams, and fragments of the dominant culture. Although each of the scenes involving Carmen, Victor, or Clint Eastwood is structured as a dialogue, these scenes do not function in a traditional dialogic manner, for the two parties in the conversation do not represent separate points of view. Instead, they function as monologues, demonstrating in theatrical form the split identities of the central characters. The following scene between Dee and Carmen shows this:

> CARMEN: Your husband's going crazy.
> DEE: (Dee looks at her) Just who does he think he is?
> CARMEN: *Loco. Loco. Loco.*
> DEE: After all I've put up with from him.
> CARMEN: Rearing his two kids.
> DEE: Exactly.
> CARMEN: Giving up your career.
> DEE: Exactly.
> CARMEN: I tell you, Dee, we can never please these men.
> DEE: Never ever. (48–49)

Dee and Carmen share the same thoughts and speech patterns. Their dialogue seems more like a call and response than an actual conversation. Although Dale's conversations with Victor are more confrontational, they too have little actual conflict, as the following scene reveals:

> VICTOR: August Sprints . . . Sure could use some company. Sure could use a ride.
> DALE: Can't do that, Vic.
> VICTOR: What you gotta do so much in August? What you gotta do so much you can't?
> DALE: Gotta fix my car. Gotta get her up to par.
> VICTOR: To look at her?
> DALE: I enjoy looking at her.
> VICTOR: She's a race car, brother.
> DALE: For me, she's strictly leisure.

VICTOR: You can't turn a race car into a thing of leisure. You'll break her spirit every time. (*Then.*) Why don't you race behind her? (31)

On one level, this scene functions as a conversation between two individuals in which one attempts to persuade the other to do something that he does not want to do. On another level Victor serves merely as the voice of Dale's own doubts and desires. The scene enacts the war between Dale's need to drive fast and his feelings of responsibility toward his family.

Deborah Geis, in *Postmodern Theatric(k)s: Monologue in Contemporary American Drama,* argues that dialogues which function as monologues have existed as long as theater itself: "One traditional feature of Greek tragedy is the repeated 'debate' sequence, or agon, in which the protagonist (prompted by the Chorus) arrives at a revelation or decision. On one level, the agon constitutes a dialogue between the speaker and Chorus, rather than a genuine monologue. But the Chorus's ability only to react and to feel, not to act, means that its members serve as surrogate audience members of sorts rather than simply as characters" (16).

Victor, Carmen, and Clint Eastwood too can only react, not act. They serve as devil's advocates and dream vehicles but can only persuade Dale, Dee, and Nita to do what those characters already want to do. They are embodied and articulate fragments of identity, splinters of self. If *monologue* (from the Greek *monos* and *logos*) means solitary speech or speech with oneself, the ghost scenes strangely combine elements of dialogue and monologue.

The split identities of Dee, Dale and Nita reflect the non-holistic world in which we live. Dale both "aint Victor" and is Victor. He struggles to escape Victor, yet refers to him frequently. He loves the same woman as Victor, claims the same daughter, but Victor remains eternally a young and successful race car driver while Dale is an aging longshoreman. In the same way, Dee is both Carmen and not Carmen. When Carmen sings, Frazier hears Dee. "You have a singer's voice," he says (65). Carmen and Victor are husband and wife: Carmen calls Victor "Hermano in the spirit world" and Victor calls Carmen "Sweet Dee" (99). Carmen remains fixed: eternally single, eternally sensual, while Dee increasingly identifies herself as a frustrated wife and mother. Nita, too, is both Clint Eastwood and not Clint Eastwood. She kisses Clint Eastwood by kissing her own arm. But she controls him in a way she can't control her own life, saying to him, "Your life's on my wall." Realizing that she can destroy him, Nita says, "Mr. Clint Eastwood, you don't even know me" (75).

Although Nita laments that by talking to Clint Eastwood, "I've been walking around making a modern day crazy of myself" (75), she's actually been making herself a postmodern character. Deborah Geis argues that "the postmodern modern subject—that is, the split, multiple or contradictory 'I'—is thus a decentered one, and so the notion of 'character' is no longer holistic" (34). Nita and her parents represent on stage the "contradictory I," the postmodern self. The device of monologue, too, reflects postmodernity. Self-consciously theatrical, artificial, nonrealistic, monologue was seldom used by realists because it disrupted the linearity of narrative and ruptured the illusion of the stage world as a real world. Many contemporary artists have embraced monologue. Solo performances, such as those by Laurie Anderson or Anna Deveare Smith, are inherently monologic. But a monologue that is also dialogue starkly epitomizes the postmodern slippage of self, for it gives theatrical form to the schizophrenic nature of character. Dee, Dale, and Nita hear voices and the voices are their own.

Playwright Porter and, indeed, the potential audience of the play, share the schizophrenic world represented by the monologic dialogues of *Tripping*. No one can be or ever has been a member of a single category. Contradictory impulses that argue with each other and confound definitive essence define us. Postmodernism recognizes that an infinite number of incomplete borrowings, of fragments of categories, compose identity. With *Tripping*, Porter places this schizophrenic world in opposition to the traditions of the well-made play, creating a work both linear and fractured, interior and exterior, modern and postmodern.

Notes

1. The text used in this essay is the version performed at Wooly Mammoth Theatre Company in April 1997.

Works Cited

Barranger, Milly S. "Southern Playwrights: A Perspective on Women Writers." *Southern Quarterly* 25.3 (1987): 5–9.

Carlson, Marvin. *Performance: A Critical Introduction*. New York: Routledge, 1996.

Collins, Patricia Hill. *Black Feminist Thought: Knowledge, Consciousness, and the Politics of Empowerment*. New York: Routledge, 1990.

Fultz, Lucille. "To Make Herself: Mother-Daughter Conflicts in Toni Morrison's *Sula* and *Tar Baby*." *Women of Color: Mother-Daughter Relationships in 20th Century Literature*. Ed. Elizabeth Brown-Guillory. Austin: U of Texas P, 1996. 228–34.

Geis, Deborah R. *Postmodern Theatric(k)s: Monologue in Contemporary American Drama.* Ann Arbor: U of Michigan P, 1993.

Mahone, Syndé. Introduction. *Moon Marked and Touched by the Sun.* New York: Theatre Communications Group, 1994. xiii-xxxi.

Perkins, Kathy A. Introduction. *Black Female Playwrights: An Anthology of Plays before 1950.* Bloomington: Indiana UP, 1990. 1–15.

Porter, Regina. *Tripping through the Car House.* Manuscript dated March 19, 1997. Collection of the author.

16

Southern Women Playwrights and the Atlanta Hub: Home Is the Place Where You Go

Linda Rohrer Paige

Home is the place where, when you have to go there,
They have to take you in.
　　　　　　　　　—Robert Frost, "The Death of the Hired Man"

Move over, Humana. Atlanta takes center stage. This city of the "New South" teems with excitement and women playwrights definitely want to go there: "The city is home to dozens of playwrights whose scripts are being produced here and elsewhere, from Washington, D.C. and Charleston, S.C., to Dublin, Ireland, and Edinburgh, Scotland," reports the *Atlanta Journal and Constitution* (Kloer, Crouch, Fox, and Sherbert). This new, transformed Atlanta has become a mecca for new voices—where Old South meets Gay Pride, where female playwrights break rules as fast as box office records, and where politics, quite often, flavor the plays. Atlanta's stages bustle with activity from these Southern women playwrights who choose to live and work in the city. In Atlanta, they feel most exposed to humanity's diversity.

In the 1960s and 1970s, this new metropolitan city absorbed a wave of enthusiastic newcomers as an unprecedented building boom swept over the city, and into this fertile field, women actors and playwrights planted "roots." Opportunities for dramatists, those "homegrown" or "imported," increased, and like roots stimulated to greater growth when transferred to a larger pot, these women flourished. Women who acted on the stage, as well as those who aspired to write for it, relished the possibilities inherent in living in an area that supported their many talents.

As early as 1985, the *Atlanta Journal and Constitution* celebrated a $20,000,000 NEA check to fund the arts, as the city hailed its corporate leaders for recognizing the value of the arts to the community: "I don't know whether Atlanta would have boomed economically as much as it has in the last decade if it had not been for the corresponding boom in the arts," declared Endowment Chair Lawrence L. Gellerstedt, Jr. (qtd. in Smith, "The Arts"). By 1986, the *Journal* excitedly boasted the fruits of a changing South as new plays and festivals dotted the landscape like dogwoods in spring:

> In recent years, Atlanta has gained a reputation as an exciting place to see live theater. The city is home to about 40 professional and avocational theatrical organizations, including half a dozen stages in the thriving Peachtree theater district. Among them are the Alliance Theatre, the state's largest resident theater; Academy Theatre, which has launched many important new works; Jomandi Productions, one of the city's most adventurous black theater companies; and Center for Puppetry Arts, one of the nation's most creative puppetry theaters. (Kloer et al.)

Besides providing a forum for classical drama, the city invited new and experimental forms of theater. By the 1990s Atlanta settled into its new image as arts advocate, comfortable with its varied activities, its "levels of productions—from readings, to shakedown stagings, to polished productions" (Hulbert, "Atlanta's Rising"). Critic Dan Hulbert notes that "The '90s also have witnessed a slow, steady output of Atlanta works that can hold their own in any theater city" ("Atlanta's Rising").

In June of 1999, the television program *The Georgia Week in Review* (GPTV) assembled a panel of theater artists and directors to report on Atlanta's theaters. Diagnosing a favorable "playbill of health," the panelists echoed a similar refrain: "Diversity," "Diversity," "Diversity"—that's what distinguishes Atlanta's stages! The city's theater critics concurred: "We are witnessing the rise of new Southern playwrights—black and white, urban and rural, Jewish and Gentile, sacrilegious and spiritual. They are playwrights who tenaciously examine questions of morality and social justice in black-and-white terms—good versus evil—however unfashionable that might be today in such citadels of hipness as Los Angeles and New York" (Hulbert, "Playwrights").

For female playwrights in the region, this overt gesture towards inclusion meant entry to a stage previously dominated by men and access to other playwrights whose interests and concerns diverged from, yet variously complemented, their own. Importantly too, these convergent voices furnished playwrights with a forum for discussion, evaluation, and repair of plays in progress. Praising this "transition," Dan Hulbert of the *Atlanta Journal and Constitution* proposed that the old definition of Southern drama must be "reinvented . . .

from its old, narrow frequency on the national radio dial to a broad, cacopho-nous band of diverse viewpoints" ("Playwrights"). With this chorus of oppor-tunity, no wonder that women playwrights found Atlanta a suitable home!

As more dynamic projects and festivals decorated the streets, Atlanta emerged as a nucleus of theatrical activity—a *play-writing hub,* if you will—not only because of its central location but also because its theater houses, similar to spokes on a wheel, have radiated to the city's suburbs. Small theaters in the city proper have acquired much needed renovations and new building projects are booming. People continue to be drawn to the magnet-city, and women play-wrights have followed the lights of the stage.

Though it is impossible here to review three decades of female playwrights whose roots may be traced to Atlanta's stage, any exhaustive list would surely include Valetta Anderson, Sabina Angel, Pearl Cleage, Sandy Corley, Sandra Deer, Margaret Edson, Shirlene Holmes, Marsha A. Jackson-Randolph, Barbara Lebow, Patty Lynch, Dianne Monroe, Pamela Parker, Bonnie Pike, Rebecca Ranson, Nicky Silver, Pamela Turner, and Shay Youngblood. From among this roster, many names deserve to be underscored, for these playwrights' impressive works have propelled them far beyond regional theater, garnering them recog-nition across the country and abroad. This essay, however, seeks to illumine the lives—and a few of the works—of only four playwrights who typify the spirit of Atlanta's theater: Shirlene Holmes, whose play *A Lady and a Woman* gained acclaim in *Amazon All-Stars: Thirteen Lesbian Plays* (1996); Sandra Deer, author of the Southern Gothic comedy *So Long on Lonely Street,* which enlivened the-aters in 1985, and whose current play, *Sailing to Byzantium,* has been published by the Oregon Shakespeare Script Series (1998); Barbara Lebow, perhaps best known for her play *A Shayna Maidel* (1988); and last, Pearl Cleage, author of Flyin' West *and Other Plays,* a collection recently published by the Theatre Communications Group (1999). Cleage's hit *Blues for an Alabama Sky* high-lighted the 1996 Olympics in Atlanta.

Not all of these women exclusively identify themselves as "Southern play-wrights"—or for that matter, even as "playwrights"—yet their craft, undoubt-edly, owes a debt to their new (or old) "Atlanta roots." Though "a sense of place" still permeates their works, many Southern women playwrights ac-knowledge that "as Southern culture grows, there is sometimes a tendency to identify less with the region" (Kloer et al.). Thus, a playwright such as Barbara Lebow might prefer a Caribbean island (as in "Cyparis") or set her tale about survival and home in New York City (*A Shayna Maidel*) just as easily as she might locate her play in the South. Nonetheless, the South wields its influence on Southern women dramatists.

Just as other Southern writers have come to recognize that their "artistic strengths" lie in their diversity, these playwrights identify with "their own Southern roots" as well as with "the black diaspora" (Kloer et al.). Beginning to equate its "difference" with "strength" as traditional themes of home, family, and Southern heritage became incorporated into larger, universal themes and issues, the theater community enhanced its repertoire, introducing themes of survival, extended family, reunion, and "invalidism," for instance. Female characters noticeably grappled with societal norms as they attempted to shape—or failed to shape—their own identities. The resulting product of this transformation made for a "new Southern drama."

Accentuating Atlanta's diversity, the work of teacher/playwright Shirlene Holmes has fared well in this premiere city of the New South. Holmes peoples her plays with complex women, fierce yet gentle, characters who subvert the status quo and battle multiple oppressions of race, class, and gender. *A Lady and a Woman* recounts the story of two African American women in 1890 who fall in love. The romance, highlighted by motifs of deliveries (of babies) and deliverance, revolves around Flora, an owner of a small town inn, and Biddie, a hog cutter, recently arrived in town looking for work. Enamored of Miss Flora's beauty and attracted by her facial scar—the mark of a battered wife—Biddie declares Flora's former wound a "medal," a badge of dignity, something deserving respect:

> MISS FLORA: When we got married my granddaddy say to me, "Flora, if he raise his hand up make sure he go to jail, but if he bring that hand down, make sure that you go to jail." That's what happened the night he hit me in my face and I went back into the wall mirror. The doctor wanted to stitch up my face, but I wouldn't have it. When I got my mind back, I was sitting in jail and he was gone; ain't seen him since.
> BIDDIE: So that's how you got that long scar on your face?
> MISS FLORA: Doctor say I'm lucky I got sight; I said he lucky he still got a behind. We both ate a lot of glass that night. (188)

Willa Taylor maintains in her introduction to the play that theater has provided Holmes a tool, supplying her an effective outlet to deal with oppression. Indeed, Holmes would agree, for the struggle for a "voice" and selfhood—apart from those produced by relationships with men—figure prominently in the lives of her protagonists. According to Taylor, "Oppression is having other people tell your story. This is why Shirlene Holmes's play, *A Lady and a Woman,* is so important. It is very rare to find a play about being Black and lesbian. . . . That's not to say there haven't been Black characters in gay plays, and sometimes—albeit rarely—gay characters in Black plays, but often these are caricatures, one-dimensional exotics peripheral to the story. They are, however, almost always gay men" (183). "Black women," Holmes reminds us, "are not seen as much on the stage, and their voice will not always be welcomed"; however, she predicts that if they are "given the stage," then audiences will come to recognize and appreciate "that African-American women have written some poignant dramas about the complexity of being a woman and being black" (qtd. in Cauley). Both Flora and Biddie find happiness in each other by allowing each her personal space and freedom. Taylor argues that *"A Lady and a Woman* continues where [other] plays [leave] off":

> Focusing on the blossoming relationship between a butch and femme, Holmes' play melds the southern folklore of early Black theater with the exploration of sexual roles, desires and discovery that so often informs queer and lesbian theater. For a new generation of Black lesbians whose only media images are straight actors playing gay, this is a piece to be admired for its honesty. For an older generation accustomed to looking [at] ourselves in the images of others, it is a play to be cherished. For anyone interested in good drama, it is a play to be treasured and performed. (185)

In "What It Means to Be a Black Woman: 'Unwelcomed Voices' Explores the Work of 14 Playwrights," H. M. Cauley, like Taylor, infers that Holmes as an activist playwright intends the exercise of power. Cauley quotes Holmes herself: "They can't stop you when you're saying it, even though they may be mad afterwards. . . . I guess that's why I see it as such a rebellious thing to be a playwright."

Unlike Holmes, Sandra Deer lacks interest in politics, but on the subject of Atlanta, her views coincide with those of her sister playwright—the environment seems conducive to her work. "Yes," says Deer, "I feel the South is home, and although my first play, *So Long on Lonely Street* is intended as a loving satire of southern gothic comedy/romance, I would consider myself a playwright whose roots are southern, but not a Southern playwright" (Personal Interview).

Growing up in Decatur, an Atlanta suburb, Deer exclaims, "I love the city, its diversity, its beauty, its activity. I live in mid-town across the street from Piedmont Park where I walk everyday and feed the ducks on Lake Clara Meera. It's a very urban life. As I write this, I can hear music and crowds cheering at the Gay Pride concert in the park" (Personal Interview). Indeed, Atlanta encapsulates for Deer the best of the Old South—the idyllic, pastoral scene of a lake brimming with wildlife, yet thriving on the same plane as a Gay Pride concert. This "music" of Atlanta inspires the playwright.

Not only does Deer acknowledge Atlanta as home, but also she credits it with encouraging her writing: "my work has found welcome homes here at the Alliance Theatre and at Actors Express" (Personal Interview). In "Humor and Heritage in Sandra Deer's *So Long on Lonely Street*," Linda L. Hubert maintains that the playwright "maximized her relationship with a significant regional theatre to gain the requisite opportunity and support for her work," following a course similar to the paths of Beth Henley and Marsha Norman, both of whom had earlier found Actors Theatre of Louisville receptive to their plays: "The success of *Lonely Street* was clearly dependent upon a spirited collaboration between Deer and others working with Atlanta's Alliance Theatre as the play developed through productions. The work has gone through the process of maturation and development from platform reading to New York production, and it has grown with each step of this progression" (108). *Lonely Street* broke box office records in Atlanta and then travelled to Massachusetts, where it "sold out" "for an entire six-week run" (Sherbert, "Taking"). Capitalizing on Southern lore and quirkiness, the drama introduces the Vaughnum family—the living and the dead. Annabel Lee, a black woman, has lived all her life at Honeysuckle Hill, at the behest—or so she thinks—of the family patriarch. When a spinster aunt dies, Annabel insists that an old will leaves her the estate. Chaos ensues as the family bickers over who will be the "legitimate" heir. Deer's satire runs the gamut of traditional themes associated with Southern stereotypes: ties to the land, the encroachment of the past on the present, miscegenation, incest, libidinous sexual appetites, degeneration, and family dissolution.

Admitting that *Lonely Street* revels in melodramatic moments, Hubert posits that the playwright, nevertheless, deserves commendation for her "compelling" characters (105) and her "comic vision" (107). Indeed, Hubert's point seems apt, for at her best, Deer's humor matches that of a Beth Henley, especially in her depictions of the Southern grotesque. Annabel, the play's most eccentric and "insanely sane" character—and possible heir to the family estate—refuses to relinquish the body of her dead half-sister, Pearl, thus smacking the sensibilities of her greedy relatives, Clarice and King. They mourn and moan, but not because their grief overwhelms them:

CLARICE: Does it smell?

KING: It was starting to just a little, but I aired it out. Now, don't look at her.

CLARICE: Has she turned black and stiff?

KING: She hadn't been dead but a few days. She looks 'bout like she always did. Only more. (*Crosses left, places stand near coffin*)

CLARICE: Seems like to me a body would start to decompose pretty quick in the middle of August.

KING: Not when the air conditioner in her room is running full blast twenty-four hours a day. I hate to think what that utility bill is going to look like. (17)

Obviously more concerned with calculating the amount of the utility bill than with mourning the loss of Pearl, the modern couple represents the heartless "invalids" of the South, those without value of tradition or family. Indeed, King intends to sell the estate in order to facilitate the building of a shopping center. To succeed, he must first dispose of Annabel by having her "committed" to a home, thus conferring upon the old survivor an invalid status. Not only will the commitment paper—in the hands of King—displace Annabel from her home, but, simultaneously, it will insinuate that she lacks the capacity to make *valid* decisions.

Ultimately King's schemes fail as Deer validates "cousin" Annabel by presenting her quirkiness as "Southern normal" (appreciative audiences accept the character too). Periodically, Deer interjects gothic humor into *Lonely Street*, for example, in the memorable scene in which Anna wanders into her dead sister's room and recites a poem:

Pretty little Pearl
Pretty little Pearl.
How's it feel being dead? *(Sound of a car* [Clarice and King's] *outside.)*
Here they come. Both of 'em. Don't let 'em talk you to death. (17)

When Annabel, aided by another relative, Ruth, lifts the dead body of Pearl, she suddenly plops it down, complaining that no one will help her to dress the corpse:

ANNA: You don't have to touch her. Just hold the dress so I can get her arms through the sleeves.

RUTH: I'd better go get dressed myself. They'll be here, and I'll still be standing here looking like something the cat drug in. I think I hear a car now. Why don't you just lay the dress on top of her? I mean, nobody's going to see her from behind. *(RUTH runs up the stairs. ANNA looks after her a second, then returns to trying to get the dress on Pearl.)*

ANNA: Hold still, now. (69)

The humor in the scene lies in Annabel's insistence on interacting with the lifeless Pearl, a body that she assumes capable of both boredom and uncooperativeness.

Though appreciated in Atlanta, the New York critics mercilessly blasted Deer's *Lonely Street*—with Clive Barnes leading the fray, referring to it as "preposterous hokum—Southern fried chicken without the chicken" (Sherbert, "Taking"). Atlantans ignored Barnes's remarks and flocked (like chickens?), feeding on the performances and spotting humor where the New York critics saw nothing but fried dough. They appreciated the implicit ironies in "the Southern character" and the resolve with which *Lonely Street*'s heroine, Annabel, refused to be displaced from her heritage. Indeed, critic Helen C. Smith retorts that the New Yorkers proved "condescending at best" and "vicious at worst," assaulting personally the playwright, the director, the cast, and Atlanta itself: "There's also a lot of feeling that the War Between the States still rages, usually to the detriment of the South. There's paranoia in that, but also a grain of truth. . . . Tennessee Williams bombed as often as he triumphed in New York. Lillian Hellman got—still gets even after death—her share of barbs from the New York press" ("Hooray"). Smith—and others in Atlanta—countercharged, asserting that New Yorkers have "long scorned" Southern playwrights and submitting that the critics' preconceived notions about what to expect from a Southern woman's play colored their judgments and blurred their critical lenses; further, they levied accusations that their attempts at wit—at the playwright's expense—kept the critics from appreciating the intricacies of Deer's satire ("Hooray").

Certainly, Sandra Deer got slammed on the New York court, but *Lonely Street* proved anything but lonely as crowds across the country filled the theater houses to capacity. Deer's reputation remained intact. In 2000, Alliance Theater continues to enjoy the playwright's versatility. Her adaptations of material for children's plays, as well as for production successes like "Gal' Baby," indicate the breadth of her oeuvre: "I think the themes and characters in my plays, certainly the two most recent, *Sailing to Byzantium* and 'The Daimon Lover,'" she remarks, "are more concerned with beauty, destiny, and desire than with any other values" (Personal Interview). *Sailing to Byzantium*, concerning the life of poet William Butler Yeats, premiered in 1997 at Actors Express in Atlanta, under the direction of Chris Coleman, who also directed the Oregon Shakespeare Festival production of the play.

Another rising playwright on the Atlanta scene, Barbara Lebow, writes plays ranging from poignant and complex "homecomings," tinged by history and annihilation, to ones about cross-dressing and female cowboys, as in *Little Joe Monaghan*. Lebow's innovative Holocaust tale, *A Shayna Maidel* (Yiddish, meaning "a pretty girl"), presents a story of loss and reunion. Two sisters, separated by time, culture, and pain, meet again in 1946. Before the war, one sister had escaped Poland with her father, thereby not personally observing the death pall shadowing Europe and Hitler's "cleansing" of the Jews. Immersing herself in American culture once she settles in New York, Razel—whose name is changed to Rose—starkly contrasts with her sister, Lusia, who has borne witness to the almost total annihilation of her race. Gulfs greater than Lusia's broken English or the body of water previously dividing the two impede their communication. In a scene in which Rose presents Lusia with what she thinks is an appropriate gift, Lebow poignantly highlights these barriers:

ROSE: Here. This is for you.
LUSIA: (*holding the present as if it might explode, staring at it.*) Thank you.
ROSE: Well, open it up.
(*Rose starts to help LUSIA undo the wrappings. LUSIA still staring at the gift, brushes ROSE's hands away and continues opening it on her own. She takes out a beautiful and elegant nightgown.*)
I didn't know what you had.
(*She is suddenly sombre, embarrassed.*)
What they gave you. I thought you might like it.
LUSIA: *Shayn.* Pretty. Too pretty.
ROSE: Oh nothing can be too pretty!
LUSIA: I mean to say, how much pretty.
ROSE: So pretty, then. "So," not "too."
LUSIA: So pretty. To sleep with. I cannot believe. So pretty.
ROSE: I'm glad you like it. Now, why don't you go wash up, I mean bathe, and I'll fix something to eat. I'll bet you're hungry, really. And you wear

the nightgown. There's a real nice robe in the closet you can use to go with it. I have extras, honestly. And while I'm making lunch—I know it's the middle of the night, but it feels like lunch to me—you can freshen up and wash away all your travelling. You've come so far, in such a short time. I know you're tired, but we need to fatten you up a bit and get those roses back in your cheeks. (14–15)

In "Toward a Feminist Perspective in American Holocaust Drama," E. R. Isser explains that Lusia's problems entail more than just "adjusting to an American lifestyle," for the "experiences during the war" leave her "emotionally shattered" (144). Isser's comment intimates the impossibility of "wash[ing]" away all of Lusia's "travelling," for the girls have travelled in two different worlds. The sisters—and the family—must integrate their fragmented selves and come to recognize their "oneness." Lebow's play celebrates finding home and wholeness despite seemingly insurmountable barriers.

Like the aforementioned playwrights, Lebow feels a bond with Atlanta. What inspires the playwright's prodigious output, works which include *The Keepers, Tiny Tim Is Dead,* and *Little Joe Monaghan,* as well as *A Shayna Maidel*? Certainly, environment must be a contributing factor, and Lebow makes clear that she lives and works in the city by choice. Now the Academy Theater's resident playwright, and winner of numerous play-writing awards, Lebow has settled into her new home and enjoys the view: "I don't see premiering a play at the Academy as a 'try-out,'" she says. "This is where the population of the country is, in the regions. I've watched one of my plays *A Shayna Maidel,* which premiered here, move to five other regional theaters—it has played off-Broadway, too, but now I view New York as yet another region" (Giles 78).

Another playwright of distinction who relishes her Atlanta perspective is Pearl Cleage. Barely remembering how long she has resided in the city—"some thirty years," she surmises—Cleage confesses to being a transplant from the North, but hastily declares, "Atlanta is home" (Personal Interview). Her penchant for writing extends beyond her ability to write drama: her essays in *Deals with the Devil and Other Reasons to Riot* and *Mad at Miles* are thoughtful and thought-provoking, and *The Brass Bed and Other Stories* attests to her insight into human foibles and ultimate strengths. Of her latest endeavors, the novel *What Looks Like Crazy on An Ordinary Day* (1999), has risen to become a bestseller, endorsed by The Oprah Winfrey Book Club. Challenging social stereotypes of race, class, and gender and triggering people's consciences to demand action, Cleage especially writes about the African American experience: *Chain,*

Hospice, Late Bus to Mecca, Flyin' West, Blues for an Alabama Sky, Bourbon at the Border, to name a few, all emphasize determined black folks pitted against society.

Calling herself "less of a Southern writer" and more a writer of a national movement, Cleage embraces politics, considering herself as one who has caught the rising wave of the "national African-American community" (Personal Interview). Politics, not surprisingly, first brought Cleage to the region when she became involved with the transition of Atlanta's first black mayor, Maynard Jackson: "Atlanta was making changes," she says, especially for black people (Personal Interview). Her voice electric, the playwright recalls the period when she first relocated to the city, a region especially attractive to her because the "majority" [of the population] was African American (Personal Interview).

Anchored joyously to her heritage, Cleage vows to be "always in touch with [her] race," the "overarching" factor of her identity, she affirms (Personal Interview). Under this arch, the playwright glides freely, like a ship hoisting an abundance of colorful sails, intent upon docking at many "ports of issues." Her work reflects an insistence upon a multiplicity of causes, interests, fights, and one of her most noted plays, *Flyin' West,* typifies Cleage's ability to mesh these pursuits. *Flyin' West* tells the story of a black family's escape from the racial injustice of the South as its members push west to homestead, establish an all-black community in Nicodemas, Kansas. Here, Cleage interweaves themes of lost inheritance, racism, miscegenation, and self-hatred with issues of domestic violence and questions of identity. Like her character Sophie in *Flyin' West,* Cleage refuses to tolerate injustice. Her heroines are *actors,* not *acted upon*—and the playwright acquaints audiences with their struggles, these figures who exude sometimes stoic determination as they skillfully bolster strength in others through their community and sisterhood:

> SOPHIE: You know as well as I do there are no laws that protect a woman from her husband. Josh beat Belle for years and we all knew it. And because the sheriff didn't do anything, none of us did anything either. It wasn't a crime until he killed her! I'm not going to let that happen to Min. I'm going to watch him prance across this yard and then I'm going to step out on my front porch and blow his brains out.
>
> FANNIE: And then we'll be savages just like he is!
>
> SOPHIE: No! Then we'll be doing what free people always have to do if they're going to stay free. (*Flyin' West* 63)

Atlanta welcomes Cleage's challenging determinedness, for here the playwright finds like-minded friends. There's a "community of theater people here," she asserts, and "I have no problem getting my work done" (Personal Interview). Praising the friendships promulgated through her theater connections—good working relationships all—Cleage expressly commends her collaboration with Kenny Leon, actor, and artistic director for the Alliance Theatre (Personal Interview). In "Atlanta's Rising Playmakers: Writers Finding Ways to Put the City's Unique Spirit Onstage," Hulbert interprets Cleage's phenomenal success with *Flyin' West,* which premiered in 1992, as a sign for all Atlanta playwrights: it "show[s] that it is possible for local playwrights to heat up box-office phones."

Cleage's reputation as a playwright extends beyond the confines of the city though she concedes her preference for the "completely different world" and "perfect size" of Atlanta to Los Angeles or even to New York, a scene which the author characterizes as discomfiting for a writer because it presents a "kind of pressure": "I don't find myself competing with peers in Atlanta" as "my New York friends do," Cleage explains (Personal Interview). Speaking with pride of her home in an "all-black neighborhood" in the southwest part of the sprawling city, the playwright appears to have located her "Nicodemus, Kansas." She surveys the houses, savoring the sight of black faces greeting her, and then acknowledges her debt to the neighborhood: "I feel it keeps me grounded," she says.

The South infuses Cleage's themes and plots: "All of my works, have a Southern something," a "consciousness of the past"—indeed, she confesses, "right now I'm looking out the window at the magnolia tree" (Personal Interview). For Atlanta, Cleage exclaims, "I have a home feeling" (Personal Interview). When reminiscing about her initiation to the South during her second week in Atlanta, the playwright narrates her encounter with a local utility man: "You all must be Yankees," divined the man as he turned on the gas at Cleage's new house. Up north, quips Cleage, the term "Yankee" was "good," but here, it implies something else, something undeclared: "In the North when people refer to 'the War,' they're talking about Vietnam. . . . Here," she chuckles, "they mean the Civil War" (Personal Interview). Despite the vitality that the author draws from Atlanta, Cleage denies that her writing must be "bound" to the city. Though they may embrace Southern characters, her plays defy margins, borders.

Nonetheless, the playwright's ear stays attuned to the voices of the city's inhabitants. "Southern voices are in my plays," Cleage emphatically states as she alludes specifically to *Flyin' West, Blues for an Alabama Sky,* and *Bourbon at the Border.* The playwright stores a "lot of Southern stories in [her] head," figuring that she has just enough time to write them before she dies: "Already I am carrying most of the stories in me that I have time enough to write" (Personal Interview). Some of those tales from the playwright's memory silo already have been mined, marketed, and passed on to others. *Chain* and *Late Bus to Mecca* Cleage designates as her "morality plays," for they "intimate the values needed if black women are to survive in society" (Paige 70–71). One might speculate that all of Cleage's dramas investigate values to one degree or another: *Hospice,* for instance, unfolds a complex relationship between a terminally ill woman and her daughter and *Blues for an Alabama Sky,* set in the Harlem Renaissance of 1930, recounts the story of Angel (originally played by Phylicia Rashad), a woman "accustomed to living in search of someone to take care of her": eventually, as one critic asserts, Angel's irresponsibility, her inability to "[shape] her own destiny" effects change in others (Giles 726). Set in 1925, *Bourbon at the Border* typifies the playwright's awareness of personal and societal issues. The play pivots around Charlie and May, "survivors" of the black voter registration drive of Mississippi in 1964: "During the thirty years since Freedom Summer they have tried to help each other cope with wounds that could not be healed, outrage that could not be quelled, and [their own] guilt. . . . They live in a small apartment near the Ambassador Bridge which connects Detroit, Michigan, with Windsor, Ontario. Their odyssey to escape their pain had led them there, 'like desperados drinking bourbon at the border and planning [their] getaway'." (Giles 726). Giles hypothesizes that *Flyin' West, Blues for an Alabama Sky,* and *Bourbon at the Border* "bring us to grips with our American past and . . . help us to understand and acknowledge its impact on present conditions, especially with regard to issues of race and gender" (725). Cognizant always of her race and gender, Cleage responds favorably when referred to as a "woman playwright." "Absolutely!" she states, and then as if "conjugating her identity," taking it through various forms of her essence, the author chortles that she distinguishes herself "always . . . in specifics": "I am specifically a woman—more specifically, a middle-aged black woman playwright. I want all my specifics in there" (Personal Interview).

As for her future, Cleage underscores her talent for versatility: "What things make me a good playwright came as a good writer," she remarks. Reiterating that Atlanta serves as a kind of fount for her own versatility, she adds, "You can live here and write well . . . and not do plays at all" (Personal Interview). Ultimately, Pearl Cleage writes to please herself, her inspiration internal. Eschewing "having to write to please people," which "makes [one] crazy," she declares that "[her] challenge is to be disciplined enough to write those stories [the ones brimming from her stored-up memories] in an organized fashion" (Personal Interview).

Slowly, the phrase "'new work by an Atlanta playwright' is losing 'its old stigma of tailbone-taxing ennui,'" says the *Atlanta Journal and Constitution,* for in its past, the city's theaters seemed so "committed to the ideal of local playwrights that the quality of the scripts seemed like an afterthought" (Hulbert, "Atlanta's Rising"). No longer does this appear the case. Besides a penchant for truth-telling and social consciousness, Atlanta's "play-writing" women, artistically and socially, share community. Drawing together, they discuss play-writing, repairing and revising, and staging, thus continuing to support one another, their craft, and the city that has beckoned them. Not surprisingly, the 1999 Pulitzer Prize went to Atlanta's newest "import," Margaret Edson, for her play *Wit*—which merely signals a green-lighted future for Atlanta's play-writing hub.

Voices varied and messages diverse, Southern women playwrights have found a home in this Atlanta microcosm of America, an area where many cultures and many aspects of humanity converge. Indeed, all over the South, women playwrights continue to gather, telling their stories. Their lives, in an odd way, have something in common with a character from Robert Frost's "The Death of the Hired Man." This poem tells the story of Silas, a farm laborer, who periodically returns to a rural farm that he has somehow "adopted" as home. One character says, "Home is the place where, when you have to go there, / They have to take you in" (30). His wife replies, more gently, "I should have called it / Something you somehow haven't to deserve." As both imply, home offers comfort, stability. Many talented playwrights deem Atlanta both comfortable and inviting, a place where they want to go. But they are only accepted there because they have proved they deserve it. Though not out of necessity, Atlanta welcomes *home* its diverse group of Southern women playwrights.

Works Cited

Cauley, H. M. "For City Life, What It Means to Be a Black Woman: 'Unwelcomed Voices' Explores the Work of 14 Playwrights." *Atlanta Journal and Constitution* 21 Nov. 996: D/09. 12 June 1999. Http://stacks.ajc.com

Cleage, Pearl. *Blues for an Alabama Sky.* New York: Dramatists Play Service, 1999.

———. *Chain. Playwriting Women: Seven Plays from the Women's Project.* Ed. Julia Miles. Portsmouth, NH: Heinemann, 1993. 263–96.

———. *Flyin' West.* New York: Dramatists Play Service, 1995.

———. Flyin' West *and Other Plays.* New York: Theatre Communications Group, 1999.

———. *Hospice. New Plays for the Black Theatre.* Ed. Woodie King, Jr. Chicago: Third World, 1989.

———. *Late Bus to Mecca. Playwriting Women: Seven Plays from the Women's Project.* Ed. Julia Miles. Portsmouth, NH: Heinemann, 1993. 297–322.

———. Personal Interview, telephone, with Linda Rohrer Paige. 30 June 1999.

———. *What Looks Like Crazy on an Ordinary Day.* New York: Avon Books, 1997.

Deer, Sandra. Personal Interview, e-mail. 27 June 1999.

———. *Sailing to Byzantium.* Oregon Shakespeare Playscript series. n.d.

———. *So Long on Lonely Street.* New York: Samuel French, 1986.

Frost, Robert. "The Death of the Hired Man." *Selected Poems of Robert Frost.* New York: Holt, 1963. 25–30.

Georgia Week in Review. With Bill Nigut (Political Reporter, WSBTV) and guests: Chris Coleman, Artistic Director, Actors Express; Jessica West, Theatre in the Square, Marietta; and Richard Garner, Georgia Shakespeare Festival. GPTV (Atlanta) 25 June 1999.

Giles, Freda Scott. "The Motion of Herstory: Three Plays by Pearl Cleage." *African American Review* 31 (1997): 709–12. Online. Galileo. 8 June 1999.

———. Rev. of "Bourbon at the Border" by Pearl Cleage. *African American Review* 31 (1997): 725–26. *Periodical Abstracts.* Online. Galileo. 8 June 1999.

Holmes, Shirlene. *A Lady and a Woman. Amazon All-Stars: Thirteen Lesbian Plays.* Ed. Rosemary Keefe Curb. New York: Applause, 1996. 186–207.

Hubert, Linda. "Humor and Heritage in Sandra Deer's *So Long on Lonely Street.*" *Southern Quarterly* 25.3 (1987): 105–15.

Hulbert, Dan. "Atlanta's Rising Playmakers: Writers Finding Ways to Put City's Unique Spirit on Stage." *Atlanta Journal and Constitution* 16 Jan. 1994: N/04; 12 June 1999. Http://stacks.ajc.com

———. "Playwrights Change the Script as Values and Philosophies Collide in the Region."

Atlanta Journal and Constitution 17 Jul. 1988: G/01. 12 June 1999. Http://stacks.ajc.com

Isser, E. R. "Toward a Feminist Perspective in American Holocaust Drama." *Studies in the Humanities* 17.2 (1990): 139–48.

Kloer, Phil, Paula Crouch, Catherine Fox, and Linda Sherbert. "Southern Arts Blossoming." *Atlanta Journal and Constitution* 12 June 1999. Http://stacks.ajc.com

Lebow, Barbara. *The Keepers.* New York: Dramatists Play Service, 1995.

———. *Little Joe Monaghan.* New York: Dramatists Play Service, 1995.

———. *A Shayna Maidel.* New York: New American Library, 1988.

———. *Tiny Tim Is Dead.* New York: Dramatists Play Service, 1993.

O'Briant, Don. "Strong, Emerging Southern Voices Ensure That a Literary Tradition

Thrives—for Now." *Atlanta Journal and Constitution* 08 Apr. 1990: N/01-02. Http://stacks.ajc.com

Paige, Linda Rohrer. "Pearl Cleage." *Significant Contemporary American Feminists: A Biographical Sourcebook.* Ed. Jennifer Scanlon. Westport, CT: Greenwood, 1999. 66–72.

Sherbert, Linda. "Taking Her 'Baby' to N.Y.: Mitchell's Big-City Debut a Familiar Role." *Atlanta Journal and Constitution* 24 Mar. 1986: B/01. 12 June 1999. Http:// stacks.ajc.com

Smith, Helen C. "THE ARTS: $20 Million Endowment Check Gets Arts Center Season Off to Flying Start." *Atlanta Journal and Constitution* 15 Sept. 1985: J/03. 12 June 1999. Http://stacks.ajc.com

———. "Hooray from Our Side for Two Artists!" *Atlanta Journal and Constitution* 27 Apr. 1986: J/02. 12 June 1999. Http://stacks.ajc.com

Taylor, Willa J. Introduction. *A Lady and a Woman,* by Shirlene Holmes. *Amazon All-Stars: Thirteen Lesbian Plays.* Ed. Rosemary Curb. New York: Applause, 1996. 183–85.

Contributors

Claudia Barnett, Associate Professor of English at Middle Tennessee State University, is the editor of *Wendy Wasserstein: A Casebook* (1998). Her work has appeared in *Modern Drama* and in *Theatre Journal.*

Elizabeth S. Bell is currently the John and Mary Grew Palmetto Professor of American Studies at the University of South Carolina at Aiken. Author of three books, *Words That Must Somehow Be Said* (1985), *The Short Fiction of Kay Boyle* (1992), and *Sisters of the Wind: Voices of Early Women Aviators* (1994), Bell has written numerous articles on composition pedagogy and on women authors.

Elizabeth Brown-Guillory is Professor of English and Associate Dean of the College of Humanities, Fine Arts, and Communication at the University of Houston. A playwright and performing artist, she is the author or editor of three books on women writers of color: *Their Place on the Stage: Black Women Playwrights in America* (1988), *Wines in the Wilderness: Plays by African-American Women from the Harlem Renaissance to the Present* (1990), and *Women of Color: Mother-Daughter Relationships in 20th-Century Literature* (1996).

Sally Burke, Professor of English and Women's Studies at the University of Rhode Island, is the author of *American Feminist Playwrights: A Critical History* (1997).

Carlos L. Dews, Associate Professor of English at the University of West Florida, is the founding president of the Carson McCullers Society and the editor of *Illumination and Night Glare: The Unfinished Autobiography of Carson McCullers* (1999).

J. Ellen Gainor is Professor and Director of Graduate Studies in Theatre at Cornell University. Author of *Shaw's Daughters: Dramatic and Narrative Con-*

structions of Gender and the forthcoming *The Plays of Susan Glaspell: A Contextual Study,* she has edited the volumes *Imperialism and Theatre* (1995) and *Performing America: Cultural Nationalism in American Theater* (1999) and has published widely in scholarly journals and reference works on British and American theater.

Janet L. Gupton received her B.A. and J.D. from Wake Forest University in Winston-Salem, North Carolina, and her M.A. and Ph.D. in Theater from the University of Oregon. Janet has taught at Bowling Green State University in Ohio as well as worked as a director and theater artist in New York City. She is currently an Assistant Professor of Theater at Linfield College in McMinnville, Oregon.

Judith Giblin James, Associate Professor of English at the University of South Carolina, has written or edited three books on American fiction, including *Wunderkind: The Reputation of Carson McCullers, 1940–1990* (1995), and is completing a study of dramatic adaptations to be titled *Dramatizing Difference: The American Social Novel on Stage.*

Mary Lamb, a doctoral candidate in English at Texas Christian University in Fort Worth, specializes in rhetoric and composition studies. Considering the cultural work of reading groups in her dissertation, she pays special attention to the current phenomenon of "Oprah's Book Club." Other research and teaching interests include feminist rhetoric and composition, twentieth-century American women's fiction, and African American women's fiction.

Donna Lisker serves as Director of the Duke University Women's Center in Durham, NC. She teaches women's studies at Duke (and previously at Virginia Tech and the University of Wisconsin-Madison) and has published articles on violence against women and on women's center administration.

John Lowe, Professor of English at Louisiana State University, is the author of *Jump at the Sun: Zora Neale Hurston's Cosmic Comedy* (1995); editor of *Conversations with Ernest Gaines* (1995) and *Redefining Southern Culture* (forthcoming); coeditor of *The Future of Southern Letters* (1996); and the current President of The Society for the Study of the Multi-Ethnic Literature of the United States (MELUS).

Robert L. McDonald is Associate Professor of English and Associate Dean for Academic Affairs at Virginia Military Institute. He regularly teaches courses in American drama and Southern literature. His publications include *The Critical Response to Erskine Caldwell* (1997) and *Erskine Caldwell: Selected Letters, 1929–1955* (1999), as well as essays and conference presentations on Tennessee Williams, Beth Henley, and Paula Vogel.

Betty E. McKinnie currently lives in Panama City, Florida, where she is Assistant Professor of English at Gulf Coast Community College.

Theresa R. Mooney, born and raised in the South, has taught at Loyola University of New Orleans since 1992. She coordinates daily operation of Loyola's Writing Across the Curriculum Centers and teaches a range of writing and literature courses; previously, Dr. Mooney taught at Fordham University and at Harvard Business School.

Linda Rohrer Paige, Associate Professor of English, teaches literature and women's studies courses at Georgia Southern University. With major interests in female playwrights and women in film, Paige has essays appearing in journals such as *Papers on Language & Literature, The Literature/Film Quarterly, Studies in Short Fiction,* and *The Journal of Popular Film and Television.*

Mary Resing serves on the faculty of Georgetown University, where she teaches theater and drama. She also works as a freelance dramaturg. Her essays have appeared in *New Theatre Quarterly, Theatre History Studies,* and *Censorship: An Encyclopedia.*

Carolyn Roark is a Ph.D. student focusing on theater history and literary criticism in the Department of Theatre and Dance at the University of Texas, Austin. She currently edits the journal *Theatre InSight* and researches Chilean puppet theater.

Alan Shepard is the author of *Marlowe's Soldiers: Rhetorics of Masculinity in the Age of the Armada* (forthcoming) as well as essays on early modern literature and contemporary Anglo-American drama, and coeditor of *Coming to Class: Pedagogy and the Social Class of Teachers* (1998). He is Associate Professor of English at Texas Christian University in Fort Worth.

Index